DRAMATHERAPY AND DESTRUCTIVENESS

Dramatherapy uses the healing aspects of drama and theatre as part of the therapeutic process and is increasingly required to supply evidence of its effectiveness. This book aims to provide an evidence base for practice with destructive clients, and raise the profile of dramatherapy as a distinct therapeutic intervention in this field.

Dramatherapy and Destructiveness discusses working with those suffering from conduct disorders, mood disorders, schizophrenia and personality disorders. Divided into three parts, topics of discussion include:

- theory and research underpinning the understanding of working with destructiveness
- in-depth case studies of dramatherapy with a wide range of clients
- analysis and evaluation of the evidence base for dramatherapy with these clients
- guidelines for best practice

Dramatherapy and Destructiveness covers a wide range of client groups, settings, methods and therapeutic approaches. As well as being an invaluable resource for dramatherapists, this book will be of interest to other therapists, health professionals, social workers, teachers and artists.

Ditty Dokter is professional lead and head of arts therapies at an NHS foundation trust in adult and older people's psychiatry. She works as Pathway Leader for the MA Dramatherapy at Anglia Ruskin University, Cambridge and lectures widely, both nationally and internationally.

Pete Holloway is a consultant dramatherapist and area lead for a psychological services team within an NHS community mental health setting. He is also a Senior Lecturer on the MA Dramatherapy programme at Roehampton University.

Henri Seebohm is Programme Convenor of the MA in Dramatherapy at Roehampton University and Senior Dramatherapist and Supervisor in adult forensic psychiatry for an NHS mental health foundation trust.

Contributors: Ditty Dokter, Pete Holloway, Jane Jackson, Phil Jones, Maggie McAlister, Emma Ramsden, Henri Seebohm, Rose Thorn, Eleanor Zeal, Lia Zografou.

DRAMATHERAPY AND DESTRUCTIVENESS

Creating the Evidence Base, Playing with Thanatos

Edited by Ditty Dokter, Pete Holloway and Henri Seebohm

LONDON AND NEW YORK

First published 2011
by Routledge
2 Park Square, Milton Park, Abingdon, Oxon, OX14 4RN

Simultaneously published in the USA and Canada
by Routledge
711 Third Avenue, New York NY 10017

Routledge is an imprint of the Taylor & Francis Group, an Informa business

British Library Cataloguing in Publication Data
A catalogue record for this book is available from the British Library

Library of Congress Cataloging-in-Publication Data
Dramatherapy and destructiveness : creating the evidence base, playing with Thanatos / edited
by Ditty Dokter, Pete Holloway and Henri Seebohm.
p. cm.
ISBN 978-0-415-55850-1 (hardback) – ISBN 978-0-415-55851-8 (pbk.)
1. Drama–Therapeutic use. 2. Self-destructive behavior. 3. Violence–Psychological aspects.
I. Dokter, Ditty, 1958- II. Holloway, Pete, 1965- III. Seebohm, Henri, 1967-
RC489.P7D724 2011
616.89'1523–dc22
2010044325

ISBN: 978-0-415-55850-1 (hbk)
ISBN: 978-0-415-55851-8 (pbk)

Typeset in Times by Garfield Morgan, Swansea, West Glamorgan
Cover image, Big Bang, by Charlotte Baynes
Paperback cover design by Andrew Ward

CONTENTS

LIST OF CONTRIBUTORS

Ditty Dokter is professional lead and head of arts therapies at an NHS foundation trust in adult and older people's psychiatry. She works as Pathway Leader for the MA Dramatherapy at Anglia Ruskin University, Cambridge and lectures widely, both nationally and internationally. Her research interest is in intercultural arts therapies practice. She has taught and published extensively, both nationally and internationally. Previous edited publications are *Arts Therapies and Clients with Eating Disorders* (Jessica Kingsley, 1994), *Arts Therapists, Refugees and Migrants* (Jessica Kingsley, 1998) and *Supervision of Dramatherapy* (with Phil Jones; Routledge, 2008).

Pete Holloway is a consultant dramatherapist and area lead for a psychological services team within an NHS community mental health setting. His own clinical specialisms are the areas of personality disorder, offending behaviour and child protection concerns as a result of parental mental illness. He is also a Senior Lecturer on the MA Dramatherapy programme at Roehampton University.

Jane Jackson is a dramatherapist and supervisor. She has worked with many client groups but has specialised in working with adults with all levels of learning disability, in a variety of settings. Jane is a freelance practitioner, works with the Dramatherapy charity Roundabout, and has extensive experience within the NHS.

Phil Jones, Reader, Leeds University, has written and lectured internationally on the arts therapies and on childhood. His sole-authored books include *Rethinking Children's Rights* (Continuum, 2010), *Drama As Therapy* (Routledge, 2007) and *The Arts Therapies* (Routledge, 2005). His edited books include *Drama As Therapy*, Vol. 2 (Routledge, 2009), *Dramatherapy Supervision* (with Dokter; Routledge, 2008) and *Childhood* (with Moss, Tomlinson and Welch; Pearson, 2007). He is Series Editor for *New Childhoods* (Continuum).

Maggie McAlister trained as a Jungian analyst at the Society of Analytical Psychology (SAP), London, and is also a dramatherapist and supervisor. She works as a highly specialist forensic adult psychotherapist at West London Mental Health Trust and previously worked there as a senior dramatherapist for 12 years. She has taught and published extensively on dramatherapy, psychosis and offending. Her latest publication is on psychotherapy and homicide, *Murder: A Psychotherapeutic Investigation*, R. Doctor (ed.) (Karnac, 2008). She is involved in teaching at the SAP and has a private practice.

Emma Ramsden is a practitioner and researcher at Leeds Metropolitan University where she is in the final phase of writing up her doctoral thesis, 'A Study of Children's Psychological Voices in Dramatherapy'. Emma also works in education with primary school-age children and in high secure forensic psychiatry, where she has developed a speciality in working with perpetrators of violent crimes and sexual offending. Emma has written several chapters about her dramatherapy practice in publications focusing on the ethics of consent with vulnerable populations, therapist as supervisor and clinical processes in forensic psychiatry such as therapeutic approaches to 'victim empathy'. Emma is a clinical supervisor and has a private practice based in South East London.

Henri Seebohm is Programme Convenor of MA in Dramatherapy at Roehampton University and Senior Dramatherapist and Supervisor in Adult Forensic Psychiatry for an NHS mental health trust. She is particularly interested in the relationship between early trauma and the onset of psychosis, personality disorder and offending behaviour and examines how the therapist can manage to tolerate manifest destructiveness in the therapy space. Henri has been using therapeutic theatre and action methods for the last 15 years in facilitating workshops, training, consultancy, conflict resolution and team- and community-building work in Europe.

Rose Thorn is a dramatherapist who has worked with a variety of people, all from a range of socio-economic, ethnic and cultural backgrounds. Her clinical experience is with adults and children with learning difficulties and people who have experienced mental distress. She currently works in a forensic medium secure unit with male and female offenders and at Studio Upstairs, a therapeutic artists community. Rose is a visual artist and a committed performer; she is one of the founding members of Breathing Fire – a black women's playback theatre company.

Eleanor Zeal works as an on-site dramatherapist in a special school for excluded adolescents and young offenders. She has a particular interest in the complex issues surrounding looked after children. Currently she is a visiting lecturer at Roehampton University and UK Coordinator/ Trainer for David Read Johnson's Developmental Transformations.

Lia Zografou, MA (Dramatherapy), is a dramatherapist and supervisor currently living and working freelance in Thessaloniki, Greece. She trained at Roehampton Institute and specialises in work with addicts in both rehabilitation settings and private practice with clients with eating disorders and drug and relationship addictions. She also teaches on the Diploma Course for Creative Supervision offered by the London Centre for Psychodrama and is a founding member and actor of the Hellenic Playback Theatre company.

FOREWORD

This thing of darkness I acknowledge mine.

(Shakespeare: *The Tempest*, 1: 275)

I am grateful to the editors for an opportunity to write a foreword to what I think is an important book for any psychological therapist working with those who 'offend' – against themselves or others. I have some particular reasons for saying this that I will explore briefly here, as a way of introducing a book that I think will be a rich source of reflection and therapeutic advice for the reader.

An important common theme in what follows is the importance of bringing something into being that was not there before. We think of those who offend generating their offences precisely because they cannot create symbols of experience: they cannot bring into being a verbal articulation of what they are thinking and feeling. We can call this 'alexithymia' or 'failure of mentalisation or symbolic function': whatever we call it, the upshot is that instead of a metaphor which communicates meaning, we have a bodily action that communicates:

Speak, hands, for me!

(Shakespeare: *Julius Caesar* III, 1: 76)

The hands enact something too awful, too overwhelming for the brain and mind to articulate. Affects are 'stuck' in the body and cannot make the move from the somatic to the verbal, let alone to the narrative level of experience (McAdams and Pals 2006). For many, this will be because traumatic experiences of neglect and adversity in childhood have adversely affected their brain development, especially in those areas of the brain that underpin affect regulation and the development of a sense of self (Schore 2001; 2003).

Psychological therapies that assume a reasonably normal capacity to articulate thoughts and feelings are not likely to be able to reach many such patients. This is particularly the case for cognitive therapies, which require a level of mentalising capacity *a priori*; to some extent, the same is true of psychoanalytic work, which assumes some capacity to symbolise and an interest in doing so. This may explain why engagement is so complex and problematic in forensic work and in work with those who harm themselves. The other problem is that for many of the patients we meet, cognitions are all they can do: it is the absence of an affective and empathic stance (towards others or oneself) that has led to the violence that they do.

Psychological therapies, that primarily engage the body, and physical expression of feelings may be meeting the emotionally inarticulate where they are – on what I think of as the Via Dolorosa that is life after the commission of serious violence, whether it be enacted against the self or others. In a magisterial review, McGilchrist (2009) describes how the right hemisphere of the brain organizes our emotional 'take' on the world, and especially how it supports the articulation of feelings through both an awareness of bodily feeling and the generation of metaphor. He reviews the evidence that music came before language in evolutionary terms; and is still the primary way that people all over the world express feeling. Visual art allows for both symbol making and physical engagement, and both drama-therapy and dance movement therapy offer the possibility of re-experiencing the body in a different way. What McGilchrist describes theoretically, from the perspective of neuroscience, this book will describe from the point of view of skilled clinicians and theorists in the field of dramatherapy.

Reading this book, I was struck by the relevance to an idea that disturbed and dangerous patients need to create a tragic narrative if they are to transform what they have done and what has happened to them into a story with a future. In a recent presentation (Adshead 2010), I drew on Aristotelian ideas about tragedy as a device that helps us understand dreadful events by calling attention to the feelings of those involved. I was particularly thinking of the criminal court, where different versions of the 'horror' story will be told. The prosecution will depict the defendant as a monster; the defence will try to portray him/her as a person who has lost his/her way in life's dark wood, who, on a quest, made mistakes and metaphorically lost 'sight' of what was happening or the true import of what he/she did. The same may be said of those whose offences are played out upon themselves, or against some abstract 'other' – where the narratives of diagnosis and unvoiced experience may both lead to an attempt to frame a particular understanding of dreadful events.

As psychotherapists, we meet the offender later. We know these other versions of the story but we want to hear the offender's own account. We think that if a person can find their 'voice', they may be able to acknowledge the 'dark things' that caused them to be violent or to act out their pain and, once acknowledged, can be worked into a personal narrative of experience. It is at the level of personal narrative that we also meet the moral identity, the voice of the 'kind of person I want to be'.

The creative therapies offer ways of accessing those deeper, non-verbal parts of mental function that are essential for regeneration and repair: the bringing of something new and growing into a barren and damaged internal landscape. The evidence of dramatherapy at work in this book, with its focus on experience, embodied metaphor, symbolisation and relationship, helped me to think more deeply about my work with damaged people – and in such work, we need all the help we can get.

Gwen Adshead

INTRODUCTION

Pete Holloway, Ditty Dokter and Henri Seebohm

To say that the forces of destruction and manifestations of destructiveness run rife in the world is to state a self-evident truth. From the geological to the socio-political, from the cultural to the domestic, from the interpersonal to the intrapersonal spheres, destruction, destructiveness and self-destructiveness abound in a myriad of guises – both in terms of the historical and cultural environment we inhabit and in terms of the capacity we have as human beings to act destructively, be it toward self or others. Nowhere is this more starkly evident than in the experiences which bring people into therapy. The stories our clients carry with them, that their sense of self has been shaped or disturbed by destructive forces, or the very real threat of their capacity to enact their destructive potential on themselves or others, are never too far away from the dilemmas of human existence that are explored within the therapeutic space.

For the dramatherapist and other creative arts therapists, who hold at the centre of their practice the idea that human beings have an innate capacity for creative imagination and creativity in their action upon their world, the experience and manifestation of destructiveness presents a distinct challenge, in its apparent opposition to all that is productive, generative and creative of new possibilities, whilst for the settings and institutions in which dramatherapists go about their work, the combination of destructive clients and dramatherapy presents another kind of challenge – a fear that a therapeutic practice based on enactment may only serve to encourage the 'acting out' of violent, aggressive and dangerous material. Yet in the genesis and development of arts therapies in general, and dramatherapy in particular, much clinical work has been located in settings and institutions where manifestations of destructiveness are woven into the clinical problems faced by clients and staff. For the moment, then, let us consider the historical development of arts therapies practice and how practitioners have come to define their practice.

1

Arts therapies: a historical framework

The first books considering the history of the four arts therapies, as recognised separately in the UK, were published very recently (Jones 2005; Karkou and Sanderson 2006). Jones (2005) shows a pattern of development where a small group individual pioneers, in collaboration with others, developed practice, training and governance of each distinct arts therapy discipline (Waller 1991; Jones 1996; Payne 1993, Priestley 1975; Nordoff and Robbins 1971). Jones' emphasis on trained individuals is a more recent development. Individuals from one country train in another and return to their country of origin to establish the profession (Waller 1998; Dokter 1998).

The European Consortium for Arts Therapies trainings has aimed to create a regional European arts therapies network. Its biannual conferences and publications provide an overview of different European practices and training. Waller (1998) researched this area in relation to art therapy and critically reviewed both the UK (1991) and other European countries (1992, 1995), with a reference to the diversity within each country and its different socio-political and health service contexts.

Many studies indicate diversity without boundaries; chosen theoretical and political directions are seldom made explicit, although they may have great implications for the development of the profession. Karkou and Sanderson's (2006) research provides a UK overview through target informer interviews and surveys, whilst Jones (2005) uses literature review and interviews to study commonalities and differences across arts therapies practice worldwide.

Jones (2005) shows how different subgroups arrive at their own description and definition. Some identify themselves by their theoretical orientation, others by their practice context. Jones provides an overview of settings where arts therapists practise. He indicates that 'the extent of practice can be limited by attitude, availability of therapists and systems of healthcare, alongside the economic and political situation' (Jones 2005: 19). Whilst arts therapists practise in similar settings, there can be a difference in emphasis in the modalities (Karkou 1999).

Karkou's research involved 40% of arts therapists, registered in the UK through their professional associations. The sample comprised 51.6% of art therapists, 21% of music therapists, 19% of dramatherapists and 7% of dance movement therapists. Of the respondents, the main working environment for 48.5% (many arts therapists work part-time in a variety of settings) is the health service; 16.5% work in education, 12.7% in voluntary organisations, 12% in community settings, 7.6% in private practice and 2.8% in other settings. Almost half of the sample work in the health service, while half of all arts therapists in the UK are art therapists.

Karkou and Sanderson (2006) shows how UK arts therapy definitions have changed over the years between 1989 and 2004. Waller (1998) also refers to changing definitions for art therapy in a European context, as do Bruscia (1998) and Wigram et al. (2002) on a worldwide basis for music therapy. The current UK definitions provided on the professional association websites are:

- *British Association of Art Therapists* (BAAT website). Art therapy is the use of art materials for self-expression and reflection in the presence of a trained art therapist. The art therapist is not primarily concerned with making an aesthetic or diagnostic assessment of the client's image. The overall aim of the practitioners is to enable the client to effect change and growth on a personal level through the use of the art materials in a safe and facilitating environment.
- *British Association for Dramatherapists* (BADth website). Dramatherapy has as its main focus the intentional use of healing aspects of drama and theatre as the therapeutic process. It is a method of working and playing that uses action methods to facilitate creativity, imagination, learning, insight and growth.
- *Association for Dance Movement Psychotherapy UK* (ADMP UK website). Dance movement therapy is the psychotherapeutic use of movement and dance through which a person can engage creatively in a process to further their emotional, cognitive, physical and social integration.
- *British Society for Music Therapy* (BSMT website). There are different approaches to music therapy. Fundamental to all approaches, however, is the development of a relationship between the client and the therapist. Music making forms the basis for communication in this relationship.

The changing definitions reflect an ongoing debate within the professions about whether or not arts therapies are primarily forms of psychotherapy or artistic modalities (Karkou and Sanderson 2006). Inter-arts modality comparisons (Karkou and Sanderson 2006) show that art therapists place a particular emphasis on psychoanalytic/psychodynamic theoretical underpinnings in comparison with music therapy and dramatherapy; dance movement therapists and dramatherapists value the humanistic framework more in comparison with music therapy, and dramatherapy emphasises the humanistic orientation more than art therapy. Dramatherapy emphasises artistic/creative practices more than the other arts therapies. The eclectic/ integrative approach is relevant to all arts therapies, but not as important for music therapy.

Dramatherapy and destructiveness

This book is a modest attempt to explore the phenomenon of destructiveness as it arises and is worked with in the dramatherapeutic encounter.

Given that the practice of dramatherapy, as highlighted in Karkou and Sanderson's (2006) research, is best described by the majority of its practitioners as drawing on humanistic and psychodynamic traditions, creative process-based and eclectic/integrative, the contributions to this book and the overall editorial style aim to reflect such a stance. Many authors in this field also draw explicitly on psychoanalytic and systemic frameworks, so that the term 'eclectic/integrative', as identified by Karkou, appears to be the appropriate stance to adopt. Contributors examine the phenomenon within its philosophical, cultural and clinical contexts, with the aim of producing a body of practice-based evidence that documents the challenges and possibilities faced by the dramatherapist when working with clients who are seen as destructive to themselves and others. The first three chapters identify existing and emergent thinking and practice in the field from cultural theory, psychotherapy and arts therapies perspectives.

Thus, in the opening chapter the editors consider ways in which different strands within cultural and psychotherapeutic thought construe destructiveness, and posit an alternative arts-based view based on the aesthetics of destructiveness and its multilayered relationship to artistic creativity.

Phil Jones (Chapter 2) explores dramatherapists' accounts of their encounters with destructiveness and creativity. Utilising a discourse analysis approach, Jones considers both how dramatherapists articulate their work in this field and how they attempt to frame and/or explain the effectiveness of such work.

Ditty Dokter, in Chapter 3, discusses the practice-based evidence/ evidence-based practice issues when attempting to develop and document clinical work. She goes on to detail the current state of the evidence base in relation to arts therapies and dramatherapy interventions with client groups who demonstrate levels of destructiveness.

The subsequent chapters explore ways of working with destructive potential in relation to specific clinical areas or particular presenting problems. In Chapter 4, Ramsden looks at working in a primary school with young boys who have been identified with emotional and social behavioural needs and for whom intergenerational trauma can be played out in the dramatherapy space. In Chapter 5, Zeal presents working in a pupil referral unit with adolescents whose challenging behaviour has resulted in their exclusion from mainstream schools. Dokter's Chapter 6 focuses on the self-harm of a 17-year-old young woman with the emerging presentation of borderline personality disorder (BPD), whilst engaged in treatment in therapeutic community-based arts therapy groups. Jackson continues on the theme of self-harm, but in the setting of working with severe and profound learning disabilities; in particular, she interviews dramatherapists to ascertain their differing views on the meaning of self-harm. Zografou works in private practice with a group of adults who are members of Narcotics Anonymous. She employs the 'hero's journey' (Rebillot 1993) to explore resistance and hope in recovery from substance misuse. Seebohm goes on to explore the concept of being held hostage in the therapy space of a forensic setting, the hostage being either the therapist, the medium or the feelings of the patient. She maintains that the challenge is to keep possibilities alive through creative play and thinking. She also suggests that when this has been temporarily suspended through manifest destructiveness in the dramatherapy space, the supervisor might be the only one left to help free the hostage. Thorn explores the theme of race as a dramatherapist working with a black female patient in a forensic medium-secure setting and how this is both organised by and organises the wider staff team. She describes an extended assessment process and refers to her countertransference, linking it to theoretical material to show her individual client's struggle in making an attachment. McAlister explores the role of symbolism in a dramatherapy group of particularly resistant patients within a forensic setting. She advocates supporting the recovery of symbolic processes to help psychotic patients in the treatment of both offending behaviour and mental illness. The clinical chapters end with Pete Holloway's description of a specific framework (using a dramatherapy approach informed by psychodynamic observation and existential theories) when working with suicide survivors.

In Chapter 13 the editors draw together the themes that have been explored in the clinical chapters, in order to demonstrate some of the ways in which dramatherapy practice can keep open the possibility of creative responses to destructive presentations. This culminates in an invitation to dramatherapists, and other professionals with whom they collaborate, to grow their confidence in terms of reporting on and evaluating the work they are doing in this field, and to make their own contribution to the evidence base.

Acknowledgements

This introduction would not be complete without us stating our enormous gratitude to the individual contributors, who manage to develop innovative practice and keep open creative possibility in the face of, at times, overwhelming despondency, fear and pessimism – on the part of their institutional settings, as well as that experienced and expressed by their clients. We are similarly indebted to the foresight and determination of the British Association of Dramatherapists and its Chair, Madeline Andersen-Warren, in commissioning the Evidence-Based Practice Research Project, which has helped to underpin the rationale behind this book. We express enormous appreciation for the tireless efforts of David Tatem and Richard Seebohm, who helped to bring the final document together. However, most gratitude is reserved for the clients themselves, whose courage and creativity in enduring and surviving external destructiveness, and learning to tolerate, mediate and contain their own capacity to destroy, is a tribute to a simple, yet profound and essential, humanity.

Part I

DESTRUCTIVENESS AND DRAMATHERAPY

1

UNDERSTANDINGS OF DESTRUCTIVENESS

Pete Holloway, Henri Seebohm and Ditty Dokter

> Destruction, hence like creation, is one of Nature's mandates.
> (Marquis de Sade)

Brief overview of chapter

This first chapter aims to explore historical and contemporary constructions of the phenomenon of destructiveness as it is manifested in the psyche and in wider culture. The chapter will provide a critical commentary on psychodynamic, cultural and artistic perspectives in an attempt to develop a lens through which the subsequent clinical chapters may be viewed and appraised.

Introduction

'Destructiveness' as a word – a linguistic signifier of socially constructed and culturally negotiated meanings – has an apparently straightforward denotation, thus:

1. The quality of destroying or ruining.
2. (psychology): the *faculty* supposed to impel to the commission of *acts* of destruction; propensity to destroy.
   (Online Medical Dictionary 1998; www.mondofacto.com)

Were we to interrogate the word a little further we would see that 'destruction' (according to Webster's English Dictionary) is defined as:

> The act of destroying; a tearing down; a bringing to naught; subversion; demolition; ruin; slaying; devastation.
> (Webster 1913)

9

And 'to destroy':

> To damage something so badly that it does not exist or cannot be used.
>
> (Cambridge Online Advanced Learner's Dictionary 2008)

When we start to think, however, about destructiveness as it manifests itself in *experience* and *behaviour*, we see a much wider multiplicity of connotations than these relatively straightforward definitions indicate. Thus, there are indeed destructive forces and acts of destructiveness – such as tsunamis, earthquakes, terrorist attacks and successfully executed murders and suicides – that do 'damage something so badly that it does not exist or cannot be used'; but there are also other acts of destructiveness which damage, maim and traumatise without resulting in the complete destruction of the recipient, and indeed other manifestations of destructiveness which remain in the darker phantastical recesses of our psyche, barely causing a ripple on the surface of our intentional behaviour.

For the purposes of this chapter, and the clinical discussions which follow, it may be more accurate to define 'destructiveness' not by its *effect*, but by its internal momentum. Thus, a typhoon, for example, has such momentum of destructiveness independent of whether its course takes it through a building. Similarly, the destructive potential of the human psyche has an internal energy regardless of its effect if and when enacted upon the external world. However, in some of the clinical discussion which follows such destructiveness has resulted in real catastrophic effects, such as arson, homicide and suicide; but in others of the clinical settings discussed it is the immanent energy of destructiveness that carries potency, rather than the actuality of destructiveness having totally obliterated something.

We will therefore consider 'destructiveness' as primarily a *propensity* within the psyche, and within relationships between people. This propensity may at times be clearly manifest in acts of aggression, violence and verbal abuse; at other times this propensity may inform, or drive, our external behaviour but is not necessarily directly expressed as a destructive act, such as sulking, boredom or withdrawal. In other contexts such energy may bubble away at a truly subterranean level – experienced as far too potent and toxic by the individual to be ever given vent – and what we may see on the surface is a 'passive-aggressive', overly-compliant or completely dissociative response to the external world.

Seen thus, as an internal energy or driver of external behaviour, we may attempt to locate destructiveness exclusively within the Freudian notion of 'the death instinct', later referred to as *Thanatos* by Freud's successors (Jones 1957: 295). Many theorists and commentators have discussed the human being's potential for, and enactment of, destructiveness through just such a psychoanalytic frame.

Psychoanalytic understandings: destructiveness and the death instinct

The psychoanalytic tradition suggests that although the most recognisable form of aggression is violence towards self or other, unconscious aggressive processes also find many disguises and may emerge through treatment as underlying phantasies. This is explored more fully by Perelberg (1999) in her chapter 'A core phantasy in violence' in *Psychoanalytic Understanding of Violence and Suicide*. In the first chapter to her book, 'A review of the literature and some new formulations', Perelberg states:

> . . . the term 'aggression' has been used to cover a wide variety of behaviours, from self-assertion to destructiveness. The various theories of aggression cover the plurality of psychoanalytic formulations, from drive theories to ego psychology and object relations theories.
>
> (Perelberg 1999: 20)

The drive theories that Perelberg is referring to begin with Freud, who believed that the human condition was made up of a set of 'drives' that were mobilised by either the 'libidinal instinct' (*Eros*), whose direction was towards life, or the 'death instinct' (*Thanatos*), whose aim was the extinction of life in order to reach '*Nirvana*', essentially, destruction of the self (Freud 1920). He asserted that it is the fusion and/or de-fusion of these two instincts in operation – the struggle between them – that lies at the root of all mental conflict. The 'death instinct' came from Freud's struggle to understand the human compulsion to repeat destructive patterns and it helped him to contextualise the resistances and negative therapeutic reaction in the analysis. Freud came to believe that aggression could be coupled with both of these 'drives', and saw that aggression had the potential to be both healthy and destructive: healthy in the context of being an impetus towards maturity and sexual expression, and destructive when assigned to the self-preservation instincts, particularly in a hatred of anything that was perceived to threaten the equilibrium of the psyche. Aggression, when applied to the 'death instinct', inevitably manifested itself destructively towards others and the self (Harding 2006: 6).

Melanie Klein developed ideas about the death instinct from her clinical experiences of children who presented a constant struggle between destroying and preserving their 'objects'. Comparable to the life and death instincts, the life-sustaining state of the psyche is *the depressive position* and the psyche's tendency to disintegrate is *the paranoid schizoid position*. For the healthy development of infants, they need to move from one position to the other, from the *paranoid schizoid position* to the *depressive position*, although the residue of each position is retained and can be returned to at various points in life.

When the infant is in the *paranoid schizoid position*, Klein believed that terrible anxieties are experienced, which threaten annihilation (Klein 1946). In order to defend against these feelings, a 'splitting' takes place, during which:

> . . . part of the death instinct is projected into the external object, which hereby becomes a persecutor, while that part of the death instinct, which is retained in the ego, turns its aggression against the persecutory object.
>
> (Klein 1946)

Rosenfeld adds that at the same time:

> . . . the life instinct is also projected into external objects, which are felt to be loving or idealized . . . the idealized and the bad persecuting objects are split and kept wide apart . . . simultaneously the splitting of the self into good and bad parts takes place. These processes of ego splitting also keep the instincts in a state of defusion.
>
> (Rosenfeld 1971)

Projective identification takes the projection process one step further, where unwanted aspects of the self are not just projected onto, but *into* the external object. In projective identification the individual enables the other person to feel (emotionally/physically) the feelings which s/he cannot tolerate to bring into consciousness (Jenkyns 1996).

In looking at the literature, it is possible to see that some psychoanalysts adopt the 'death instinct' as an integral part of what informs them theoretically, whilst others, such as Robert Royston, suggest that the death instinct should be viewed with suspicion and used only as a metaphor. He describes it as 'a necessary fiction' and concludes:

> Even if there is constitutional destructiveness, another level exists. Here destructiveness operates powerfully and its original impetus towards self-damaging behaviour comes from toxic experiences with caretakers.
>
> (Royston 2006: 36)

Towards attachment theory: destructiveness and development

Winnicott would agree with Royston's argument that the 'abusive or negligent childhood object' is the source of toxicity. He traced most origins of clinical manifestations of destructive tendencies to emotional deprivation in infancy and early childhood. In developing Klein's idea of object relations, Winnicott saw aggression as something that we are born with. However, he departed from Klein in that he viewed aggression as a way of defining what is self and not self. He saw it as representing the dramatisation of inner reality, which is experienced as too bad to tolerate. When children have no space in their personality for containing the aggression and destructiveness, their capacity for playing is replaced by acting out (Winnicott et al. 1984). By acting out the destructive role, the control that they are unable to find internally will be enacted by an external authority. In this way, Winnicott believed that a delinquent act was the expression of a desire to return to the moment of deprivation in an attempt to experience the good object providing external control and security.

In her book *From Pain to Violence*, De Zulueta welcomes the break that attachment theorists made from a theory based on instincts to one based on relationships. She describes the Freudian instinctual theory as 'untenable' (De Zulueta 2006: 120), although she begrudgingly acknowledges a need for it to be understood. She places object-relations theory as the founding platform for attachment theory and, in keeping with Winnicott's view, emphasises that 'the experience of deprivation of our basic attachment-related needs leads to destructiveness' (De Zulueta 2006: 54). In her review of psychoanalytic theory, she pays particular attention to Fairbairn, who openly rejected Freud's instinct theory, believing that the human is 'essentially object-seeking, that is to say relationship-seeking, and not pleasure-seeking' (De Zulueta 2006: 128).

When looking at different attachment patterns, in particular disorganised attachments, De Zulueta relates the 'splitting' identified above as seen in people suffering from a range of dissociative disorders ranging from borderline personality disorder to dissociative identity disorder (De Zulueta 2006: 97). Skogstad, who works with people with severe personality disorders (SPD), identifies that these patients tend to use action instead of thought, actively getting rid of thoughts or feelings that are experienced as too painful by violently projecting them outwards. He asserts, as cited by Welldon:

> . . . more often than not these actions are of an aggressive and destructive kind. Many patients turn their destructiveness towards themselves and their own bodies, which they cut, burn, bleed, starve or overdose. Others turn their destructive action towards other people and become, as offenders, abusive, sadistic or violent. Some do both.
>
> (Welldon 1988)

A recurring theme from such attachment-based theorists is that destructiveness is not so much the expression of an innate drive, more

13

that it has its genesis in failures of the attachment figure or primary-care giver to contain, mediate or de-toxify aggression and frustration in the developing child. Alternatively, the experience of profound neglect or trauma at the hands of the external world may also result in the developing child's inability to ameliorate its own aggressive responses. The context of destructive phantasy and behaviour subtly shifts within this theoretical perspective from one which is purely internal to become a relational phenomenon.

In their research conducted over the last decade, Fonagy et al. have attempted to close the circle between external experience and the internal working of the brain and functioning of the psyche, by linking attachment experiences with the neurochemical development of the brain. Their research suggests that disruptions in attachment have a profound developmental effect on the internal communication pathways of the brain as an organ, as well as on the psyche as a relational entity. Thus they have discerned, through sophisticated neuro-imaging techniques, significant changes at the level of receptor cell sensitivity and response to certain neurochemicals. This, in turn, they suggest, affects the individual's ability to mentalise, by which they mean reflect upon, process and digest relational interactions and emotional responses. They conclude that much aggressive, destructive and 'anti-social' behaviour is prompted by failures in the ability to mentalise 'affectivity', which Fonagy et al. (2002: 15) define as 'the capacity to connect to the meaning of one's emotions'. Their research also suggests, however, that positive therapeutic relationships may in turn help to remedy and rebuild some of the disruptions in neural communication pathways and hence develop a capacity to mentalise.

The 'problem' of destructiveness

Common to all the commentators and theorists discussed so far is the sense that destructiveness *per se* is an essentially negative force, construed as a problem of human existence, whether it is borne of a failure of the ego and super-ego to regulate innate drives, a failure in the internal world to build object constancy around a 'good enough' introject, or a failure in neurochemical and synaptic development. In such psychoanalytically-influenced epistemology, then, destructiveness is seen primarily as an undesirable, primitive phenomenon which should be 'regulated', 'developed beyond' or 'treated away'. There is, however, another tradition inspired by the writing of Jung, which, although it had its roots in the early psychoanalytic movement, made a significant break with its intellectual progenitors and spawned 'analytical psychology'. Jungian and 'post-Jungian' (Samuels 1985) theories illuminate a subtly different, yet significant, perspective on the phenomenon of destructiveness.

14

Analytical psychology: Jung and the Shadow – towards integration

It is not our intention to revisit the theoretical and technical disagreements that gave rise to the hotly contested schism in early psychoanalysis – this has been authoritatively discussed elsewhere by commentators such as Samuels et al. (1997). Rather, we focus our discussion on Jung's notion of 'the Shadow' archetype, its relationship to the 'collective unconscious', and Jung's proposition that it is only by integrating 'Shadow' material that the psyche can achieve 'individuation'.

Jung's simplest definition of the 'the Shadow' is that personified structure of the psyche which contains 'the thing a person has no wish to be' (Jung CW16, 1966: para 470). He contrasts this with his own concept of persona: 'what oneself as well as others thinks one is' (Jung CW9 1975: para 221) and develops his definition thus:

> The Shadow is that hidden, repressed, for the most part inferior and guilt-laden personality whose ultimate ramifications reach back into the realm of our animal ancestors.
>
> (Jung CW9 1975 ii: para 422)

Jung, like Freud, saw the evidence at play in the unconscious of destructive impulses and instincts, but as well as viewing such a propensity as intrinsic to the personal unconscious, Jung proposed that it was also formed and informed by the collective, ancestral and transpersonal unconscious – that sum total of human evolutionary experience which leads us towards combativeness, defensiveness, fear of 'the other' and of the external environment. For Jung this potential destructiveness is (to borrow a phrase from Irvin Yalom) a 'given of existence' (Yalom 1980: 5). In and of itself such potential is morally neutral and essentially inert. It is only through the active psychic mechanisms of repression and projection that its potential finds a devastating realisation. Once repressed, and confined to 'the Shadow', destructiveness or – as Jung refers to the phenomenon in a number of his post-World War II writings – 'evil' (Jung 2002) appears to draw nurture from the darker recesses of our unconscious and grow in its latent potency:

> We should, so we are told, [avoid] evil and, if possible, neither touch nor mention it. For evil is also the thing of ill omen, that which is tabooed and feared. This attitude toward evil, and the apparent circumventing of it, flatter the primitive tendency in us to shut our eyes to evil and drive it over some frontier or other . . . But if one can no longer avoid the realization that evil, without man's ever having chosen it, is lodged in human nature itself, then it bestrides the psychological stage as the equal and opposite

partner of good. This realization leads straight to a psychological dualism, already unconsciously prefigured in the political world schism and in [the] even more unconscious dissociation in modern man himself.

(Jung 2002: 109–110)

The real potency of such primitive material that we have banished to the confines of 'the Shadow', however, lies in its expression though the mechanism of projection – the capacity to hate in others that which we find intolerable within ourself. For Jung, and the post-Jungian theorists he gave rise to, the demonisation of other cultures, beliefs and practices becomes a repository for our hatred of that which lurks below the surface of our own psyche. The more we repress and deny our own capacity for destructiveness, the more magnified and vilified it becomes in others and, therefore, the more it needs to be countered, attacked and destroyed – which results in the interpersonal and international enactment of destructiveness.

Jungian and other psychotherapists have occupied themselves with the group psyche and its potential destructiveness, moving from the individual dynamic to the wider international dynamic of human relatedness. Jung equated war and revolution as an expression of group psychological pathology:

To a quite terrifying degree we are threatened by wars and revolutions which are nothing other than psychic epidemics. At any moment several millions of human beings may be smitten with a new madness, and then we shall have another world war or devastating revolution. Instead of being at the mercy of wild beasts, earthquakes, landslides, and inundations, modern man is battered by the elemental forces of his own psyche. This is the World Power that vastly exceeds all other powers on earth.

(Jung CW10 1964: para 71)

Storr (1991) sees this order of cruelty and destructiveness as specific to the human species and points out how it requires the operation of the imagination:

To be able to see fellow human beings as wholly evil, as possessing magical powers for harm, as being both despicable and dangerous, requires an imaginative capacity not present in other species . . . our innate discontent with what is . . . compels a resort to imagination to invent something better. Imagination knows no limits. Man's greatest achievements, in the arts and sciences, depend upon his imagination. But what can be used for good can also be used

16

for evil. Men are irresistibly attracted by fantasies in which reason
is abandoned.

(Storr 1991: 137)

Storr points out that we long for simplicity in a complex world, but that
this simplification may lead us to split the world into good and evil, seeing
Freud's *Eros* and *Thanatos* as one manifestation of this split. He warns that
when the world is divided between sheep and goats, what happens to the
goats is usually horrible. Others, such as Hillman (2004), however –
quoting from Shakespeare's *Julius Caesar* – also remind us that within our
collective psyche we possess a vicarious fascination for such 'horrible
outcomes':

> *Domestic fury and fierce civil strife*
> *Shall cumber all the parts of Italy*
> *Blood and destruction shall be so in use*
> *And dreadful objects so familiar,*
> *That mothers shall but smile when they behold*
> *Their infants quartered with the hands of war;*
> *All pity choked with custom of fell deeds:*
> *And Caesar's spirit, raging for revenge,*
> *With Ate by his side come hot from hell,*
> *Shall in these confines with a monarch's voice*
> *Cry 'Havoc' and let slip the dogs of war. . . .*
> (Shakespeare: *Julius Caesar*: Act 3, Scene 1)

Group analysis and the anti-group: towards a dialectic of destruction and creation

In the formative stages of group analytic psychotherapy, in the shadow of
World War II, its early practitioners (Bion 1961; Foulkes 1964; Yalom
1995) preoccupied themselves with the healing aspects of groups after
collective trauma. It is only more recently that destructive aspects in group
psychotherapy have been highlighted (Nitsun, 1996) and linked to the
potential for creative development. The benefits of groups in overcoming
individual trauma have not been supported by empirical evidence (Johnson
et al. 1999; Vardi 1999). This problematic lack of clear evidence of effectiveness has been connected to the severity of the trauma endured (Nicholas
and Forrester 1999; Solomon 1992) or to the homogeneity of the group
composition. A homogeneous group can be validating and containing
(Barnes et al. 1999) and perceived as compassionate and safe (Rozynko and
Dondershine 1991), but the more homogeneous and cohesive a group is, the
less room is allowed for individual expression and the more pressure for
denial, repression and projection of anything outside the group consensus

(Weinberg et al. 2005). It is more difficult to recover from traumas inflicted on one's group of belonging (Rouchy 1995) by another group, because traumas inflicted by others often involve unspeakable acts or omissions by fellow humans that are humiliating and act as a threat to one's individual and group identity (Rice and Benson 2005). However, a group may re-empower itself, even if the individual cannot. Freud (1895) noted 'over-determined' symbolic events in an individual's history; Volkan (1997, 1999) names the group equivalent as 'chosen traumas', where the large group chooses the trauma encapsulating the group experience, giving it meaning and group identity. A key dynamic of a 'chosen trauma' is the experience of humiliation and shame that leads to the experience of impotent rage and the desire for revenge, inflicting humiliation on others in turn and creating a shame–rage cycle. Frequent defences against the shame of helplessness, rejection or inadequacy are rage and aggression. The transgenerational effects of such traumas have been noted by many (Benson 1995; Goertz 1998; Volkan et al. 2002). Rice and Benson (2005) note that adequate grief and mourning are crucial within the collective experience of trauma, as they can reduce projections of destructiveness onto 'others' outside of the group.

Nitsun (1996), however, argues that the potency of 'destructive' feelings within the therapeutic group, such as shame, humiliation, rejection, rage and aggression, are not simply to be wished away or 'purged'. He compellingly argues that such dark forces constitute an 'anti-group' within the group's representation of itself which, through a truly dialectical process, forces the group to address and find creative solutions to those dark experiences of humanity which are otherwise all too easily projected into 'the others' or 'the outsiders'. For the group therapist (according to Nitsun), revealing and negotiating this dialectic between 'pro-group' and 'anti-group' becomes akin to an aesthetic task:

> I believe that art is meaningless without some confrontation with the dark side; similarly that the group experience is incomplete and likely to be superficial without such recognition. Holding together the constructive and the destructive potential is a major require-ment of the group therapist, as I believe it is in the artistic process . . . Sometimes the tension between the two is very great, even unbearable, but usually there comes a point of reconciliation, of synthesis, and a new form emerges. I believe this is also what happens in the group. At every moment the dialogue forms and reforms itself and within this, creative and destructive forms emerge side by side. Eventually, an understanding, an insight, a change, is achieved. Openness to the process is the creative gift of the group analyst to the group – and the gift of the group to the analyst.
>
> (Nitsun 1996: 99)

The developing lens: summary of discussion

As we have developed this synthetic review of understandings of the phenomenon of destructiveness, we have attempted to move beyond a sense of destructiveness as a simply negative phenomenon set in opposition to human creativity and the instinct towards life. Thus we can see that early psychoanalytic thought, and certain strands within the perspectives that it has given rise to, may contribute greatly to our understanding of the internal energy of destructiveness as it operates within our psyche and manifests itself in our behaviour. As we have moved the frame, however, to encompass developments in attachment theory, we can see that there is also a relational aspect to the development of such propensity to destructiveness, rather than it being simply an innate 'negative' drive. Further, through the lens of Jung's Shadow and his idea of the collective unconscious, we can see that the capacity for destructiveness is part of the human condition, both in terms of the individual and in terms of our social interactions. We can also hear echoing over the decades Jung's invitation for us to truly own those destructive aspects of our personal and collective psyche (Johnson 1991), rather than to live in fear of their potency, whereby their capacity to haunt us in the dark recesses of our mind grows ever bigger. Jung posits the possibility of integrating these aspects of ourselves, rather than experiencing them as directly toxic, negative or ultimately completely destructive. Widening the lens further, we can see that from within contemporary developments in group analytic theory and practice, the entreaty is to acknowledge, tolerate and ultimately transform the destructive potential within groups, seeing it as a dialectical force, without which there can be no creativity, maturation and human development. With this in mind, we would now like to turn our gaze to the relationship between art, culture and destructiveness, in order to illuminate the third point of the triangle that exists between client, therapist and artistic medium.

> If it has been believed hitherto that the human shadow was the source of evil, it can now be ascertained on closer investigation that the unconscious man, that is his shadow, does not consist only of morally reprehensible tendencies, but also displays a number of good qualities, such as normal instincts, appropriate reactions, realistic insights, creative impulses . . .
>
> (Jung CW9 1975 ii: paras 422, 423)

The aesthetics of destructiveness

Anyone who has ever been drawn to the demolition of high-rise flats and cooling towers, or queued to see the latest film depicting ever grosser massacres, or played ever more realistic violent video games, knows that there is an aesthetic of destructiveness. More controversially, of course, are Stockhausen's (press conference, Hamburg, 16 September 2001) and Damian Hirst's (BBC News Online, 11 Sept 2001) descriptions of the planes crashing into the twin towers as an act of 'the greatest work of art that exists for the whole Cosmos' and 'visually stunning', respectively. We could hypothesise that such fascination with demolition, horror and brutal realism enables us in some way, as Yalom (1980: 6) suggests, to mediate the perilous nature of our existence; somehow reassuring ourselves that whilst destruction reigns around us, we survive. Such an observation, of course, does not just relate to created or man-made representations of destruction but also to our fascination with the destructive potential of the natural world. The coverage of tsunamis, earthquakes and volcanoes, in no matter how far-flung corners of the world, still captures a global audience and a significant charitable financial response, even in times of economic austerity, again, maybe, assuaging a sense that we are but a tremor away from obliteration: 'there but for the grace of God . . .', as well as providing an opportunity to demonstrate solidarity and a desire for reparation and rehabilitation in response to our fellow beings.

The reciprocal relationship between human experience and artistic representation is clearly a creative process whereby collective experience is mediated through artistic expression, the product of which then becomes part of our collective experience (McGrath 1996). The artistic expression is often one which contains within it the depiction and dramatisation of the destructive potential that surrounds us and is within us (Nitsun 1996). For the artist, in whatever form of artistic enquiry, it is almost as if there can be no act of creation without something being first destroyed, rendered obsolete or becoming 'passé'. If we consider that in each new artistic movement, as well as in each original piece of art work, something transcends that which already is, and is borne of a blank canvas, an empty space, a body in motion or the impulse of the body on an instrument, we can see, in a real sense, that artistic creativity, despite King Lear's categorical assertion (Shakespeare, *King Lear*, Act 1, Scene 1) really does enable 'something to come from nothing'. If, however, we look at the darker corollary of this, we may also discern that 'something' needs to be rendered 'nothing' before a new creative possibility emerges. Thus, as Williams (1971) argues, every epoch sees a struggle for hegemony between the dominant, emergent and residual cultural forces, often sharply focused on a deconstruction of the artistic and cultural endeavours that have gone before in order that a new movement can capture the zeitgeist, which then has its profound impact on not only *what* we see, but *how* we see it (Berger 2008).

This cycle of form (destruction/deconstruction and regeneration/reconstruction) takes us a very long way from the bipolar opposition of the life instinct versus death instinct and takes us closer to Nitsun's dialectical synthesis between creativity and destructiveness. So the experience of human destructiveness, be it born of desire or fear, can inform and be contained within the artistic image, as well as being concretised in the formal process of art-making. If this is true for art forms in general, when we consider the agglomeration of artistic media that exists in drama as a particular form of art, staging as it invariably does a dynamic conflict, then from farce to high tragedy we can see that the interplay of destructive forces and creative possibilities is at the very heart of the dramatic act. Not only do we see this in the classical tragedies of ancient Greece and Shakespeare, but also in more contemporary theatre writers, such as Edward Bond, Howard Barker and Sarah Kane. From Oedipus' terrible realisation of his 'crimes', through the vicious blinding of Gloucester, through to the stoning of the baby in its pram in Bond's 'Saved', the dramatist's (and by extension the audience's) gaze cannot but help to comprehend the destructiveness within and around human existence. Similarly, from the Greek comedies, through commedia del arte to Ayckbourn and Fo, the threat of impending chaos engulfing and subverting our best attempts to make order of our world is what drives the comic action. If, as George Bernard Shaw reputedly said, 'conflict is the essence of all drama', then drama as an art form, as a medium of making sense of our world, may enable us to better explore, contain and achieve a dialectical synthesis of the conflict between destruction and creativity.

Introducing arts therapies and destructiveness

Our aim now is to link our observations on the process of drama and art-making and its relationship to destructiveness with the earlier theories, which related to dyadic or formal group verbal psychotherapeutic processes. What the arts therapies bring in particular to the field, alongside the body of knowledge from psychotherapy, is the art-making process which, when applied by the arts therapist, becomes an actualisation of Winnicott's (1991) 'transitional space' in the form of the particular artistic medium.

This triad (client–therapist–medium) enables the opening of a direct avenue for creativity. The emphasis can be on the client responding to the opportunities, stimuli or challenges of three things: the relationship with the materials or expressive forms, the creative and therapeutic opportunity presented by the space and by the potential relationship with the therapist (Jones 2005). In any of these three arenas there is the potential for the 'reframing' (Watzlawick et al. 1974) or 'reconstruing' (Kelly 1955) of destructive impulses and experiences as expressions of the dialectic of creativity in action.

In contrast, verbal psychotherapy relies on a *narration* of experience and actions which may go beyond that frame (such as becoming emotionally overwhelmed, or overly withdrawn, or physically responding to distress), it is frequently construed as 'acting out' and can become a threat to the

21

Without fiction, therapy can be too overwhelming.

therapeutic relationship. Analysis practises 'suspended action' (Foulkes 1964) rather than direct action, or 'enactment'. Dokter (1988) hypothesised that dramatherapy and group analysis in their ways of intervention aim at different levels of thinking. Stamp (2008), in her reflections on containment in forensic dramatherapy supervision, also distinguishes this primary and secondary process thinking accessed through the arts. Dramatherapy uses symbols and actions as communication with primary process thinking, whilst both therapy models use words as communication, with the secondary process thinking. Bion (1967) distinguished between primary and secondary process thinking as two separate mental developments. In the development of thought it is necessary to go through preconceptions, conceptions and finally concepts; the latter have names and therefore thoughts attached to them. Bion links the development of thought with the ability to tolerate frustration. This is similar to Freud's notion of the reality principle as a crucial factor in developing the ability to think (Freud, quoted by Fenichel 1946). Anticipation of action becomes thinking proper and consolidates consciousness. In secondary process thinking, the reality principle demands the transfer from action to thinking, followed by verbalisation (Bion 1967). The inability to tolerate frustration destroys the development of thinking; the thought becomes a bad object to be evacuated. In this primary process form of thinking there is a striving for discharge; there is no apparatus to anticipate action. It is a magical, archaic type of thinking represented by symbols (Fenichel 1946).

Acting out in the analytic sense can occur in both arts therapeutic and analytic treatment. The client repeatedly performs acts or undergoes experiences similar to past ones in an attempt to find belated gratification, or at least some relief from tension (Fenichel 1946). The group or individual is not able to recognise the experience in relation to its source – the past – or its repetitive character. The therapist often sees it as a resistance to reflection and thinking (Dokter 1994).

Within arts therapies in general, and dramatherapy in particular, the encouragement to simultaneously enact and narrate – 'to be actor and critic/director within the same chronological and corporeal frame of experience' (Holloway 1996: 138) – enables the destructive act, potentially, to be contained and reflected upon *within* the creative process.

2

CREATIVITY AND DESTRUCTIVENESS: A DISCOURSE ANALYSIS OF DRAMATHERAPISTS' ACCOUNTS OF THEIR WORK

Phil Jones

Brief overview of chapter

This chapter explores dramatherapists' accounts of their practice, as published in the literature, to examine what they reveal about *how* dramatherapists view the tension between creativity and destructiveness. It will identify what themes and issues emerge concerning their beliefs and experiences of creativity and its opposites. The chapter looks at the cultural context of such ideas in order to examine how these are reflected in the discourse dramatherapists engage in within their clinical accounts. Drawing on the practice of discourse analysis, the ways in which clinical encounters with clients are framed in terms of creativity and its opposites will be explored. The aim of this is to clarify what it is about creativity and its relationship to opposite states that dramatherapists see and value within their accounts of what is effective about their practice.

Introduction

One of the often-stated tenets of dramatherapy is that it draws on the benefits of creativity and uses the healing potentials of creative, artistic processes. One of the tensions within the literature concerns dramatherapists' accounts of clients in relation to creativity and destructiveness. Reports on clinical practice frequently feature a tension between clients who are initially seen as experiencing a dearth of creativity, or who express resistance to engagement with creativity in the therapy, and a later state where they are described as engaged and creative as the therapy progresses. This oppositional state is often described in ways that connect together withdrawal, distress, refusal and destructiveness within clinical accounts of dramatherapy (Jennings 1997; Johnson 1999; Jones 2005, 2007; Langley 2006). This tension – between a state of engaged creativity and a state of resistance, destructiveness or an absence of the creative – is something that is so common in the way therapists describe practice that we often take it for granted.

Discourse analysis and professional practice

Discourse analysis concerns 'the way in which meaning is constructed' within texts through the analysis of the language used (Woods 2006: xi). In her discussion of the uses of discourse analysis in examining the ways professions write, Woods identifies that 'every profession has its own way of speaking and writing: its own particular styles of language . . . and its own conventions for the construction of discourse' (Woods 2006: xvi). The discourse in the ways professionals write is seen to reflect attitudes, trans-actions and positions. Willig (1999: 2) adds to this idea, noting that 'there is always more than one way of describing something and our choice of how to use words to package perceptions and experiences gives rise to particular versions of events and reality'. Barker and Galasinski (2001: 65) echo this when they say 'discourse is a system of options from which language users make choices'. They talk about an approach based in the 'close analysis of discourse within specific texts whether spoken or written . . .' (Barker and Galasinski 2001: 62). This chapter examines dramatherapists' 'discourse'. It looks at the ways a selection of dramatherapists describe, respond and think about how dramatherapy is used by clients. It focuses on the par-ticular ways the therapists' discourse reveals how they see creativity and its opposites in relation to their work. The texts have been selected to reflect a range of encounters with contexts and client groups identified by a review of dramatherapy literature.

A review of literature: destructiveness and creativity

Destructiveness as negative, creativity as its opposite

There are two main ways in which destructiveness is often approached within literature in fields as diverse as psychoanalysis and learning theory, neuroscience and the arts. The first tends to encounter it as a *purely negative phenomenon*: the second sees it as more *complex and ambiguous*. This section examines these two frameworks as a way of understanding the cultural discourses of destructiveness within which dramatherapy operates.

Within the first approach, then, destructiveness is often positioned as something which has one meaning, is primarily, or exclusively, negative, and reflects problematic situations, encounters or experiences. Such analysis of destructiveness in humans has been undertaken from a number of fields, such as psychoanalysis, and its proposals concerning object relations or 'personality organisation' (Klein 1946; Kernberg 1976), cognitive neuroscience (Ward 2006) and political science and sociology (Guillén 2001). These disciplines, variously, often situate destructiveness in relation to phenomena such as being a negative part of instinctual drives (Livingston 1967), allied with evil in spiritual battle (Ellens 2004), as a problem in learning processes (Ellis 2001) and as reflected in violent, immoral political events (Fromm 1973). The following undertakes an analysis of examples of this negative positioning in order to propose *a cultural framework* to help understand what is often brought to the dramatherapy space, in theory and in practice.

Fromm, for example, powerfully reflects this singular meaning:

> The most ample – and horrifying – documentation for seemingly spontaneous forms of destructiveness are on the record of civilised history. The history of war is a report of ruthless and indiscriminate killing and torture . . . destruction in which neither conventional nor genuinely moral factors had any inhibitory effect . . .
>
> (Fromm 1973: 361)

Here Fromm creates interdisciplinary connections between psychoanalytic perspectives of sadism and object relations, social psychology and understandings of large group behaviour in order to engage in historical analysis. In *Neuropsychiatry and Behavioural Neuroscience*, Cummings and Mega (2003) frame self-destructiveness in relation to violence, behaviour and medication:

> Self-destructive behaviour may occur along with violence directed at others in any of the syndromes presented in the previous sections. In a few disorders, however, self-inflicted injury may occur as a prominent or even as the dominant behavioural disorder. In children with . . . autism, self-injury may occur in the course of head banging . . . Likewise, self-harm may occur as a result of some of the irresistible compulsive urges that occur in some patients with Gilles de la Tourette syndrome . . . The most important principle involved in the evaluation of the violent individual is that violent behaviour is rarely the result of a single circumstance. Rather, violent behaviour is the result of neurological, toxic, characterological, social, and situational factors that conspire at a point in time to produce a violent act.
>
> (Cummings and Mega 2003: 366–367)

Here the discourse of neuroscience sees destructiveness and violence as allied. They are presented in opposition to 'hope of successful treatment'

(Cummings and Mega 2003: 367) and the worker's positive, curative actions such as their investigation of areas of neurological history which may diagnose the production of these destructive phenomena. The treatment depends on 'a thorough investigation of all possible elements', including 'birth trauma, head injury . . . systematic illness, drug or alcohol ingestion' (Cummings and Mega 2003: 367). A part of the response to such destructiveness by Cummings and Mega is to list medication, which is seen to oppose and reduce the destructive, violent phenomena (Cummings and Mega 2003: 367–368). Here destructiveness is clearly placed as purely negative and as oppositional to the way neuropsychiatry is framed by the authors as curative and positive.

In all these examples from different fields, the discourses concerning destructiveness place it as clearly seen as purely negative, allied with individual and group violence, distress and illness. The discourses from the different fields involve actions which take the form of interventions designed to combat or eliminate it.

Destructiveness and creativity as complex and socially constructed

In contrast to this common way of seeing destructiveness and creativity, I am going to argue that it is useful to approach the concept of destructiveness *not* as something that has an absolute or singular meaning. If we see destructiveness as something that is constructed, and as having different, often conflictual meanings and significances, then this can help elicit the particular ways that dramatherapists and their clients reflect upon their experiences in therapy. Destructiveness becomes something that is constructed out of a number of different interacting perspectives and forces.

So, for example, destructiveness can be seen as something that might be constructed or experienced out of a combination of cultural, social and political ways of understanding. However, if we look at destructiveness in a way that allows more complex meanings and tensions, it can be seen as being in ambivalent tension within the process of art making, or as a close ally in a cycle of creativity – part of a creative cycle, the destroying of one set of ideas or forms to innovate or challenge by creating a new combination or way of expression. As Gerard (1952: 251) sees it in his writings about the biological basis of imagination, 'the dissonances of a mere generation ago are consonances to ears of today'. Differences within a culture, or between different cultures, might, in this way, see different creative ways of working as destructive. In addition, the context within which 'destructive' or 'creative' acts are being engaged with will also affect the ways we see them or encounter them. For example, as we will see in relation to acts such as dynamiting a shed, an act that takes place in a studio or theatre might be seen as creative, whereas the same act undertaken in a street might be seen as destructive and illegal.

From this perspective, destructiveness can hold more than one meaning or significance in any one encounter – depending on whose perspective you are looking at, or who is the dominant narrator or meaning maker in a situation. Grenier's curating of *Big Bang: Creation and Destruction in 20th Century Art* (2005) talked of the main role of contemporary arts as concerning destructiveness and creativity:

> As modern artists, such as Annette Messanger, increasingly confront the dark matter of these terrorised times – an artistic instinct – diverse movements of art . . . return to an essential understanding of creation and destruction, and the realisation of dark matter, the subject matter of today.
>
> (Grenier 2005)

So, for example, Cornelia Parker's *Cold Dark Matter* (1991) can be seen in this way. It involved the army using explosives to blow up a garden shed, which was then reconstructed and shown as part of a major exhibition at the UK's Tate Modern Art Gallery, with the following explanation:

> A terribly British institution, the shed functions as a place of refuge, a safe place, a place for secrets and fantasy. By blowing up the shed Parker is taking away such a place, throwing doubt on all it represents. Its contents are revealed, damaged in the process and yet somehow more eloquent. We get an 'exploded view' which creates a vast new space for our own mental activity.
>
> (Watkins, Director of Ikon Gallery, Birmingham, 1999)

> The challenge for me was to arrange the explosives in such a way as to achieve the disintegration of the shed (easy), while distressing and distorting as many of the items as possible without destroying them (more difficult) . . . I was stunned when some months later I walked into the Chisenhale Gallery and saw the final installation. The single light bulb, now in my mind representing the core of the explosion, threw out the debris that in turn projected dramatic shadows onto the stark white walls, floor and ceiling – such a powerful image. I had never considered modern art before, but if this was it, I was a convert.
>
> [Hewitt (Major, Senior Instructor, Army School of Ammunition) 1999]

This illustrates the ways destructiveness can be given different meanings. Here the complexity and ambiguity of destructiveness and creativity is shown: how the exploding of a shed in a non-art space would be illegal, in an arts space it is seen as creative. The examples of the discourses from different perspectives are included to show the importance of acknowledging this complexity: of the viewpoints of curator, army major and artist. The value of this way of exploration is that a phenomenon such as the 'destructive' can be seen as a part of different discourses or ways that we make meaning together out of phenomena we encounter. Destructiveness here is not viewed in a singular way – as negative – but as complex and as having different significances. By analysing these discourses we can try to look closely at what is experienced by people. We can also stand apart and try to look afresh at phenomena or ways of looking at things that we are so familiar with that we take them for granted. This approach tries to see what is happening by identifying the ways different discourses exist within the way professions or disciplines approach a phenomenon and what looking at the discourses can tell us.

The following shows that creativity, also, cannot be assumed to be always positive. As with destructiveness, it is important to recognise it as constructed, as dependent upon its context. Writing about theatre in Nigeria, Soyinka (1996: 341) argues that, rather than being inherently positive forces in society, drama and theatre can be allied to oppression and destructiveness. Culture, he observes, 'is always a primary target of assault by an invading force . . . its destruction or successful attrition reaches into the reserves of racial/national will on a comprehensive scale'. Drama interacts and is created in relation to its context and can be used by oppressor or oppressed in the development or destruction of a culture. Soyinka points out how the Christian Europeans set about the destruction of the live cultures of 'indigenous people' in a number of ways: the 'excesses of the Christian cultural imperialism, such as the embargo on African instruments and tunes . . . and the prohibition of drumming on tranquil Anglican Sundays' (Soyinka 1996: 349) and how they 'closed their churchyards and schools' to forms of drama that challenged their hegemony (Soyinka 1996: 350). He follows the development and evolution of drama, theatre, song and ritual produced by oppressed groups to the emergence of new forms, such as Duro Ladipo (Soyinka 1996: 354), which are a response to this attempted destruction. Here he shows drama to be part of complex forces concerning colonial destructiveness, but also to be a part of survival and the challenging of oppression: 'how certain creative ideas are the very offspring of historic convulsions' (Soyinka 1996: 354). He is illustrating the complex nature of destructiveness and creativity and that their meaning and relevance is constructed by the contexts they are a part of: that drama can be allied both with the destructive and oppressive and with the 'resistance and survival' of a culture or society.

This way of looking at destructiveness and creativity sees them as neither wholly positive nor negative, but as complex and defined by factors such as their context. It sees them as socially constructed. The approach illustrates the value of *not* giving a single meaning to destructiveness, for example, but instead looking at meaning as situation-specific, and of seeing it as express-ing and reflecting tensions and opportunities between different disciplines or power groups. This approach can be useful to look at dramatherapy's relationship to destructiveness. The next section will use this approach to look at the frameworks within which destructiveness and creativity are constructed in dramatherapy. What values do dramatherapists *bring* to their work concerning destructiveness and creativity? What value do they *put* on destructiveness and creativity?

The ways in which dramatherapists encounter destructiveness and creativity

The themes and tensions identified in the above review of literature will now be used to develop an analysis of published accounts of dramatherapy literature from journals and textbooks. The discourse analysis will aim to identify how dramatherapists conceive of the role of creativity and its 'opposites' in their understanding of change and benefit in dramatherapy. This is based on a review of literature from different approaches to drama-therapy (Anderson-Warren and Grainger 2000; Cattanach 1999; Emunah 1994; Holloway 1996; Hougham 2006; Jennings 1997; Johnson 1999; Jones 2005, 2007; Karkou and Sanderson 2006; Langley 2006; Milioni 2001; Pitruzzella 2004; Radmall 2001/2002). The literature has identified a number of different frameworks which are used to describe and understand change in dramatherapy (Jones 2005; Karkou and Sanderson 2006). The selection of accounts does not attempt to be exhaustive given the length of the chapter, but to represent three diverse elements of this: a developmental approach using the concept of embodiment–projection–role, myth method and role.

Generally, dramatherapists view creativity in *opposition* to the elements of difficulty or negative experiences that clients bring to therapy. A position is seen as 'difficult' or causing problems for the clients and drama is set up as in opposition to this.

From a developmental perspective, for example, they see creativity as an assisting force in balancing or counterforce to processes which have resulted in clients' problematic encounters or experiences with development (Cattanach 1999; Emunah 1994). So, for example, a developmental block may have occurred because a client has not been given appropriate support in making a developmental step or engaging with a developmental process. This might be due to their differences from a norm that is served by usual ways of a step being taken. So, for example, someone with a learning disability might not have available to them the appropriate means to enable their development. This negative effect of the absence of support is seen to have a destructive effect on their lives, and the creativity and language of drama and the client-centred space and relationship in dramatherapy are seen to offer a counterbalance to this. Hence, dramatherapy is positioned as oppositional to negative forces of a disabling society that does not provide appropriate process, language and empowerment. Similarly, processes of social exclusion that result in clients receiving prejudice are seen to be opposed by the combination of drama and therapy.

From a psychodynamic point of view, destructiveness is often allied to, or reflective of, unconscious anger or resulting affects, such as depression (Clarkson and Nuttall 2002). Here a dynamic relationship between the conscious, unconscious and language process and relationship of dramatherapy is often seen within a pattern or relationship building, processes of creativity and space to enable the encountering and working through of such a knot of negativity to arrive at a working with, working through and resolution (Jones 2005: 181; Langley 2006). Here destructiveness is seen to be allied with negative early relationships experiences and introjected parts of the self; dramatherapy is allied with a positive outcome, moving the client from self-destructiveness or destructive attitudes.

From a position of role work, the dramatherapy space, relationship and process is seen as part of expressing and relearning, so that negative or destructive roles are engaged with and reworked or resolved. Dramatherapy is here allied with learning and opposition to destructive patterns. Creativity is allied with cognition, thought and learning processes.

The following gives three specific analyses of the discourses of dramatherapists' accounts to understand the different ways destructiveness and creativity feature in the way they frame why and how their practice is effective. Each draws on the different relationships described above.

Discourse analysis 1: embodiment projection role (EPR)

The following excerpt is from a clinical account concerning a patient in a maximum secure hospital for the treatment of offender patients (Jennings et al. 1997: 84), diagnosed as living with paranoid schizophrenia and admitted to the hospital after killing his mother. The extract is from their conclusions about the dramatherapy's efficacy:

> Patient B illustrates a dramatherapeutic process through the stages of embodiment, projection and role. Whereas he struggled with physical prowess, nevertheless he gradually took more risks. He clearly identified with the disillusion as told in the story of Pinkie, and Pinkie, too, went on journeys as he had attempted to do as a young man. However, his journey had ended in frustration and eventual breakdown. It would seem that through the characters of Aegeus and Oberon he was able to address his violent rage, and importantly was able to be his angry father looking for a son to live up to his expectations. With Patient B there is a recurring

theme of leaves, on and off trees and on his mask. Leaves had taken on a diabolical significance during his offence, and it would seem that there was some normalisation of the leaves within the dramatised story and pictures . . . The clinical view is that the dramatherapy enabled him to accept inwardly the anger of his own father by putting himself in his father's place, i.e. by being father both as Aegeus and as Oberon. He was also able to explore and accept his own anger, something which had always been difficult. This process allowed him to find the inner strength to deal with his father's marriage to another woman.

(Jennings et al. 1997: 109)

Relationships between creativity, therapy and destructiveness can be seen behind the descriptions the therapists make of their client's use of drama-therapy. Two positions are seen within the the therapists' discourses about their perceptions of change. One concerns disillusion, difficulty breakdown, violent rage, legal offence and the diabolical. The other concerns develop-mental processes, expressing the previously unexpressed through creating roles and acting with them, addressing negative feelings connected with the client's offence of killing and to redress 'difficulty' in expressing and accept-ing his own feelings. Opposites are often constructed within this account. On the one side are the destructive, killing rage and held unexpressed feelings; on the other are creativity, expression, exploration and acceptance. For example, the client's breakdown and violent rage are framed by lost journeys ending in frustration and breakdown, whereas the creative work in dramatherapy is set up by opposition to these negative 'journeys': in the dramatherapy he 'finds' strength through the creative acts, he meets and encounters 'his own anger' in positive exploration.

Here we can see the kinds of oppositional constructs described earlier. On the one hand, destructiveness is set apart from creativity: it is seen as oppositional. However, these are not seen as *separate* states which cannot exist *together*. Analysis of the therapists' discourse reveals that the creative, therapeutic act is seen to be able to *engage* with the destructive: to find a language which can meet and express it. The therapists see dramatherapy as enabling the client to express what previously he had experienced as inexpressible about his destructive experience. Past destructive experiences are brought into the present of the dramatherapy processes of embodiment, projection and role. In this way the *destructive past* is connected with the *creative present* of the therapeutic space. This is seen to be linked to being able to explore what previously was unseen and unseeable. Patient B has previously been unable to 'express and accept his own anger' or, to phrase it differently, to explore and 'own' his anger. This is seen to be positive and curative. To summarise, whilst the destructive and creative are seen to be oppositional, the dramatherapy process and space allow for connection and a relationship between the two to occur. In this way the combination of the creative and the therapeutic can transform the destructive. This is connected to the creative therapeutic space being able to *represent, hold, explore and resolve* the destructive.

Discourse analysis 2: myth, symbol and the self-regulating psyche

Dramatherapists such as Lahad (1992), Silverman (2004) and Watts (1992) all draw on myth and narrative in discussing dramatherapy and efficacy. Watts, in her discussion of metaphor and myth in dramatherapy, for example, describes the process so that 'a sense of meaning' is created:

> . . . through drama, and especially perhaps through work with metaphor, we offer a vehicle for finding again and recreating that which was incomplete . . . communicating in an intelligible way that which could not be communicated before.
>
> (Watts 1992: 49)

Rawlinson (1996) describes her work with a client, Janet, living with depression and anxiety, in a way that reflects the discourse dramatherapists often bring to creativity and destructiveness in relation to this area of work:

> Janet continued working with the sandtray, which in turn stimulated the imagination, producing fragments of dream material, enabling her to begin to build bridges between the unconscious and conscious areas of her psyche . . . Janet discovered another way of expressing her anger and frustrations through the exploration of creative movement . . . she could both celebrate and mourn the essential aspects of the feminine that were lost for her.
>
> (Rawlinson 1996: 164)

Her rationale talks of the dramatherapist and client being 'required' to 'respect' images and links this to the role of art as mediating images that 'flow' from a source (Rawlinson 1996: 178) and which oppose destructive elements and experiences in a client's life. Hougham's (2006) rationale concerning how dramatherapy work that draws on myth is effective for clients also asserts the connection between myth as a container for 'eternal truths' that 'offer a "narrative form" for the unconscious' (Houghan 2006: 5–6). The aim of this work is 'to activate the self-regulation of the psyche of the patient through the opportunity to work with archetypal images and themes' (Houghan 2006: 5–6). The discourse in this second approach is less oppositional than the first. The 'destructive', in the form of problems and challenges, is balanced against acts of offering creative 'backdrops' and opportunities. A client such as Janet's individuality is set in contrast to a different level of awareness or being, described variously as 'archetypal', 'the human condition' or 'eternal' (Hougham 2006: 5–6). Rawlinson (1996) draws on an image that is often used in this kind of discourse in drama-therapy: the arts in therapy facilitate a positive 'building of bridges' between the archetypal and the individual. So, for example, individual problems and 'challenges' are seen to be transformed by contact with certain aspects of the creative and the 'psyche'. These aspects are frequently connected to what is described as the 'unconscious' and include myth or symbolic images. The *general* is offered within the creative, and this movement away from *individual* problems to meet a *broader* perspective is frequently cited in the discourse as essential to the therapeutic process. In Hougham's (2006) account we are given the idea of contact with a broad amplified 'matrix' beyond individual experience, a 'collective backdrop', the movement away from the 'personal' to the 'symbolic' and a space or 'world' away from the 'mundane' and the 'familiar'. Here creative activities are seen to move the client from one frame – that of 'problem' or 'challenge' – to this broader space or frame. The image of the creative arts as mover or bridge is used: drama and movement are 'natural' *carriers*; play, drama, improvisation and ritual enactment are '*bridges*' to a 'world' away from the mundane – that of 'symbol' (Hougham 2006). This inter-relationship between the general, archetypal and collective through creative processes is seen to offer transformation of the singular meaning (vs. 'multiple mean-ings'), the mundane and familiar' (vs. the 'innate qualities' of the archetypal and the world of the 'other'), and the problematic (vs. myth, story and fairy tale as the 'collective backdrop').

Here, then, the creativity in drama and movement is seen to form a bridge enabling access to the transformative potential of symbolic, arche-typal experience. The core of this is seen to offer the client access to the 'self-regulating psyche', which is beneficial and contrary to the problematic or negative experiences that bring the client to therapy. Again, we can see, at first, a seemingly oppositional state between the problematic or destruc-tive in the client or client's life and creativity, in a therapeutic framework, as offering health or resolution. As in the discourse of the first example, though, the relationship, once examined, is more complex than this. Here destructive elements of the client's life are changed or 'transformed' by creativity, but in this discourse the key relationship surrounds *access*. It is as if the arts create access to aspects of the client's 'psyche' that have previously been unavailable or inaccessible to them. This inaccessible arena is typified by the general, archetypal, group or collective and this is seen to take the form of symbolic expression through drama and movement. Once this access has been created through the creative process, then the *connection* is seen to be potentially able to resolve the problems or diffi-culties. In this discourse, then, the therapist sees the relationship between the destructive and the creative to be potentially therapeutic through a relationship of bridging or access from the particular and individual to a symbolic, collective and archetypal domain.

Discourse analysis 3: role

The following relates to role-based accounts of dramatherapy, and draws on two accounts of why role method is effective:

> Despite the archetypal, dramatic, social and genetic determining factors, human beings are still creators of their own identities, at least in part. George and Mackey in the many examples above were pictured as active players of their various roles, rather than passive takers of some predetermined substance. Implicit in dramatic playing is the sense of the player as creative. Even if roles are, to a large degree, predetermined, each individual must still choose those roles that are most appropriate to a given circumstance and most meaningful to that individual. Each role chosen and played must be done for a purpose, whether to survive, express a feeling, or meet a need. And each act of role taking and role playing is creative in the sense that one is building a piece of one's identity . . . (like children) . . . struggles with role lie the seeds of our struggles as adults who live on the other side of the looking glass but sometimes imagine what it would be like to venture forth again through that magical window.
>
> (Landy 2008: 10–11)

The clinical example of 'Sam' (Landy 1997) is an example of dramatherapy within this framework. The client is initially presented in the following way. His roles included a key figure that had been 'tortured, wounded in some extreme ways by external and internal forces . . .' and the therapist suggests exploring aspects of Sam's role 'system', for example, 'the murderous, exploitative father who is not what he appears, of women who are split into children, seductresses and aggressors, of bravery and fear, of gatekeeping and setting boundaries' (Landy 1997: 130–131). An analysis of the outcome of this approach to dramatherapy sees efficacy in the following way:

> I found that at the end of treatment Sam had discovered a way to integrate his many confusions and reconstruct a viable role system. For one, he returned to playing and composing music, reclaiming the artist role with commitment and confidence. He approached his ability as an artist with a healthy respect for his disability, accepting the possibilities of slipping into manic and depressive phases.

> The full rediscovery of the artist role led Sam 'to assert the creative
> principle, envisioning new forms and transforming old ones'
> (Landy 1993: 241). This principle would guide his recovery from
> not only an aesthetic crisis, but also a moral and spiritual one.
>
> (Landy 1997: 139)

In this third example of discourse analysis, role is seen to be central in forming a framework to enable the activation of particular aspects of creativity. Whereas in the second example creative access to the archetypal was seen to be at the heart of change, here the relationship is seen to be different. Creativity is actually set *against* the archetypal, as this is seen as a determining factor – allied to negative constricting forces, and the clients being 'passive takers' rather than active makers of their identities. Here the destructiveness is seen to be connected to this act of constriction and limitation. Creativity in the dramatic form of an individualistic taking of roles or playing is allied to a broader framework of creative living. Choice is seen to be central to creative living and to health and to the client as active creator of their own individual roles and identity.

The discourse sets apart the destructive, linking it with limiting and imposed roles and creativity connected to the client as 'player', the image of a 'builder' actively creating roles with a sense of their own 'purpose'. This is positively linked to survival, expression and the meeting of needs. Destructive role images of torture, wounding and murderous exploitation are set against a creative engagement and empowerment of the client as active meaning maker and role taker in their lives. Here the discourse contrasts the passive recipient of distorting and fragmented roles which are imposed on the client and which the client cannot integrate or find an active, creative response in their role repertoire to one where they are a creative, active player and builder. The relationship with destruction here sees role and creativity as at the core of well-being, and the role of the dramatherapy is to enable the client to express, explore and creatively improvise and extend their roles until they have a creative, flexible, 'fit' of their roles, rather than a destructive relationship with roles that they experience as distorting and ill-fitting.

Here creativity is not set against a destructiveness seen as a developmental process which can express, contain and transform destructive experiences, as in the first example, nor as something that provides a symbolic bridge to archetypal arenas which can be transformative. The relationship between the destructive and the creative here is one that sees role as the means of understanding destructive and creative forces in an individual's life: that drama can be a therapeutic means of enabling the client to become a more effective player. The qualities of the ways they negotiate their relationship with role are seen as a way of encountering destructive and creative forces in their lives. The therapy focuses on the way they can change how they handle the roles they inhabit in engaging with this mediation of the destructive and creative pressures they encounter.

Conclusions

Table 2.1 below presents some of the key ways in which the dramatherapy discourses analysed reveal the diversity of the ways they see the relationship between destructiveness and creativity in terms of efficacy.

On closer examination, then, none of these align themselves with the cultural perspective identified in the review of literature at the start of this chapter, which saw the destructive as having a singular, negative meaning.

Table 2.1 Dramatherapy discourses: destructiveness and creativity

Discourse example	Discourse of destructiveness and creativity
1. EPR	• Developmental processes expressing the previously unexpressed through embodiment, projective work and role creative therapeutic work addresses negative feelings connected with the offence of killing and to redress 'difficulty'
	• The destructive past is connected with the creative present of the therapeutic space
	• Dramatherapy process and space allows for connection and relationship between the destructive and creative to occur and for the creative to transform the destructive
	• The creative therapeutic space being able to represent, hold, explore and resolve the destructive
2. Myth and symbol	• Dramatherapy can offer mediating images and processes to engage with negative or destructive client experiences: these are located within the client's psyche, but are not accessible in ways that serve the client well
	• A relationship is facilitated between symbolic, collective material and the individual experiences of the client in a way that offers creative, transformative possibilities to destructive or negative life experiences, patterns or ways of seeing the self
	• The dramatherapeutic space and relationship offers access and connection, a 'bridge' with archetypal, collective material from within a 'self-regulating' psyche
3. Role	• Role as the means of understanding destructive and creative forces in an individual's life
	• Drama can be a therapeutic means of enabling the client to become a more effective player
	• Focus on the way therapy can change how clients handle the roles they inhabit in engaging with the destructive and creative pressures they encounter

The therapists do not concur with a cultural position that frames the act of therapy as in opposition to 'destructive'. They see destructiveness as complex and as constructed of different factors. Creativity is not seen as the opposite of 'destructiveness', but can be identified as a way of encountering, reframing and enabling dialogue between areas that are often positioned as opposites.

The value of this analysis is that it offers the field a sense of how creativity and destructiveness are seen, and illustrates how discourse analysis can assist in developing a critical awareness of how therapists understand the dynamics at work in making their practice effective for clients. The analysis has revealed the specific nature of these responses and has helped to articulate how dramatherapists see their work bringing benefit to clients in the domains of destructiveness and creativity. This examination of dramatherapists' discourse has shown the different ways destructiveness is constructed and the perceived value of creativity within dramatherapy in relation to destructiveness. The chapter has examined how dramatherapists see deficits of creativity, absences of creativity and opposition to creativity in their accounts of their work. In this way, the analysis has looked at how therapists conceive of creativity and its impact on clients. It has illustrated how therapists conceive of the role of creativity and its 'opposites' in their understanding of change and benefit in dramatherapy.

3

PRACTICE-BASED EVIDENCE: DRAMATHERALY AND DESTRUCTIVENESS

Ditty Dokter

Brief overview of chapter

This chapter introduces the debates around evidence-based practice and practice-based evidence in the arts therapies. It outlines the first stage of a systematic review of dramatherapy evidence commissioned by the professional association, and analyses the outcomes for dramatherapists working with manifestations of destructiveness. The phenomenon is considered in relation to particular client groups and settings, but also to clinical presentations, including violence against self and others. When appropriate, attention is given to particular dramatherapeutic interventions used. Gilbody and Sowden (2000) call for disciplines to define their own evidential standards, to make decisions about what constitutes 'good' or 'poor' evidence and which levels are appropriate for their discipline's research profile. In the chapter conclusion, the state of the art of the current evidence is evaluated. In the final chapter of the book, the editors revisit this evidence and make further recommendations for research to develop the evidence base for dramatherapy in this area.

Arts therapies evidence: an historical framework

The UK Department of Health introduced the Effectiveness Initiative in 1995. Its objective was:

> All health care staff to work together and in partnership with patients to increase the proportion of clinical services shown by evidence to be effective.
>
> (Davidoff et al. 1995)

Evidence-based practice (EBP) is characterised by a cycle of activities that seek to guarantee that all interventions are effective, based on rigorous research, and to ensure that services are delivered in the most efficient and economic way (Gilroy 2006). Its paradigm is contested, because EBP has created a situation where the methodology of the randomised control trial (RCT) is privileged as evidence above all others. The NHS hierarchy of evidence (Mann 1996: 16) rates:

A. RCTs.
B. Other robust or observational studies.
C. More limited evidence, but the advice relies on expert opinion and has the endorsement of respected authorities.

The Parry and Richardson (1996) review showed how EBP can be developed in the psychological therapies. Together with Roth et al. (2004), they showed how EBP research should be developed from clinical practice, but they do not include qualitative research. This has been critiqued by arts therapists (Gilroy and Lee 1995; Gilroy 2006; Jones 2005), but there is also an acknowledgement that:

> . . . art therapists have no choice but to engage with EBP, but . . . should do so in full awareness of the principles and policies that situate EBP in the UK public sector market place.
>
> (Gilroy 2006: 25)

Arts therapies do not yet have the critical mass of outcome research required by EBP. Various authors (e.g. Gilroy and Lee 1995; Payne 1993; Wheeler 1995; Aldridge 1996a; Smeijsters 1997) wrote about research methodologies potentially useful to arts therapists. Most of this literature concerned qualitative research written with the aim of describing and analysing arts therapies processes. Some arts therapists, the majority of them music therapists, did quantitative research. They published the controlled trials and correlational studies recognised as experimental research in journals such as *The Lancet* (Hoskyns 1982) and the *Journal of Rehabilitation* (Bolton and Adams 1983). Other researchers (Meekums and Payne 1993; Aigen 1995) advocated new paradigm research, allowing for subjectivity, participatory and holistic knowing and knowledge in action (Reason 1988). Gilroy and Lee (1995) stressed the necessity for outcome studies if arts therapists were to demonstrate that their work is effective.

The new paradigm critiqued traditional experimental research as divorced from the subject and the real world of the clinical environment (Meekums and Payne 1993). Single case study research (Smeijsters 1993, 1997; Aldridge 1993, 1996b) was offered as a viable alternative closer to the clinical environment and existing practice. Some single case study research-ers advocated the combination of quantitative and qualitative research methodologies to give wider evidence of effectiveness (Lewith and Aldridge 1993; Smeijsters 1997; Langenberg and Frommer 1994; Aldridge 2005).

A critical appraisal of arts therapies research needs to acknowledge that the evidence-based practice criteria of medicine's evidence hierarchies (Jones 2007; McLeod 2001) would exclude most of the available arts therapies research. Indeed, Roth and Fonagy (2005) did not include them, while Parry and Richardson (1996) only made a short reference to their existence. Several arts therapists discussed evidence-based practice-related concerns for arts therapies research (Gilroy 1996; Jones 2005; Edwards 1999; Grainger 1999; Wigram et al. 2002). Gilroy proposed an alternative for the evidence-based practice (EBP) hierarchy of evidence. She suggested that as criteria for inclusion, studies need to be relevant, effectiveness-oriented and methodologically rigorous.

Recent guidelines from the National Institute for Health and Clinical Excellence (NICE), such as the guidelines for schizophrenia, acknowledge arts therapies evidence, but more in the area of 'supportive' interventions (NICE 2008). There is also a passing reference in the borderline personality disorders guideline, when it refers to the use of combination therapy tailored to what engages the interest in creativity in individuals. The self-harm guidelines do not mention the arts therapies, as they focus on management rather than treatment strategies.

Evidence-based practice or practice-based evidence in the arts therapies?

Wigram et al. (2002: 261) identified which music therapy evidence is available in the EBP hierachical structure, but recognised that for many of these levels there is no evidence available. The majority of evidence is available in the last three categories (case studies, qualitative studies and expert opinion).

As mentioned earlier, Gilroy (2006) advocated a different hierarchy of evidence:

- Evidence from at least one RCT, or evidence from at least one controlled and/or quasi-experimental study.
- Evidence from other research, for example case studies, phe-nomenological, ethnographic, anthropological, art-based or collaboarative studies.
- Evidence from other academically rigorous texts.
- Evidence from expert committee reports or opinions, or clinical experience of respected authority or both.
- Evidence from local consensus or from user representatives.

(Brooker et al. 2005)

Gilroy argues that clinical governance is key; the secondary sequence of evidence-generating activities within the EBP cycle, where practitioners can demonstrate that the primary evidence from research and other forms of evidence are informing practice. Arts therapists can show they have engaged with the cycle if they have conformed to the criteria of evidence-based disciplines, because they will have:

- Adopted clinical guidelines for standard practice.
- Ensured that guidelines are informed by research and service evaluation.
- Specified the client groups for which the service is appropriate.
- Monitored the outcomes of innovative treatments.
- Audited the key elements of standard practice.

(Parry 1996)

Gilroy (2005) emphasises the need to synthesise art therapy's evidence base through systematic reviews. The aim of a systematic review is to articulate what art therapy's best evidence (its research, academically rigorous literature and expert practitoner and user opinions) says about different approaches with different client groups, according to explicit criteria and evidential levels devised by the profession.

BADth systematic review

The British Association of Dramatherapists (BADth) commissioned a research project aimed to address Gilroy's short-term strategy. This strategy aims to develop local and national processes to synthesise and articulate art therapy's research, knowledge and experience as represented in the literature and embodied in practice (2005). The BADth project aimed to do so by establishing regional groups to collate outcome measures currently in operation, but also to establish reading groups for critical review of the available literature. In order to complete a systematic review, the following steps were taken:

1. Definition of database topics.
2. Establishing expert panels on the topics, nominated by BADth.
3. Search of the literature (all published dramatherapy UK or English language literature), collated through expert panels, reading groups, regional groups and involving MA literature search material.
4. Critically review the literature in reading groups, using a standardised checklist (adapted from Gilroy 2005).
5. Compilation of systematically reviewed evidence into a database.

(Dokter and Winn 2009)

We looked at Parry's (1996) treatment choice in psychological therapies and counselling to identify the range of clients, such as depression and post-traumatic stress disorder (PSTD), as well as those excluded. The range was compared and contrasted with the employment patterns of dramatherapists (Dokter and Hughes 2007). To cover the main dramatherapy employment areas, it was decided to include clients with learning disabilities across the age range, children and adolescents in educational settings and separate mental illness in over 65s. The topics for inclusion thus became:

- Psychosis: adults.
- Personality disorder (including BPD): adolescents and adults.
- Addiction: adolescents and adults, including drug, alcohol and eating disorders.
- PTSD: all ages.
- Mood disorders: all ages.
- ASD/Asperger's and learning disabilities: all ages.
- Functional and organic disorders in clients over 65.

Dramatherapy and destructiveness: the state of the evidence base

The understanding of destructiveness in relation to these topics is particularly pertinent to the psychosis, personality disorders, addiction and PTSD evidence, many of which presentations overlap with research undertaken in forensic settings, and new evidence in these areas is included in this volume. For those areas where there is little or no evidence in the existing literature relating to dramatherapy and destructiveness, this volume aims to contribute to the evidence base. The mood disorders topic includes literature on child and adolescent education-based work with school-excluded young people and those labelled 'emotionally and behaviourally disturbed', and therefore relates to Chapter 5 in this volume. Similarly, Chapter 6 relates to new evidence in the field of self-harm in clients with learning disabilities. Destructiveness in the work with dementia sufferers will remain an area for further research, as there is currently too little evidence at the time of the systematic review.

Overview of evidence

In the area of destructiveness and psychosis the reader groups evaluated as best evidence (rated 8–10 on a scale of 10) articles by Ruddy and Dent-Brown (2007) and Yotis (2006) on schizophrenia, Casson (2004) on working with hearing voices and Grainger (1990, 1992) on thought disorder. Dramatherapists working with psychotic clients in forensic settings have found the work by Stamp (1998), Jennings et al. (1997) and Smeijsters and van Cleven (2006) extremely useful. Older research by Johnson (1980) and Nitsun et al. (1974) is also still judged relevant as evidence.

There is an overlap with the evidence for personality disorders in Jennings et al., Stamp and Smeijsters and van Cleven, as they work with mixed diagnostic groups. In the personality disorders review, additional evidence evaluated as excellent was work by Bergman (2001), Brem (2002), Dent-Brown and Wang (2004), Duncan et al. (2006) and Moffett and Bruto (1990). The last article overlaps with substance abuse in its evaluation of therapeutic theatre with personality disordered substance abusers. The addiction evidence only includes Moffet and Bruto as excellent in substance abuse and Dokter (1996) on eating disorders.

PTSD evidence applies mainly to work with children and adolescents, i.e. to the work with abused children (Bannister 2003; Herman 1997; James et al. 2005); Attention deficit hyperactivity disorder (Chasen 2005); effects of terrorist attacks (Lahad 1996; Long and Weber 2005; Haen 2005) and recovery from neurotrauma (McKenna and Haste 1999; Haste and McKenna 2010).

Psychosis

Returning to the reader group's evaluation of the psychosis evidence, Ruddy and Dent-Brown (2007) and Yotis (2006) provide recent reviews of the evidence for dramatherapy and schizophrenia. The Ruddy and Dent-Brown study illustrates the difficulties around EBP, when only RCT evidence is considered as evidence. The readers commented about the Ruddy and Dent-Brown study that it is based on a meta-analysis of existing RCT research in dramatherapy, psychodrama and social drama as it relates to work with schizophrenia and schizophrenia-like illnesses. The methodology of the review excludes all data not gathered from RCTs. Of the 183 research papers reviewed by the study, only five studies meet this criterion: one dramatherapy, one social drama and two psychodrama papers. Based on the dearth of available evidence and the differences in the five studies presented, the authors conclude that use of dramatherapy should continue to be evaluated, as its benefits are unclear. The paper presents a suggested design for future RCTs. The readers felt that the study was limited in practical application. Although it clearly details the methodology used in each of the five reviewed studies, it does not offer discussion of specific interventions.

Yotis (2006) discusses the hypothesis that creative psychotherapeutic approaches may risk further disorganisation of clients' thought disorders and emotional instability, as well as research advocating psychotherapeutic handling of the schizophrenic condition as a meaningful human experience (Silver and Larsen 2003). It is interesting to note that the existing dramatherapy research addresses these concerns: Johnson (1982a) practised and researched the use of role playing to establish clients' boundaries (Johnson and Quinlan 1985), as well as studying theatrical performance to address secondary symptoms of isolation and withdrawal (Johnson 1980). Other studies showed improvement in verbalisation and conversational skills (Spencer et al. 1983). These studies seem to have been adopted by NICE in their guidelines for schizophrenia (NICE 2008) when advocating the use of the arts therapies in the treatment of secondary symptoms. Grainger (1990, 1992) and Casson (2004) address primary symptoms, such as thought disorder and hearing voices. Grainger's research (1990) highlights the use of dramatherapy to improve cognitive structuring of reality, while Yotis' doctoral research focused on the use of theatrical performance for clients with schizophrenia to improve interpersonal relationships and verbal processing (Yotis 2002). Casson's research (2004) focused on the primary symptom of hearing voices and construing these as part of the meaningful experience of the schoziphrenic condition.

Yotis' (2006) review advocated a mixture of quantitative, qualitative and theatre-based methodologies, while Ruddy and Dent-Brown delineated the RCT methodology, both very useful for further dramatherapy research in this area. The Yotis article was scored higher by the profession in its usefulness to application with clients, as was Casson's and Grainger's work. The Ruddy and Dent-Brown meta-analysis fitted more within the medical model evidence base paradigm. Yotis fitted more within the psychotherapeutic paradigm, whilst stressing the importance of the creative arts modality in its methodology. It is interesting to note that, in terms of clinical practice, all of the dramatherapy research reviewed with this client group was group therapy-based.

Forensic settings

As in psychosis, where Yotis and Ruddy and Dent-Brown provided useful pre-existing review evidence for the BADth systematic review, a Dutch review of arts therapies forensic work provided useful pre-existing evidence for the critical readers here.

Netherlands creative therapies context

Smeijsters and van Cleven (2006) reviewed the literature for working with destructive aggression in forensic settings. Their study included all arts therapies, but the systematic review focused on dramatherapy findings in particular. Critical readers reported: 'The emphasis on more cognitive, here and now treatment goals helps therapists to feel more confident and focused about the beneficial aspects of their intervention. The paper helps to set a protocol for future research and measuring outcomes', and 'This paper is of clear use to therapists working in the field. While the outcomes presented are therapist-reported rather than gathered directly from patients, this paper provides an interesting account of the different approaches of arts therapies in forensic settings'. The Smeijsters and van Cleven qualitative inquiry involved 31 experienced arts therapists working in 12 forensic institutions in the Netherlands and Germany. They were interviewed face to face, using semi-structured questionnaires and focus groups. Their implicit knowledge about indications, goals, interventions, effects and rationales were compared and integrated into consensus-based treatment methods for destructive aggression in psychosis, addictions and personality disorders in a forensic setting. In the Dutch tradition all arts therapists are united in one national association. The arts therapies are researched and developed within the same methodological format and compared to each other. They are a regular part of multidisciplinary teams in forensic settings and approximately 10% of arts therapists work in forensic settings. Within the treatment programme, arts therapists focus on particular goals. In the Netherlands over the last decade they have developed from insight-oriented therapy, taking the personality as a focus, to changing ways of feeling, thinking and behaving. The arts therapies have become more re-educative, training the client to change feelings, cognitions and behaviours in one so-called problem area. DSM-IV (2000) diagnostic categories are complemented by a treatment focus on these problem areas, which are related to the diagnosis and the offence. Various authors mention problem areas such as lack of impulse control, aggression, low social functioning and lack of structure; tension, aggression, impulsivity, power, control, lack of boundaries/structure/expression and inadequate perception. Factor analytic research shows factors for social perception, assertiveness and non-verbal behaviour as problem areas for this population (Woods et al. 2001). An important rationale for arts therapies in forensic psychiatry is their orientation to action. Underpinning theories are in line with Stern's developmental psychology (Stern 1985, 1995). Smeijsters has linked the vitality affects of the psyche to dynamic expression in the arts form (Smeijsters 2003). By experiencing vitality affects in arts forms, clients can work through unarticulated layers of experiences and develop consciousness of their cognitive schemas (Johnson et al. 1999; Timmer 2004).

UK/US forensic contexts

The Netherlands review evidence was experienced as useful and applicable to UK contexts. One difference is that in the Netherlands dramatherapy is often used as a primary treatment in CBT contexts (Smeijsters and van Cleven 2006), whilst in the UK dramatherapy is more often used in non-CBT contexts. Dramatherapist involvement in CBT treatments is a growing area, however, which could be usefully followed up in further research. Developmental transformations as a model of working was introduced by

David Johnson (1982b) in the USA and is slowly being introduced in European dramatherapy, but this is another area for development in the UK context.

Landers (2002) focuses on playing both victim and offender to help clients acquire a more varied role pattern, while Smeijsters and van Cleven (2006) help clients make the connection between the here and now and past history by encouraging them to enact different life stages, including the ones that led up to the offence. Thompson (1999a) is more reductionist in his cognitive behaviourally-oriented rationale – rehearsal of appropriate roles in real life. Smeijsters and van Cleven use rationales adopted from gestalt, self- and developmental psychology as well as transactional analysis. Landers' American case study (2002) was difficult to translate to UK contexts for the readers. The reviewers evaluated: 'This paper aims to provide a theoretical rationale for the use of developmental transformation (a specific model of dramatherapy) with violent men. It places the victim–perpetrator cycle within the patriarchal society and aims to address both individual and social difficulties. It does not address clinical diagnostic issues, which may be problematic in its use as evidence. The case described is meant to illustrate the theory and is used to argue the need for further research. As such it is interesting for dramatherapists to inform their practice, but may be less useful as evidence for non-dramatherapists'.

Sally Stamp's (1998) chapter highlights similar areas. Her group dramatherapy settings include high-security male prisons, adolescent secure units and a regional secure unit for psychiatric offenders (men and women). Her dramatherapy methodology involves role-play, improvisation, story-building, tableaux, scene enactment and Moreno's social atom. She studies commonalities and differences between drama teaching and dramatherapy. The reviewers identified that the article has elements of heuristic and action research, as it is based on the author's experience of working with a particular client group. Her rationale for the effectiveness of dramatherapy is that the distancing potential of dramatic structures enables the potential to develop thinking capacity. She also identifies links between fictional and autobiographical material in dramatherapy.

The Jennings et al. (1997) research focuses on improving self-image as a problem area. The treatment consisted of a 6-month programme, with 3-hour sessions at 3-weekly intervals at Broadmoor maximum secure hospital. The dramatherapy methodology involved embodiment–projection–role developmental work (Jennings et al. 1997) in group treatment: six patients plus core staff. The aim of the research was to test the preliminary hypothesis that participation in dramatherapy workshops would improve self-image. The clients were directed through a process of growing self-awareness in enacting *A Midsummer Night's Dream*, using masks. Pre- and post-testing used the Haward body barrier test (HBBT), the body cathexis scale adapted from Jourard and Secord, and repertory grids (Kelly) measuring change in patients' ways of thinking about themselves. The findings showed a positive outcome in improvement of self-image. Clinicians involved were in no doubt that dramatherapy was a useful tool in accessing aspects that may be inaccessible by other means, in particular through the use of distancing. Some results were inconclusive in this ever-changing setting. Clients were moved or discharged and it was therefore difficult to monitor other potential influences. It is interesting to note that this study in its methodology and aims was different from many other dramatherapy interventions for this client group, as reported by Smeijsters and van Cleven. British–Netherlands differences in dramatherapy orientations, interventions, theoretical influences and settings may play a role. Smeijsters and van Cleven also focus their research on changes in destructive aggression, rather than self-image. The rationale from Smeijsters and van Cleven's research is that dramatherapy facilitates distancing, which enables cognitions to be recognised before and during agression. Clients can thus reach insight into external/internal stimuli, their cognitions and their inner conflicts about status and (self) respect. All arts therapists sampled identified lack of aggression regulation as an indication for treatment.

Co-morbidity, diagnostics and other modalities

Four studies outside the parameters of the Smeijsters and van Cleven review, but rated as excellent evidence by UK dramatherapists in their systematic review, are the studies by Moffet and Bruto (1990) on personality disorder (PD) overlapping with substance abuse, Brem (2002), in a case study on borderline personality disorder (BPD), Dent-Brown and Wang (2004), on storytelling as a diagnostic tool for BPD, and Duncan et al. (2006), who conducted a systematic review of group interventions in forensic psychiatry. Brem provides an in-depth individual case study, which the reviewers rated highly. They evaluated it as very useful object relations based evidence focusing on feelings of abandonment of a borderline psychotic self-harming client, during breaks in therapy and therapist measures to contain them. The author shows a correlation between self-harming acts and thoughts during breaks in therapy. She indicates strategies within the dramatherapy intervention to manage these frustrations. The reviewers critiqued the Brem study, as well as the Dent-Brown and Wang (2004) study, for lacking comparison studies and limited sample size. The reviewers felt that Dent-Brown and Wang's use of the six-piece story method was a useful method of assessment, as few dramatherapy methods are part of a systematic diagnostic assessment. Smeijsters and van Cleven stress that diagnostic assessment is undertaken by the psychiatrist, but in the UK new ways of working in psychiatry more and more involve multidisciplinary team assessments at intake.

Duncan et al. (2006) provide a context for the proliferance of group interventions in forensic settings. Although not specifically focusing on arts therapies or dramatherapy, the reviewers found it useful underpinning evidence. Their systematic review found that group interventions are especially effective with mentally disordered offenders. The effectiveness is noticed in three areas: problem solving, anger management and self-harm. More research is needed, developing from reporting of clinical practice to more robust methodological research. The Duncan et al. findings therefore support the Smeijsters and van Cleven findings as a wider evidential framework. They do not, however, give a rationale as to why group interventions may be more effective. Moffet and Bruto provide some indications, which require further research.

Moffet and Bruto (1990) employ therapeutic theatre interventions, where making and using video footage provided a sense of community, enabling participation and consistent attendance. Users were enabled to relate to 'immature defences' within themselves via role usage. The intervention focused on the mechanisms of empathy within the process, and the realisation of ego within the addictive personality cycle. Moffet and Bruto focused more on substance abuse than personality disorder and as such provide better evidence for this client group. They provide a generic explanation, based in psychoanalytic understandings, of the aetiology of defences for the 'substance abuser'. Whilst not specific to dramatherapy, it was relevant in explaining the therapeutic theatre project in its context. The gaps the reviewers identified were a lack of academic rigour in cross-referencing to other work. In terms of the project, it relied on author reporting and author opinion and would have benefited from comparative references to other work.

Dokter (1996) also used a psychoanalytic framework for her eating disorders case study of a 6-month dramatherapy group in psychiatric unit with a mix of complex and chronic anorexic and bulimic clients. The group showed high drop-out rates congruent with other psychological group therapy interventions. The author suggested that treatment was effective as part of an integrated team programme with the dramatherapy approach focusing on underlying causes and interpersonal relating. The key findings were that offering non-interpretative groups with limited direction, using projective work with objects, placing emphasis on active reflection and the use of methods such as continuums could be beneficial for this client group. The therapist's role as container involved using limited direction, so that the themes of control and manipulation were not destructively re-enacted. The critical readers felt that more detail about the creative interventions would have been beneficial as potential guidelines for practice, but summarised that the creative methods employed seemed to contain the projections and enabled reflection, whilst the emphasis on the self in the work for the clients and limited direction by the therapist were important for the return to self-control (in areas other than food). The author and readers identified the need for further research to identify the possibilities and limitations for generalisation from this case study.

PTSD

The final topic area for evidence appraisal was that of PTSD, a notoriously broad category, with a wide diversity of aetiological factors, symptoms and age groups. Bannister (1995), for traumatised children, and Winn (1994), on working with PTSD in adults, are both rated highly as providing a good grounding in the subject area. Most of the highly rated individual case study evidence about children was found in the American volume edited by Weber and Haen (2005) and in the Israel-based work by Lahad (1996). Reviewers state that the context and interventions used (such as developmental transformations in Chasen 2005) can make the work difficult to generalise to a UK-based setting, although rating the evidence as excellent. Terrorist attacks and their aftermath, as well as sexual abuse, are regretfully common human experiences. International exchange and comparative research would enable further identification of effective interventions. Intercultural psychotherapy research provides a pathway to identify suitable adjustments to the cultural and national context.

Conclusion

As stated in the introduction to this chapter, this conclusion summarises the state of the art of the evidence and identifies the gaps in the area of dramatherapy with destructiveness.

The chapter shows that a narrow definition of evidence, which privileges particular types of evidence, does not enable practitioners to use available research with their clients. A wider engagement with practice-based evidence proves an excellent opportunity for dramatherapy practitioners to evaluate evidence as to its suitability for their client work.

The reader group rates that the evidence for group interventions with psychosis is very good in helping clients to establish personal boundaries and alleviating secondary symptoms such as isolation and withdrawal. Evidence has also been identified in alleviating/giving meaning to primary symptoms such as thought disorder and hearing voices. Group interventions were also found to be most effective for clients with personality disorders, especially in reducing destructive aggression and expanding a narrow role repertoire. The rationale for the use of dramatherapy in this context is that the distancing potential of dramatic structures enables the development of thinking capacity. There are individual projects showing the usefulness of dramatherapy assessment as a diagnostic tool and a workshop based intervention to improve self-image. Overall, however, interventions targeting problem solving, anger management and self-harm were evaluated as the most effective.

Part II

CLINICAL PRACTICE

4

JOSHUA AND THE EXPRESSION OF MAKE-BELIEVE VIOLENCE: DRAMATHERAPY IN A PRIMARY SCHOOL SETTING

Emma Ramsden

Brief overview of chapter

This chapter adopts a single case study approach to explore an 11-year-old boy called Joshua's conscious and unconscious re-enactments of inter-generational patterns of experience in a dramatherapy group for boys with identified emotional and social behavioural needs. It explores how replaying experience is holding and healing for Joshua. The chapter enables the reader to gain insight via parent interviews of the potential for trauma to be replayed through the generations and identifies tensions and concerns for Joshua's future health and well-being.

Introduction

Joshua, the pseudonym chosen by an 11-year-old boy, who described himself as a 'kind person, angry and that's it', has a myriad of support lenses that frame his psychological and educational care. Over the past 5 years, one of these lenses has been individual and group dramatherapy sessions. A child and adolescent mental health services (CAMHS) assessment 14 months ago led to a diagnosis of attention deficit hyperactivity disorder (ADHD). This resulted in treatment via oral medication methylphenidate, aimed to improve mental activity. A diagnosis of ADHD occurs following a dominancy of persistent features in the categories of inattention, hyperactivity and impulsivity which '. . . cause impairment . . .' (DSM-IV-TR 2000: 66), preventing the child being able to '. . . remain focused and naturally attend to tasks' (Chasen 2005: 154). In his assessment Joshua displayed many of these features, which his mum reported experiencing at home and which staff reported experiencing in school (e.g. 'Hyperactivity (b) often leaves seat in classroom or in other situations in which it is inappropriate . . .' (DSM-IV-TR 2000: 66). The deputy headteacher, a great champion and innovator of pastoral and psychological intervention in the school, described Joshua as '. . . defiant when challenged by adults with whom he does not have a relationship'. The chapter analyses Joshua's situation by exploring some of the lenses, i.e. therapy, family, school and outside support. It draws on evidence gained from post-intervention taped interviews with Joshua, his parents, key school staff and the diversion manager from the Youth Offending Service, along with clinical observations captured via session process notes. It focuses on his inclusion in a drama-therapy group which engaged with the core processes of playing, life–drama connection, witnessing and role play (Jones 1996) as a way of transforming experience and developing well-being. Key factors taken into account in his developing identity include the impact of his ADHD drug treatment, along with familial themes relating to his father's extensive criminal history and his parents' own special educational needs. Reflections of Joshua's under-standing of destructiveness are explored and commented upon through exploration of a clinical vignette from the dramatherapy group.

The mainstream primary school referred to in this chapter is in an inner city area, identified in the most recent (government) Ofsted report as having high levels of social deprivation and learning needs. It operates an inclusive practice policy in line with both local education authority (LEA) and national standards. The policy promotes health and well-being, access to education, overall '. . . ensuring the needs of every child are fully met . . .' [Department for Children Schools and Families (DCSF) 2003]. The school offers a range of educational and pastoral interventions for children requiring additional input. These include the work of a full-time learning mentor, who offers emotional health, behaviour management and nurture groups alongside curriculum-based support. Dramatherapy has been offered for 2 days per week since 2001, with 1 day of art therapy being introduced in 2009. The art therapy post is funded by a locally based educational trust, while the dramatherapy post is funded directly out of the school's budget.

The dramatherapy group: referral, consent and session structure

The group was established in response to growing adult concerns about difficulties experienced by five boys aged 9–11, who persistently struggled to thrive in their environments in and out of school. The difficulties manifested in ways such as fighting in the playground, using negative and abusive language in exchanges with peers and staff and refusing to do work or stay in the classroom. The behaviour was mirrored in the home context in an increase in the intensity of arguments and fights with siblings and adults, an inability to contain feelings of anger and leaving the home without permission. Incidents of theft, shoplifting and contact with the police had occurred in some cases. Most of the boys were in contact with older children known in the community for trouble-making and contact with law enforcement agencies.

Following parental consent, each child was invited to a 20-minute creative assessment, during which they could either agree to join the group or not. All boys presented as excited and gave permission eagerly. The group consisted of 35 weekly sessions of 50 minutes each, spanning an academic year (September to July). Attendance was high; four out of five boys stayed until the end. One boy was transferred to a special unit for emotional and behavioural difficulties part-way through the academic year and could no longer attend due to geographical logistics.

The dramatherapist provided session boundaries with an opening and closing structure, which focused on being together as a group. Each person was encouraged to share in the opening check-in something from their day or week. In the ending reflection they were asked to comment about the roles played during the session, feelings experienced and a commitment to hearing and witnessing the reflections of others. The aim of this structure was to enable the group members to begin and end each session with clarity and safety, whilst developing skills of naming experiences, active listening to others and building empathic exchanges. It would also enable each child to connect with their choices of roles. Landy suggests that:

> . . . each individual must . . . choose . . . roles that are most appropriate to a given circumstance and most meaningful to that individual. Each role chosen and played must be done so for a purpose, whether to survive, express a feeling, or meet a need. And each act of role-taking or role-playing is creative in the sense that one is building a piece of one's identity.
>
> (Landy 1995: 26)

In between the opening and closing boundaries, the group were free to play, explore and experiment with their experiences and feelings, so long as they offered respect and care to each other, to the dramatherapist and to the play objects in the room. By and large, this respect was upheld; however, some objects did become irreparably damaged through the gusto and energy of the playing. The concept of play is placed into a theoretical context, followed by a clinical vignette which illuminates a moment of playing in the work, in which the core processes of playing, life–drama connection, witnessing and role-play (Jones 2007) are at work.

Play, dramatherapy and a clinical vignette

Identities are developed through play. From a young age children act out and take on aspects of the roles available to them in their lives – the children and adults who inhabit their everyday world (Landy 1995). A belief in play as a naturally occurring medium for communication, self-expression, learning and exploration (West 1996) was a supporting theoretical theme for this group:

> [Play] . . . is free, is in fact freedom . . . It is a stepping out of 'real' life into a temporary sphere of activity with a disposition all of its own. Every child knows perfectly well that he is 'only pretending . . .'.
>
> (Huizinga 1955: 8)

In this setting, an environment is fostered where natural play can be both witnessed and engaged in. The aim is to develop inter-relational exchanges, to facilitate a deeper understanding with the child about their communications. Throughout the violent and destructive themes re-enacted in the dramatherapy group, there was never a real fight, nor any breaking of the play boundaries. Whatever Joshua may have been enacting of perceived real-life events relating to his father's offending and his experiences of being a member of his family, there was a safety in his knowledge of pretence.

Dramatherapy shares with play the lack of a correct or incorrect way of 'doing'. It draws on a wide and eclectic range of creative and therapeutic principles where the:

> . . . intentional and directional use of drama . . . [has] . . . the expressed purpose of effecting constructive change. One of the advantages of dramatherapy is that there is no right or wrong way of doing it, apart from the confines of confidentiality and boundaries common to all psychotherapies.
>
> (Langley 2006: 2)

These notions were central for the boys, who had so often given and experienced negative and hurtful attention from children and adults. They collectively presented with low self-esteem, limited concentration and a pervasive self-knowledge of being 'stupid', which often presented itself through self-effacing humour. Referring to his therapy group with children affected by the event of 11 September in New York, Haen (2005: 398) defines group therapy as providing its members with '. . . a forum in which to connect to others who have been traumatized and, together, experience a lessening of shame, isolation, and fear'.

The following clinical vignette focuses on a moment approximately 6 months into the 11-month process. In it, Joshua and the group replay a familiar theme of a bank robbery. What we see in this vignette is that in 'acting out' roles in the dramatherapy play space, in a creative and playful way, Joshua and the others can be destructive without causing 'harm'.

A bank robbery was the most popular theme for the group to re-enact. Using role-play, the group made use of the play-money, play-guns and play-handcuffs. Invariably the dramatherapist was asked by the group to play the bank manager, or person who was going to be 'robbed'. The boys would equip themselves with as many play-guns that they could find, ending up with at least two each. Some guns fired rubber sucker bullets and others simulated shooting noises. Often Joshua would cast himself as the chief bank robber. A lot of energy, laughter and chatting would be present between the boys, who would display strong communication and some team-work skills in their play as they discussed and agreed a strategy for stealing the money. The 'bank manager' would be handcuffed, sworn at and sometimes play-punched. The money would be taken with play-force or handed over. The 'bank robbers' would 'run off' and either stick together as a group and share out the money, or have a disagreement and split into two sub-groups, where a gun-fight would follow. The victorious side would often gather all the money together. Sometimes the 'bank manager' was spared and at others she would be play-shot. Occasionally she would be freed and then asked to take on the role of a 'baddie'. Joshua described a baddie as 'someone who wanted to take all the money and shoot everyone'.

This sequence and its variations would be recreated from week to week during the group's life. However, one bank robbery a few months into the group was very different in terms of Joshua's role taking and enactment. In this session, the 'bank manager' was handcuffed and seated on a bean bag, having been placed there by the other 'robbers'. Joshua was standing in front of the 'bank manager', unusually close and with his gun pointed to the middle of her forehead, almost touching her skin.

Joshua stared directly into the 'bank manager's' eyes, holding his gun to her face and shouted angrily 'give me all the money'. This was a familiar instruction, yet Joshua's piercing eye contact and fixed gaze was a different presentation. He was not blinking. His eyes were wide and pupils dilated. His face was drained of colour and he was deathly still as he held the gun in place. It was as if he was not present in the moment, whilst at the same time being intently present. The other group members, who were behind or to the side of Joshua, also held their guns towards the 'bank manager' but from a distance. They were laughing as they did so and were engaging in dialogue with each other, which compounded their giggly behaviour. They were having fun. Joshua remained fixed on the 'bank manager', placing her in the role of victim. He was not smiling or laughing and the play seemed deadly serious. He appeared to have detached himself from inter-relating to other group members, seemingly determined to succeed in his chosen objective of gaining the money. In role, the dramatherapist handed over the money after declaring, 'Here, have it all. Please don't shoot me. I've got a family at home to support'. Joshua took the money and with great speed moved to another area in the room with it, where he counted and then hid it. He did not call over the other group members, who by this time had begun play-shooting each other following an in-role disagreement of who was second in charge.

After a few moments, one of the group members displayed the fickle nature of this play by moving on to engagement in softball play. Other group members quickly followed, leaving Joshua, still focused on his own play with the money at one side of the room. After a short time, one of the other boys called him over to join in with their ball play. Joshua retrieved the money from his hiding place and put it in his trouser pockets. He then joined the others. At the end of the play part of the session, without prompting, he replaced the play-money back to the jar where it had been at the start of the session. The boys regrouped on the cushions in the soft play area of the room for the grounding and closing reflection (in grounding, the group's connections are re-established outside of playful, creative and projective processes; Jones 1996: 27). Congruent with ongoing reflective processing, positive words were attached to the session, including 'fantastic', 'brilliant', 'fun'. Negative reflections were rarely offered in relationship to role taking.

Joshua's leadership in the dramatherapy group enabled him to gain majority control over some of the bank robbery role plays. The identification for him seemed more profound than for the others, who over time lost interest in this type of role play, progressing to other play. For Joshua, the re-enactment through role playing enabled him to communicate some of these experiences, fears and concerns about fragments of stories and themes that pertained to his family narrative. His father's offending history has been briefly mentioned in these pages. Hayden (2007: 1) comments in her book on children in trouble that '. . . some parents are "in trouble" too, and may also be instrumental in the trouble presented by their children'. I will therefore contextualise Joshua's play in relation to his history in a little more detail.

Family background and intergenerational themes

Joshua is the eldest male child in the family. He has two sisters and three brothers. His parents are in their late 20s. They have been together since their early teenage years and married for the past 5 years. Both parents attended an out-of-borough secondary school for young people with learning and behavioural needs. Both were hyperactive in childhood and had educational needs, such as dyslexia. Whilst Joshua's mum's reading has improved over time, as a result of reading books with her children, his father remains mostly illiterate.

Joshua's father did not know his own father, who was addicted to illegal substances and subsequently died from a drug overdose. His older half-brothers have both served prison terms. Joshua's father describes the importance of his half-brothers' influence: '. . . that's where I got it from . . .

soon, as I got a bit older, I used to go around with some friends and we'd get in a gang and do stuff . . .'. At the age of 7, Joshua's father began what is now a prolific criminal career. Petty theft led to burglary and a first prison term served at a young offenders institute (YOI). Illegal substances imbibed from age 14 onwards led to profound stimulant and alcohol addictions. He underwent a drug programme in prison in recent years which, he reports, had some success around stimulant prevention. As a prolific burglar, Joshua's father has spent more than the past decade locked in a pattern of incarceration and freedom. Whilst out of prison between 2007 and the latter part of 2009, mostly free of illegal substances, he endured periods of depression with ideation of self-harm as a result of drug cravings. These feelings were mostly anaesthetised through excessive alcohol consumption.

Mum describes a good bond between Joshua and his dad, commenting that her husband is a 'more hands-on dad now . . . before he was very distant'. Of this distant relationship with his children, dad recalls, 'I wouldn't do nothing . . . no cleaning, well every now and then I'd do it but I was always out of my head. I was always hung over. I used to come in at 2, 3, 4 in the morning and I'd sleep until 5 pm. If anyone woke me up, I'd get annoyed'. Joshua's father was present for the first year of his life before returning to prison. In this first year Joshua experienced inconsistent and therefore confusing patterns of family life, dependent upon his father's criminal activities and substance misuse. When interviewed, Joshua's dad noted, 'I never took my drugs around my kids. Coz I won't do that at all . . .'. Both parents spoke of their awareness of protecting the children from knowing about the details and spoils from various burglaries, yet inevitably, as Bowlby (2009: 114) suggests, 'Children not infrequently observe scenes that parents would prefer they did not observe; they form impressions that parents would prefer they did not form; and they have experiences that parents would like to believe they have not had'. Joshua's father describes his son as having the same 'lack of fear' that he had – which led to him taking regular criminal risks.

Over the years Joshua and his siblings will have made their own sense of what they have seen and heard in their family. As his father says, 'I would be discrete when I got home but he would see me with a lot of money'. The family's cycle of having sudden wealth then limited funds, as a result of the pattern of offending and drug using perpetrated by Joshua's father, has inevitably had effects on the behaviour of Joshua and his siblings. Despite their desire to conceal the full story around the appearance of such items, there was a knowing by the children, who may '. . . cease consciously to be aware that they have ever observed such scenes, formed such impressions, or had such experiences' (Bowlby 2009: 114). In the dramatherapy group, almost on a weekly basis Joshua would repeat something of this pattern in his play, by having no play money, then all the play money, before leaving the session with nothing once again.

All children benefit from growing from a secure base (Bowlby 2009). Joshua's parents undoubtedly love him, his siblings and each other and strive to provide what they consider to be the best care, security and consistency that they can. Joshua's father speaks of wanting to keep out of trouble, but makes it clear that if crime is the only option to protect and provide for his family, then there is no choice for him.

The role of being absent and present, played by Joshua's father, has inevitably impacted significantly on the lives of the family. It seems to manifest most profoundly in Joshua's behaviour and his ways of relating with many aspects of his world. Of note are the variety of concerns relating to four of Joshua's five siblings. These concerns include suspected autism, ADHD, dyslexia and physical disability. During the interview, his dad movingly commented that '. . . the reason why Joshua is the way he is is because of me . . . he looks up to me. When I was younger and used to have all the cars and the motorbikes, he used to climb out of the window . . . to try to get out with me, because I was out committing crime all the time'. Joshua's mum is all too aware of the threat of intergenerational patterns repeating themselves. She says, 'He would think "Dad don't work. Dad's got this money. Dad's got a stereo. Dad's got this and that". Joshua was thinking, "I want this". That is my biggest fear, him committing crime and going to drugs'. The destructive behaviour noted by teachers and other school staff mirrored the behaviour his mother describes. Joshua struggled to stay in class, preferring to 'escape' and roam around the building. This desire was no different prior to his ADHD drug treatment, suggesting it may be an imprinted desire from father to son to push boundaries.

Much relevant research has taken place in neurobiology and trauma (Wilkinson 2006). This research suggests that experiences are processed by the child in a preverbal limbic arena for which they later seek verbal translation. However, the developing brain may lock memories of traumatic experiences in the unconscious and abstract right hemisphere (preverbal, emotional, imaginative), unable to integrate them with the later developing left hemisphere (language and analytic abilities) and subsequent verbal expression. The child, now left with the locked-in trauma, expresses this over time in a myriad of acting-out behaviours. How might Joshua's acting out of make-believe violence in the dramatherapy group have enabled him to find expression through action for unintegrated traumatic experiences lodged in the right hemisphere of the brain?

Of note is the comparison of energy witnessed in his actions and expressions in dramatherapy sessions, as opposed to his lack of animation during the verbally based question-and-answer taped interview in preparation for this chapter. Joshua has a limited verbal vocabulary when invited to comment on his understanding of destructiveness. He described a single word: 'anger'. Joshua reflected that he liked the dramatherapy because, 'I get to do more things with my friends'. This kind of destructiveness was 'fun' and 'burnt energy'. What was happening in the dramatherapy group for Joshua? What role did it have in developing his identity and sense of well-being versus his destructiveness? Did it enable him to try out new patterns of thinking considering his family context and experiences without needing to focus on verbal language?

Joshua's presentation and the ending of the dramatherapy group

The check-in at the start of the dramatherapy group was a space for the boys to introduce something of themselves and their experiences. After a few months, Joshua began checking in by pretending to be intoxicated. Others would copy this in their own check-ins and the familiar sound of laughter would accompany these explorations. Around this same time, Joshua began taking his ADHD medication (see DSM-IV-TR 2000 for symptomology). He experienced changes in his body as a result of the medication – his own experience of taking drugs. Joshua commented, away from the other group members, that he did not like taking the medication as it stopped him playing. A few months later he had changed his mind and said he was 'okay' with taking it. This 'okay' was conveyed with a sense of resignation – as if he understood the limitation of choices offered to him by the adult health professionals and his parents. Joshua had commented in the early weeks of taking his medication that he wanted to be good for himself and not because the tablets made him so.

Within the play world inhabited in the dramatherapy group, Joshua could re-enact some of his thoughts and experiences via his engagement in symbolic playing – such as pretending to be intoxicated. Of interest is that his depiction of intoxication was congruent with mood suppressants rather then mood enhancers. His father's illegal drug use was self-reported as stimulant use (i.e. cocaine, speed). Joshua's ADHD medication would fall into the category of a mood suppressant. It seemed he was depicting both himself and his father's presentation through drugs in this symbolic play.

In the bank robbery role play, Joshua would remain fully focused on the play-crime and would be clear about what should happen to the bank manager (played by the dramatherapist). He would order the other boys into their respective roles of taking play-money, play-handcuffing the bank manager and making a getaway. Joshua would have the clearest narrative vision at these times. The others were keen to join in, play the 'bad men' and engage in their own imaginative thinking about the development of the story. Often, if one of the other boys wanted to free the bank manager, Joshua would be keen to shoot him. He was exploring the play seemingly in a 'them and us' framework, where no mercy was shown to the other side. What was notable was his detachment from the others in the group. In that moment, he was alone and nothing would deter him from achieving his goal. How might he have seen or imagined his father's determination at home preparing to commit crime, in order to satisfy his need for illegal substances? I wonder how this may relate to Joshua's understanding that his father must not compromise whilst on a 'job', in order not to be caught. Whatever real moment of knowing and understanding he may have been consciously or unconsciously re-enacting, based on the modelling experiences and stories of his father, were done without directly exposing his family's past. He would not betray his family honour by informing on his father's activities, or get himself into any trouble. These dramatic re-enactments were safe for him; this was shown by the way that he was able to demonstrate 'play violence'.

Joshua could have been acting out images of fragments of stories overheard or pieced together by evidence from crimes at home. He could have been angry with someone or some event in school and took this opportunity to embody his frustrations in role.

> Considerable research both in humans and animals has led to the conclusion that much of human development occurs by means of a mirroring process . . . monkey see monkey do . . . What is so striking about this for therapists and analysts is that it provides a sound neuroscientific basis for the transference/countertransference process and establishes an indissoluble link between those processes and the earliest development of mind.
>
> (Wilkinson 2006: 28)

Allowing Joshua to play out, and for this to be witnessed by the therapist, often in participant–witness role, enabled Joshua to explore some of the preverbal stories held inside him.

The four boys, who were members of the group throughout, reflected in the closing sessions that they would miss it. Three of them were heading for secondary transfer. It was not only the group that was ending, but also their primary schooling. Fears in relation to secondary school urban myths – such as being beaten up by older boys – abounded in these final sessions. Humour and boisterous energy remained a stable and safe self-protecting mechanism. Files, heavy with notes and reports on interventions they had undertaken, would accompany at least two of the boys on their onward journey. A third was unexpectedly taken to live abroad in an attempt to 'cure' his behavioural difficulties. For Joshua, as well as his file, a series of transition meetings occurred. He was referred to the local youth at-risk organisation and included in a dramatherapy transition project, facilitated by the secondary school's resident therapist.

Drawing from the past to support the future

Joshua and the other boys were referred to the dramatherapy group for the challenging and disruptive behaviour they displayed in the here-and-now of the school environment. According to the deputy headteacher, they could '. . . demolish a teacher's relationship with a class . . .', particularly if inconsistent teaching patterns were in place. It has already been discussed that '. . . traumatic events can disrupt, delay, or hinder normal courses of development . . .' (Haen 2005: 395). Brief explorations of their known family narratives reveal early significant trauma for each child, with loss as a common theme. One boy's father committed suicide when he was a young child. Another boy was taken into care, following severe neglect and physical abuse by his drug-dependent mother. Another boy had previously lived in a hostel following his mother's escape from a home life of domestic violence. For another, living in extreme poverty in a bedsit with his mother and sibling impacted negatively on his healthy developing self. Joshua experienced trauma through his father's drug use, criminal activities and inconsistent parenting due to periods of incarceration. Whilst this group were not referred for explicit reasons of 'trauma', reflecting upon the histories and presenting behaviour of these boys, these connections were possibly being worked with on an unconscious level, repetitively re-enacting through a variety of literal and symbolic play themes the feelings and experiences associated with trauma and loss (Jones 2005; Haen 2005).

The knowledge of his family history with crime and the behaviour associated with ADHD, including risk taking, places Joshua at risk of potentially becoming involved in negative and dangerous activities with devastating consequences. Joshua's father's own non-relationship with his natural father is significant in the familial narrative. His own criminal past may be traced back to the early trauma he experienced. This retracing is considered an important factor in juvenile crime (Hayden 2007).

Now in secondary school, a new set of lenses are being provided for Joshua. However, the supportive multi-agency framework continues. Transition meetings are attended by the primary school dramatherapist. She encourages an ongoing dialogue, which places Joshua in the heart of the meaning making. The inclusion manager of his new school sees a hopeful pathway, if support towards an apprenticeship when he reaches 16 years old can be consistent. However, the 'if' is incredibly weighted with the difficulties Joshua has already encountered in settling into this large secondary school, exacerbated by the recent re-incarceration of this father.

In dramatherapy, fantasies can be explored and contained within the safety of dramatic processes such as enactment and embodiment (a process where roles and ideas are inhabited and creatively expressed). The core processes of the life–drama connection, playing, witnessing, empathy and distancing (Jones 1996), provide the opportunity for children to play out, explore and express their feelings, which may include anger, frustration and aggression. These dramatic explorations are helpful and can be vital methods in order to develop and internalise healthy changes towards what

Jones (2002: 73) refers to as '. . . the building of a self that serves us well . . . Aggression has to be part of that self. It can be destructive, but it can also be directed into assertiveness, decisiveness, healthy competition and altruism'. Within the safety of the therapeutic container, which engenders trust, 'real-world' recriminations are absent. Haen (2005) identifies the difficulty in expressions of the unspeakable, the loss of language as a trauma response and the crucial role that engagement with metaphoric arts therapies processes can have on working through trauma. Dramatic acting out of the 'what if' can yield new patterns of relating, via identification with old patterns and being open to consider the possibilities of subtle but significant changes in the child's internal world.

Change and hope are still present for this family. Joshua's mum, drawing upon her own experiences of being misdiagnosed and failed by the system as a child and young person, coupled with the clear failings detailed in the description of her husband's childhood in this chapter, have instilled in her a determination to provide her children with the best possibilities that she can. As may be evident in this writing, however, she requires significant support for many years to come from the various health and educational services, to work towards this.

In this chapter, the work of the dramatherapist has been framed from a family dynamics approach. This is consistent with an increasing body of clinical practice in psychological fields in education and health, which have been influenced by and developed from the United Nations Committee on the Rights of the Child (UN 1989). The subsequent Every Child Matters initiative (HMSO 2003) encouraged participation (direct inputting into changes in policy) by direct consultation (finding out views to inform changes) with children (Hill 2006). These are key areas in developing listening skills, so that children can be active agents of their own experiences (Tomlinson 2008).

When reflecting on what changes he had noted in himself during the dramatherapy work, Joshua said that he felt more patient. Over time he had demonstrated less intensity in the features of inattention associated with his ADHD. He also displayed a decrease in extreme acting-out behaviours in school – suggesting that an expression for some of his non-verbal trauma may have taken place in the dramatherapy process. Joshua consistently expressed a desire to be free from behavioural conflicts and difficulties and to keep away from crime. When asked to think of memories to take away, he gently remarked on the importance for him of an image he had made during one session using poster paints and paper, which he referred to as 'the ladybird and the butterfly'. Joshua had requested this image be put on the wall, where it stayed for some months. He would often look at it as he arrived in the room. He was proud of the image and saw in it, I wondered, a calmness as well as pride. The ancient Greek name for a butterfly is *psyche*, meaning soul or mind. It is hoped that the ongoing support for him will enable his mind to continue to strengthen towards life-long well-being and to express his non-verbal experiences.

Key findings

- Non-verbal play supports the child's agency in working through trauma.
- Enactment and re-enactment through role play of real narratives (whole or fragmented) are key processes in working through difficulties in dramatherapy.
- Group work offers an opportunity for children to connect and explore shared themes and overcome difficult emotions via playful expression.
- Family themes, choices and patterns may have an impact on shaping brain development, attachment and role modelling.
- Destructive experiences can be contained in therapy and transformed by the client.
- Systemic models of therapy have an important place in complex family cases.

Acknowledgements

I am grateful to Joshua and his parents for their openness and honesty during the interviews. Further expressions of thanks go to the boys who took part in the dramatherapy group and also to the school's deputy headteacher and inclusion manager and the Youth Offending Service's diversion team manager for their agreement to participate in interviews in preparation for this chapter. I am grateful to each of the above-mentioned people for providing the time to reflect on their perspectives and the commitment to change and well-being that were significant features of each interview.

5

CHAOS, DESTRUCTION AND ABUSE: DRAMATHERAPY IN A SCHOOL FOR EXCLUDED ADOLESCENTS

Eleanor Zeal

Brief overview of chapter

This chapter aims to present an outline of the nature of working as a dramatherapist in a school committed to supporting excluded adolescents; the various challenges faced and how dramatherapy may be utilised. The chapter provides the theoretical orientation upon which the intervention is based, illustrated by a group and individual case vignettes.

Introduction

The work featured in this chapter takes place in a school, established as a charity, and similar to a state-run pupil referral unit. It accommodates 30–40 male and female students aged 13–16, from virtually every London borough. The students' cultural and racial backgrounds are diverse. Many of the students are 'statemented' with numeracy and literacy learning difficulties [educational statements are a way of funding extra support for children with special educational needs (SEN)]. Many of the students may also have attention deficit/hyperactivity disorder (ADHD), emotional and behavioural disorder (EBD), self-injurious behaviour (SIB), autism, cannabis addiction and self-harming tendencies. A proportion of them have been sexually abused. Several have endured neglect and the effects of living with drug-addicted or alcoholic parents, or those suffering from mental health problems. Some of the students have already served sentences in young offenders' institutions. Others have anti-social behaviour orders (ASBOs), supervision orders and a history of low-level criminal activity. A number are involved in gangs, with allegiance and identity dictated by postcode and/or race. Guns, drugs, violence and crime are usually integral to these gangs. The need for identity, purpose and something to belong to, as well as a lack of anything else to do, make gang membership an attractive option for young people living in deprived inner city areas by providing an alternative 'family' and structure. Some are in and out of care; some have arrived recently as refugees. The majority have been excluded from previous schools for physical abuse, bullying and dangerous behaviour.

With a high staff-to-student ratio, the school aims to provide education, nurture and sufficient life-skills for students to access college, or the required qualifications for work. Students are referred to the school, often as a last resort, by the borough in which they live. Due to the government's recent policy of inclusion, the students referred are increasingly those deemed impossible to place in mainstream education. The looked-after child (LAC) pupils can present the greatest challenge because they have necessarily been rejected or removed from their family and passed from foster-carer to care home. Many professionals are involved in the decision-making processes affecting their lives. A LAC may have rarely experienced a consistent, lasting relationship with any adult.

My role as a dramatherapist is to support the school's intention to provide education by meeting some of the emotional needs of the pupils. Once referred students have been accepted by the school, dramatherapy is offered as part of the provision. Group and individual sessions are available for a period of up to 2 years. Students self-refer for individual sessions and each teaching group is offered one session per week, which students choose whether or not to attend. Time-tabling is difficult, as demand far outweighs the resources of a lone therapist.

Theoretical framework – understanding adolescence

Even in normal adolescence, the teenager is subject to an onslaught of changes; physical growth, hormonal surges, changes in the neural pathways of the brain's frontal cortex. Teenagers are generally seen as moody, uncommunicative, hostile, challenging and unpredictable. Blos lists seven non-sequential areas of maturation:

1. From concrete to abstract thinking.
2. The development of judgement and logical thought.
3. The stabilisation of sexual feelings and social skills including empathy and altruism.
4. Self-image secure enough to manage criticism and stress.
5. The incorporation of a variety of internal and external roles to create an individual identity.
6. Acceptance of a changed body image so less obsessing over appearance.
7. A sufficiently strong sense of self to allow continuing maturity with less outside support.

(Blos 1962)

Mario Cossa (2006), when using psychodrama with adolescents, observes from a developmental perspective:

> . . . developmental stages are cumulative, in that unless the tasks of the earlier stages are successfully completed, the challenges of the later stages cannot be fully met. Although cumulative, the stages are not strictly linear. There is a great deal of overlap and moving back and forth.
>
> (Cossa 2006: 36)

Cossa believes that group process parallels individual developments in infancy and early childhood and can provide 'corrective emotional experience'.

Hillman states:

> Youth carries the significance of becoming, of self-correcting growth, of being beyond itself (ideals) since its reals are in status nascendi . . . Youth is the emergence of spirit within the psyche.
>
> (Hillman 1990: 189–90)

Frankl adds:

> Another important question to consider is: What kind of world does the spirit awaken to in adolescence . . . how the emerging spirit is received by the culture has significant impact on the process of becoming, an impact that has lasting consequences . . .
>
> (Frankl 1998: 50)

Winnicott (1971), from a psychoanalytic perspective, describes how the unconscious murderous fantasy of replacing parents once maturity is reached underpins the experience of growth and how the aggression of this fantasy, in part, creates the aggressive adolescent. He also stresses the need to accept and embrace adolescent immaturity, its liveliness and freshness:

> Immaturity is an essential element of health at adolescence. There is only one cure for immaturity and that is the passage of time . . . And, while growing is in progress, responsibility must be taken by parent-figures.
>
> (Winnicott 1971: 200)

My own experience finds adolescents as fragile as emerging butterflies but armed to the hilt with clanking, ill-fitting armour. Where there have been interrupted and damaged passages through childhood and there is ongoing socio-economic deprivation, those delicate butterflies are unbearably fragile, afraid and defensive and hence the problematic levels of anger, destruction and violence they display. I have found the concepts of pro-jective identification and Gilligan's 'germ theory' of violence (1996) useful for my practice:

> Projection and projective identification are viewed as two poles of a continuum of types of fantasies of expulsion of aspects of the self.
>
> (Ogden 1979: 371)

These adolescents are very good at making other people feel angry or despairing on their behalf. Professionals and parents frequently say things like: 'He just makes me want to bang my head against a brick wall' or 'She winds me up till I scream at her' or 'He's a nightmare, I could slap him'.
Gilligan believes that:

> Violence is a contagious disease, not an hereditary one. The pathogen is psychological, not biological, and it is spread pri-marily by means of social, economic, and cultural vectors, not biological ones.
>
> (Gilligan 1996: 111)

He maintains that:

> . . . the different forms of violence . . . are motivated (caused) by the feeling of shame. The purpose of violence is to diminish the intensity of shame and replace it . . . with its opposite, pride, thus preventing the individual from being overwhelmed by feelings of shame.
>
> (Gilligan 1996: 111)

Time and again, following an aggressive outburst, a young person will state that he was not treated with respect: he was 'dissed'and made to feel small. It is this loss of self that needs to be defended against. Such aggressive outbursts are often decried as meaningless by others and seen as an inappropriate response to a relatively minor slight. It should be kept in mind that the aggressor may have a severely compromised sense of self, and therefore anything he experiences as an attack constitutes a serious threat to the remaining threads of his identity. The task of the therapist is to repair these threads and the following describes how I use several models of drama-therapy in an attempt to do so: embodiment–projection–role (Jennings 1995), the creative/expressive model (Andersen-Warren and Grainger 2000), narrative and story work (Gersie and King 1990) and developmental trans-formations (Johnson 2005).

The Yellow Group

This group of eight students was an existing tutor group and, unlike their lessons, they did not have to attend the dramatherapy sessions. On average, only half that number tended to be present at the weekly dramatherapy session. This work took place over a period of 2 years, delivered over approximately 70 sessions. I was usually supported by another member of the staff team.

At the beginning, the group comprised Chloe, John, Ken, David and Omar (pseudonyms are used throughout). Chloe had recently been released from an acute adolescent psychiatric ward, where she had been admitted for anorexia, repeated suicide attempts and self-injurious behaviour (SIB). John had been repeatedly excluded from school. Due to his considerable size he posed real threats to other students, staff and furniture with his 'acting-out' behaviour. Ken, also repeatedly excluded, was a heavy cannabis user who alternated between a gentle disposition and paranoid and violent episodes. John and Ken also had serious literacy and numeracy problems. David was very bright but involved in street crime, whilst Omar presented as a diminutive gangster in full possession of all facets of criminal law and allegedly a regular on *Crimewatch*.

Early sessions

At first, territories are staked out, with individuals sitting or lying as far as possible from one another. It's probably not the best time to insist on a circle, as no one will move. My own sense of powerlessness in the face of their negativity is something I try to note but not feel overwhelmed by. My impulse to leave the room, rejected, a failure, is one of many projections the therapist encounters here. Instead, at a suitable point I try to ascertain how in control they feel of their own lives and what being excluded from school makes them think about themselves. So I persevere and talk about how they might like to use sessions. I try to bracket every session, opening and closing, with an inquiry as to how each individual is at that moment. Sometimes I'm told to 'fuck off', sometimes I am given a detailed account of a recent crisis, and sometimes I might dare to suggest that their physical demeanour indicates that all is not OK, and I would like to acknowledge that. I have often noticed that a softening or deepening of the posture, or brief eye contact, can be significant early modes of communication.

Pens and paper are always available. This is partly to reroute the desire to graffiti on the walls and also to facilitate some non-verbal communication when talking or physical expression are rejected. First we discuss tags (an individual's street persona – 'Deep', 'Nightmare', 'Messa', 'Truble') and postcodes, followed by R.I.P.s for gang-members, friends and family who have been killed or who have died.

These themes of identity and loss appear early and the group is anxious to share their experience. In a following session, large rolls of paper are used to expand the previous writings and are put on the wall. Discussion of the postcodes leads to talk of territory, lack of safety when out of one's area, how far they have to come to school, how they travel. We make a map of London and mark where we live and have lived.

There seemed to be a need for the boys to draw pictures of genitals, which led to a discussion of hormone levels in young people and how other cultures not only don't condemn but celebrate and hold sacred such imagery. This was succeeded in a later session with pictures of the Cerne Abbas Giant and his 17 foot erection, as well as some images of fertility gods and goddesses. 'The integration of genital sexuality into the adolescent's soma and psyche is one important component of adolescent development' (Bloch 1995: 141). I noted that once this need to draw attention to their new sexual potency had been expressed, no more explicit pictures were drawn. However, there is in this client group a tendency to use highly sexualized language and talk dismissively about sexually available girls – 'ho's' and 'dirts' – who are there apparently to service their sexual needs but who are despised. A girl in the school whom I knew to have been sexually abused as a child was seen as an easy route to gratification. Male and female members of the group decried her actions. Some role-play taking opposite sex roles produced insight and grudging glimmerings of reflection on responsibility, boundaries, sexism and exploitation.

A given exercise might only hold their attention for minutes but often led to further discussion. In one session I offered the 'Bubble' exercise, where each person senses how much space they like to have around them and what happens when this is encroached upon. After this, spontaneously, Omar, mini-gangster, demonstrated how he walked down the street, if it's his or someone else's. He allowed inquiries about how it felt inside as he walked: what was he thinking, what was he feeling? We experimented with imaginary places to walk without danger and the group produced scenes of what happens when they meet someone on the street – police, friend or foe.

Concentration exercises, such as trying to count to 10 as a whole group, with no number said by anyone else at the same time, or selecting a subject (e.g. food) and going through the alphabet naming different kinds of food, engaged the majority of the group in the early sessions, with one or two deliberately sabotaging, walking out or providing a running commentary of obscenities. However, in later sessions they joined in and seemed to enjoy themselves, requesting that we do a particular exercise every week (although on some days they would refuse to do anything). A particularly useful exercise with this group was the 'fruitbowl' exercise, where they discover what they have in common with each other. Normally the exercise is done in a circle with one person standing up and saying, everyone who is . . . (for example) wearing blue must get up and swap places. The standing person aims to gain a seated place during the ensuing swap. This group managed to do it from their various stations round the room and without getting up. Once it was clear that everyone had had some experience of the police, family breakdown and trouble at previous schools, a fragile bonding started to take place.

Middle sessions

Several months into the school year, the group was altered to accommodate 'impossible' combinations of students in other groups and newcomers to the school. Newcomers Joan and Amy joined the group. Joan was loud, proud and African and Amy was a quiet 'mixed-race' girl who preferred to sit and make things while slowly unfolding her complex history. Now the majority of students had African or West Indian families and the group seemed to split along racial lines, along with some truly appalling verbal abuse. The school has sanctions for such behaviour and the client-agreed dramatherapy contract also declared verbal abuse to be unacceptable. However, stopping it was like King Canute trying to control the sea. Eventually, feelings about origins and homelands and difference were explored through imaginary scenes and episodes of real life, sometimes starting with the six-part story method (Lahad 1992) and sometimes using the 'who, where, when, what, how' approach to starting a scene (Gersie and King 1990).

Joan was part Congolese, part Cameroonian, part South African and part Angolan. She had a beautiful singing voice and knew many of the rhythms and dance-styles from the countries her relatives hailed from. She was also extremely large and self-conscious and had the sharpest, most creative tongue. Her coruscating insults, often given in the form of advice, created mayhem. My attempts to stop the flow resulted in her glaring down at me and announcing, 'You are a pathetic four-eyed midget and I will not hesitate to disassemble you'. Fair enough, and I wanted to live a little longer, so I used a distraction technique. I got out a box of coloured drapes and ribbons and invited her to have a look. Shortly, the whole group were dressed up, hammering out rhythms and dancing, each still insulting each other's dance-styles, but in a good-natured way. Even the student who said he wouldn't join in sat grinning and rocking in his non-rocking chair. All good until the lighters came out and they thought it would be even more fun if some of the material was set light to. This happens frequently, especially as most students are smokers. I am aware that I am relied upon to preserve the safe space. I was told to 'fuck off' but no one actually resisted my taking away of the lighters.

Typically, if I tried to set up a similar session, it would fail; the impulse needed to be theirs. During the middle months of the group, a growing familiarity with the props and structures available for creative play enabled expression and an evident enjoyment of the freedom to do so. Although moods changed, it seemed to be generally understood that I would respond to their behaviour with firmness, warmth, permission where appropriate, interest and acceptance.

Later sessions

In the latter half of the second year, exams are a priority and everything else comes second. The pressure is unwelcome, even for young people who have no other stressors beyond those of a mainstream, 'normal' adolescence. Here, teachers and pupils become increasingly stressed and 'acting-out' behaviour increases. Staff become subject-focused and work less as a team. Therapy sessions are cancelled, when they might be most useful.

In Yellow Group (whose dramatherapy was not compulsory), Joan had just lost her father. Chloe had found her birth mother via the internet and was so traumatised by meeting her that she felt increasingly suicidal and was planning to return to a secure psychiatric unit. David was awaiting trial for armed robbery. Omar had been thrown out of his home. Amy's father was back in prison. None of them had done any course work. Two members of the group were causing staff to consider permanent exclusions.

Part of the anxiety around exams is the knowledge that an ending is looming and that the safety and support of the school will disappear. Some students became increasingly absent from school, others found excuses not to come to sessions, but when they did come there seemed to be a regression to earlier confrontational and destructive behaviours, an unwillingness to engage; openly using mobile phones, sleeping or winding up other group members. When I questioned what they wanted to get out of the group at this stage if they weren't willing to participate or cooperate, I heard variations on the response, 'Fucking leave me alone', while at the same time staying in the room and making no attempt to leave. The use of space altered dramatically; we were in a not-quite-a-circle shape, close together. The dramatherapy space appeared to be a cocoon or refuge. One member only came to school on the day of the group. Sometimes, on volatile days, I hardly dared breathe, but usually a few members of the group would start to share why they felt so irritable and to voice recent thoughts and events. We would discuss what would happen after the exams. We talked of families and childhoods that did not deserve the name. When offered beads, pens and paper, pipe cleaners and clay, objects were made and destroyed. There was a drive to create something visible and lasting, something that meant they would be remembered. This could be in the form of graffiti on a permitted wall, echoing the impulse at the beginning of the group. In one session most of the group threaded beads to represent aspects or stages or people in their lives. They decided what they needed to do. I tried to facilitate. On one occasion I was able to share some of the changes I'd seen in them: less verbal abuse, more racial/religious tolerance, less aggression, more empathy and trust, that they appeared more comfortable, less defensive.

Omar, who had once seemed so hard-bitten, was sitting nodding. He was going 'legit' now (in Omar's world, 'legit' meant no more street crime or crime with violence or drugs, although it could include credit-card fraud and handling stolen goods) and he was proud of the corner he'd turned. When asked what the group had meant for them, the response was again 'fucking shit' but said with affection and smiles. Ken even said, 'Yeah, it's really helped with my anger but don't get big-headed little smurf'. Amy noted that it had enabled them to support each other more, be like a family. John, who had once spat at me, reflected on his changed attitude towards me and the work I was trying to do; 'I hated everyone, I thought you'd be like the police but you weren't'. Not many words, no questionnaires filled in perhaps but an acknowledgement that dramatherapy had been an important part of their time at school.

Work with individuals

Some students would make use of individual dramatherapy sessions only when they had a particular crisis to deal with. Some had regular sessions over the 2 years. Certain students had to come with a friend first before progressing to individual work. My biggest problem was meeting demand.

Individual case study

Adam had a history of exclusions for violent behaviour and had spent time in care. He was quiet and withdrawn and very uneasy with his peers. He was prone to violent outbursts. Being 6 feet tall and bulky, these caused some damage. Other students bullied him because he was not 'street-wise'. He had no interest in drugs, crime or gangs and wore the same clothes every day. He was severely innumerate and illiterate.

Initially Adam came to 'talk things through'. Following our initial assessment session, he took up the offer of regular sessions. His rationale for coming was that at least once a week he would be away from his classmates. He saw the dramatherapy space as a safe refuge. In the first few weeks we worked with a variety of projective materials, as Adam was unwilling to work physically. He made 'messes' and 'creations' and started to discard adolescent awkwardness in favour of a childlike un-self-consciousness. Secure enough in our relationship, he began to gently mock me, saying what a 'failure' and/or 'midget' I was. He often repeated the phrase: 'Get over it and deal with it, you're going to die'.

When talking about his life, he was usually monosyllabic. In a lifeline exercise (in which significant events are shown on a line representing the client's life from birth to the present moment), he marked all his exclusions, his many broken bones and his time in care. He would not talk about feeling depressed but he did 'kill' all the glove puppets, mostly by hanging. Subsequently, his home situation deteriorated. His mother, a drinker, was arguing with Adam's alcoholic step-father. Adam attacked furniture with a knife and barricaded himself in his room. An extra session with me was requested in the hope that he would be able to stay at school. In this session he safely expressed his anger by thumping cushions and attacking the cardboard victim/scapegoat/indifferent object. I asked him about his barricading himself in his room and he asked if he could demonstrate by piling the cushions around me. I agreed and, when covered in cushions, I did note that it felt quite safe. Happy I had understood, he then created a cushion nest for himself until he was completely covered and went to sleep. Over the months the cushion nest became a fixture, with frequent naps, and with the addition of a cuddly toy transitional object and requests for stories. He also started sucking his thumb when in his nest.

I have found the need to regress a common feature of therapy with this client group, who often insisted on taking blankets and cushions from my room to take round with them during the school day. Sometimes, on a bad day, a member of staff, knowing I am booked up, will ask for X's pink blanket or Y's blue one. Interestingly, no student has ever mocked another student for this behaviour.

In Adam's case, such 'regressive' behaviour continued for weeks, until I sensed we were a bit stuck and wondered whether there was a need for further communication. Playfully, I removed a couple of cushions. Immediately 'Derek' the ghost emerged, covered in a sheet that Adam liked to have placed on top of his nest. Derek wanted to eat the midget and started to follow me round the room, attempting rugby tackles. Pinned against the wall of a very small room with 'Derek' demanding midget blood, I tried to work out a safe way to accommodate Adam's need for physical proximity and his desire to internalise the therapist by eating her. I had been thinking of David Read Johnson's *Developmental Transformations* (2005) in relation to my work with Adam, where very physical play is key as is the need to make the playspace safe. Speaking as myself, I indicated that we needed some more rules – beyond the ones I thought had been established between Adam and myself, i.e. for 'Derek' and 'the midget', and thankfully I was heard. 'Derek' released me and was satisfied with one midget arm for lunch. Adam was clearly hungry for affection and, by using Johnson's (2005: 13) guidelines – clear definition of play space and my own sense of what was safe and appropriate, Adam could have the reassuring hug from me he needed. Over the next few months, 'Derek' and other ghosts, who used very few words, indicated their fears, sadness and hopes, while Adam appeared to manage his peer relations more successfully and the bullying stopped. The midget was 'eaten' every week until Adam's last session, when 'Derek'

..ounced he now had the midget's power inside him and could leave. He then stuck a toy soldier on the ceiling to guard me and remind me of him.

Alongside the above, usually before the nest was made in a session, we started to use Sue Jennings' theory of embodiment, projection and role to explore Adam's need to find a voice to confront his aggressors:

> Dramatic projection enables access to dramatic processes as a means to explore. The dramatic expression creates a new representation of the client's material. The projection enables a dramatic dialogue to take place between the client's internally held situation and the external expression of that situation or material.
>
> (Jones 2007: 87)

Adam eventually found he could respond verbally and be heard before becoming physically violent. Adam was later able to reflect on his experience of dramatherapy, saying that it gave him a way to 'deal with things like anger' and to feel more confident about himself but he was not answering any more stupid questions.

Discussion and evaluation

This client group can, as seen, be very chaotic and fragmented. It should be noted that behavioural changes also occur as a result of the various contributions of the staff team. In evaluating the work, I used a modified version of Jones' adaptation of the Sutton–Smith–Lazier Scale of Dramatic Involvement (1981). My modification included use of space beyond dramatic use, i.e. how and where they chose to sit, lie, sleep, communicate or move outside of given exercises, as sometimes this was a large part of sessions. I attempted to incorporate strengths and difficulties questionnaires (SDQs) but, as any questions can inspire anxiety and hostility, the process was far from perfect. And if I asked what they had got from the group, the answer might be, 'It was fucking shit and you're fucking shit'. But, said with a smile, it might also indicate the opposite. I used my own observation of levels of trust, cooperation, confidence, tolerance, reflection and engagement. For example, with the group, staying in the room for the duration of the session indicated a positive change. One outcome was the creation of cohesion and a sense of safety where group members could be both vulnerable and relaxed. Johnson (1982b: 184) has noted that, from a developmental perspective, 'the degree of interpersonal demand which can be experienced in interactions with others' is a process that dramatherapy fosters, and I found it to be evident in both group and individual work. There was a marked decrease in abusive language and destructive behaviour within sessions, which was mirrored by behaviour in and around the school. Using Sue Jennings' (1995) EPR model and Johnson's *Developmental*

Transformations (2005), it was possible to reorient an angry individual to find his voice(s) and exert self-control as he learned a wider repertoire of roles in stressful situations. The difficulties associated with being on the receiving end of painful and disempowering projections can be seen as indications of core issues needing attention and become instead possibilities for transformation. Scapegoating is a common expression of the inability to tolerate weakness, 'badness' or vulnerability and is a key issue with this client group, whether as a victim or perpetrator. Dramatic projection (Jones 2007: 87) can ease the overloaded psyche of the troubled adolescent and allow movement where development has become stuck. Containment of the chaos became easier as individuals were offered ways to express their fears and pain and there was a subsequent reduction in anxiety and a reduced need to throw things out of the window or destroy people and furniture. In addition, the emerging adolescent spirit could progress according to its inner need, not the external criteria imposed by society and exam boards, which may mean going backwards before venturing forwards. There is often an impulse to regress with this client group and frequently transitional objects in the shape of soft toys and blankets used in sessions disappear from my room and are carried round the school for comfort or a 'corrective emotional experience'. Being a resident therapist may have advantages over appointments at a clinic or hospital; I am not a stranger in a strange place – an individual can decide to come and see me after they have assessed whether it's safe for them to do so. Roth and Fonagy (2004: 272), in their research on what treatment is efficacious for children and adolescents, have stated that the 'prevalence of . . . disorders implies that attention should be focused on the development of intervention programmes which can be integrated with educational initiatives and made as accessible as possible'.

Summary of key findings

Dramatherapy is a valuable resource in this setting, due to the variety of models and media at our disposal, the playful aspect of the work and the facilitation of physical and non-verbal expression, as well as its use as a container/transformer in group work. It is able to mirror and support the adolescent's tumultuous process safely and also provide a means to revisit earlier developmental gaps and trauma where possible. By having a dramatherapy space, the school has a designated chaos and destruction zone, which acknowledges rather than simply tries to control the behaviour of excluded adolescents.

6

SELF-HARM IN YOUNG
PEOPLE'S PSYCHIATRY:
TRANSFORMING MUNCH'S
SCREAM

Ditty Dokter

Brief overview of chapter

This chapter focuses on active self-harm during therapy. This may occur
within or between sessions, in the form of substance abuse, self-mutilation
and suicide attempts. These problems tend to be prevalent in clients with
the diagnosis of borderline personality disorder (BPD), addiction and psychosis, but tend to be extra prevalent in adolescent psychiatry. The clinical
case study is drawn from a 17-year-old young woman participating in
therapeutic community-based arts therapy groups. The theoretical orientation is group dynamic.

Introduction

As discussed in Chapter 1, arts therapists may understand the destructiveness
from an object relations and psychodynamic point of view. The integration
of the shadow aspect of the personality is an integral part of Jungian
individuation. Winnicott (1967) speaks of the discovery of the destructive self
in adolescence. Guggenbuhl-Craig (1971) points to a destructive urge which
appears with notable openness in youth. Frankl (1998) interprets these
destructive and aggressive elements in adolescence as manifestations of the
Shadow. The destructiveness of the client can evoke destructive impulses in
the therapist through defence mechanisms such as projective identification.
Arts therapists may be at risk of idealising the aesthetic, not recognising the
destructiveness potential in the arts medium (Milia 2000). In this chapter a
case example of therapeutic community group therapy for young people will
be analysed, highlighting the individual case of Sally. All names used are
pseudonyms. The subtitle, poems and images in the chapter are from the
health diary kept by the client in the case study. Munch's *Scream* was Sally's
image to sum up how she felt on a particularly 'crap' day. Figure 6.1 depicts
'Clouds', an image from her mood diary on another day, experiencing a
similar state of mind. The case study is drawn from research data studying

Figure 6.1. Clouds

the influence of cultural background variables on young people's access to arts therapies groups (Dokter 2010), although the aim of its use in this chapter is to use learning from the individual case to highlight ways of working with destructiveness. The conclusion links the understandings from the case study to the literature and systematic review guidelines.

Suicide as self-harm

Suicide is the cause of death for some 873,000 people worldwide per year according to World Health Organization estimates (Comtois and Linehan 2006). Non-fatal acts of self-harm occur in 400 out of 100,000 people in the UK (NHS Centre for Reviews and Dissemination 1998), with considerably higher rates amongst young people (Hawton et al. 2002; Meltzer et al. 2002). While deliberate self-harm may or may not involve suicidal intent, among known risk factors such acts are the best predictors of eventual suicide (Hawton et al. 2003). Between one-fifth and one-third of young people have had suicidal thoughts at least once in their lifetime; between one-quarter and one-half of those who have suicidal thoughts go on to attempt it. The best single predictor seems to be how hopeless a young person feels (Brezo et al. 2007; McMillan 2007).

Over the last decade, the Department of Health has encouraged trusts in the NHS to meet targets in suicide reduction, with particular attention to people who deliberately self-harm (Department of Health 1999; National Collaborating Centre for Mental Health 2004). Follow-up of self-harm is still only offered to 50% of incidents and of those there is a 70% attrition rate (drop-out after one appointment or failure to attend). Clients who self-harm are often met with negative attitudes by health professionals (Clarke and Whittaker 1998) and there is little available training in therapy with suicidal individuals (Comtois and Linehan 2006). Various forms of therapy focusing on suicide and self-harm prevention have been evaluated, showing a 'not proven' verdict (Hawton et al. 2002), although indicating 'promising results' for dialectical behaviour therapy for women diagnosed with borderline personality disorder, and group therapy for repeatedly self-harming adolescents. More recent studies in brief, focused, cognitive, personal construct and interpersonal psychotherapy also indicate potentially positive results (Comtois and Linehan 2006).

The British Association of Counselling and Psychotherapy (Winter et al. 2009) undertook its own systematic review of 63 quantitative and 13 qualitative studies in counselling in psychotherapy for the prevention of suicide. The review showed that therapy rather than no therapy had better outcomes. But therapist feelings of ambivalence indicated difficulties in treating the suicidal clients. These ambivalent feelings may override aspects such as therapist competence. Young people's views showed that clients wanted to be accepted, listened to, treated with respect and understanding, and they wanted the focus of the treatment to be holistic, focused on internal and external problems. Findings concerning group therapy highlight problems arising from transmission effects of self-harm, hopelessness and depression (Crouch and Wright 2004). Winter et al. (2009) emphasise in their recommendations the importance of the therapeutic alliance. Therapists who show respect, who validate feelings, who show non-judgemental understanding and do not remain silent for too long were experienced as effective by self-harming clients. Therapist hopelessness can be a detrimental factor in that alliance (Davidson et al. 2007).

The socio-cultural context of destructiveness

> Whoever studies the behaviour of human beings cannot escape the conclusion that we must reckon with the enemy within. It becomes increasingly evident that some of the destruction that curses the earth is self-destruction; the extraordinary propensity of the human being to join hands with external forces in an attack upon its own existence.
>
> (Menninger 1938: 4)

When looking at issues around self-destructiveness in dramatherapy, it is important to look at the potential for self-destruction in both the client and the therapist. In this chapter I will not focus on large group phenomena such as war (Hillman 2004), but it is interesting that in 1938, the time leading up to the Second World War, Menninger looked at a variety of ways in which human beings could be self-destructive. He distinguished chronic suicide from more focal acts, such as self-mutilation. Some thinking has changed; Favazza (1987) would certainly query whether self-mutilation should be considered as a form of suicide. Clients often exhibit a combination of self-destructive behaviours. I prefer to consider self-destructiveness on a continuum from 'socially sanctioned' to 'pathological'. Sociocultural variables play a role in this, which is why I put the sides of the continuum in inverted commas. On the 'sanctioned' side of the continuum, body piercing and tattooing have become more part of Western European fashion at the change from the twentieth to the twenty-first century. Unprotected promiscuity has moved over to the more 'pathological' side, especially since the onset of HIV and AIDS. Alcohol and food abuse tend to move along the continuum, depending on cultural, social and individual variables, while cutting, addiction and suicide tend to be seen as pathological. War is rarely seen as pathological, but weapons of war such as martyrdom/terrorism are easily pathologised and need to be considered as part of the cultural and political context in which they occur (e.g. Dokter 2008; Finklestein and Dent-Brown 2008; Stapley 2006). Physical illness and accidental injury are still rarely considered part of the destructiveness picture.

Before going into more detail about the self-destructive behaviours seen in young people's psychiatry, I want to contextualise the argument about the act of suicide. Suicide in itself is neither syndrome nor symptom (Hillman 1965). Suicide arises in life; it is more likely to occur in the home than in hospital. The points of view demanded by medicine and psychotherapy can be hard to combine. In a medical setting, psychological considerations may need to take second place. Hillman critiqued in 1965 that sometimes preventing suicide may constitute a psychological insult. Malan (1997), in a private practice context, quotes Winnicott's ruthlessness in saying to his suicidal client, 'You have a right to commit suicide'. The therapist's attitude to suicide is a crucial element in the relationship. The therapist's values can mirror the medical profession in the wish to preserve life; when working in a medical context, the therapist can be held liable if s/he does not adhere to the medical model of preserving life. The therapist's religious values may influence the stance taken. Each therapist needs to work out their own approach, but needs to take account of the possibility of destructive acting out, not only by the client but also by the therapist.

One of my early clients indirectly raised the ethical issues around the preservation of life. She suffered from very severe recurrent depression. I saw her for individual dramatherapy in an acute inpatient setting. She repeatedly attempted suicide and was also treated by heavy medication, ECT and, ultimately, at her request, psychosurgery in an attempt to protect her life. I wonder whether we as a team colluded with the client's sense of helplessness? Ultimately, after all the interventions, she developed life-threatening cancer. Menninger's reflection in 1938 about 'joining hands with external forces' can be a useful warning. The therapist's blind spots, ideological commitments and potential for active participation in destructiveness (such as withdrawing, punitive urging to take responsibility, premature termination, therapist illness and coldness) are as much a part of human relationships as the more curative factors (Yalom 1995). However, arts therapists can also take the view that self-mutilation is a form of attempted self-healing, through violent or destructive means (Milia 2000). Creation and destruction can be seen as neutral forces inherent within the creative process, operating in response to one another in an attempt to effect transformation (see also Chapters 1 and 2). In the context of self-healing, self-mutilation can be viewed as an act of transformation which opens many pathways between ritual, psychology, culture and art.

Further context: the setting and client group

The NHS young adult service provided outpatient and day treatment options. At the time of the research, outpatients were seen in individual psychological therapy while day patients received group psychotherapy treatment. The day treatment unit was modelled on standard therapeutic community settings and served a client group of 12 young adults, aged 16–25. Their average expected stay was 2 years. Over the 18 months of fieldwork, 18 clients attended the day treatment therapeutic community group.

Within the young adult unit, the arts therapies groups were part of the group programme attended by all clients. The author joined the groups as researcher/participant–observer for 18 months. The staff group consisted of a medical consultant, nurse therapists, an occupational therapist, arts therapists (art therapist, dramatherapist and dance movement therapist) and psychoanalytic psychotherapists. The arts therapies groups were co-facilitated by another staff member, often a nurse therapist. They took place 1 day per week; the morning group was co-facilitated by the drama-therapist and the dance movement therapist, whilst the art therapy group took place in the afternoon.

The arts therapies and young adult service developed during the social psychiatry movement in the 1960s and 1970s (Dokter 2001). The unit philosophy was based on psychoanalytic and medical concepts; diagnosis included psychiatric and psychodynamic formulations. The clients' problems were understood to originate in relational difficulties, which were thought to be re-enacted in the community group and addressed through group treatment of peers and staff. An analysis of the diagnoses showed that 45% of clients showed significant features of personality disorder, of which one-third met the criteria for borderline. The five cases of adjustment disorder were co-morbid with these diagnostic categories. Half the clients also suffered depression and exhibited self-harming behaviours. The co-morbidity with addiction was 45%. I would like to stress that diagnostic categories need to be considered critically here. Given that a large number of clients showed features of a variety of diagnoses, often co-morbid, these categories need to be considered as a relative way of indicating people's problems. One-third of clients had not received previous treatment, except medication, whilst two-thirds had received previous in- and outpatient treatment, indicating severity and chronicity of problems. The young adult psychiatric service added their own psychodynamic diagnosis indicating the aetiology of the clients' problems. The main identified stressors in clients' lives were parental separation and death (40%), bullying at school (30%) and sexual abuse (20%).

The research study examined, through the analysis of post-session focus groups (separate staff and client focus groups) and individual evaluation questionnaires completed following each therapy group, whether client and therapist differences in perception were linked to higher attrition rates. The research found that, in this unit, clients with significant features of (border-line) personality disorder and/or addiction problems were at greater risk of attrition. Severity and chronicity of symptoms, as well as co-morbidity, were also related to a high risk of drop-out. This reflects the literature (Roth and Fonagy 2004). Diagnoses were shown to be a relative way of categorising clients, because of the high rates of co-morbidity for 60% of clients. During their stay in the unit, the clients were asked to keep a health diary, to monitor their shifts in mood and reaction to treatment (Murray 1985). The rationale for its use was that:

> . . . the individual's response to the occurrence of symptoms is conditioned by a variety of non-medical factors of both an endur-ing (i.e. personality attributes) and a changing nature (i.e. social support). The health diary provides an appropriate method of studying the daily variations in health and illness behaviour.
>
> (Murray 1985: 827)

Research indicates that 40–60% of clients drop out of psychotherapy treatment in the early stages (Lambert 2004). There are no specific figures for the arts therapies. Comparatively, the clients in this study showed 33.3% attrition within the first 4 months, while 66.6% of clients remained in therapy.

Understanding borderline personality disorder (BPD)

This case study concerns Sally, a 17-year-old client, who was diagnosed with borderline personality disorder (BPD). In ICD10 this would be named 'emotionally unstable personality disorder', whilst any client under the age of 18 does not tend to be diagnosed with a personality disorder. As stated above, diagnostic categories are relative. Sally exhibited several of the following diagnostic criteria:

Figure 6.2. Sally's self-portrait 1

1. Impulsivity or unpredictability in at least two areas that are potentially self-damaging, e.g. spending, sex, gambling, substance abuse, shoplifting, overeating, physically self-damaging acts.
2. A marked pattern of unstable and intense personal relationships, e.g. marked shifts of attitude, idealization, devaluation, manipulation.
3. Inappropriate, intense anger or lack of control of anger, e.g. frequent displays of temper, constant anger.
4. Identity disturbance manifested by uncertainty about several issues relating to identity, such as self-image, gender identity, long-term goals, friendships.
5. Affective instability; marked shifts from normal mood to depression, irritability or anxiety, usually lasting a few hours with a return to normal mood.
6. Intolerance of being alone.
7. Physically self-damaging acts, e.g suicide attempts, self-mutilation.
8. Chronic feelings of emptiness and boredom.

(ICD10, World Health Organization 1992)

Sally used her health diary to explore her relationship with her diagnosis:

I did a lot of reading about BPD. This gave me a clearer understanding of some of the feelings I get. I was given that diagnosis, but no one ever told me about it so I didn't know if it was accurate. Now I understand it better.

This was on a day when she absented herself from the unit, read about her diagnosis and completed a self-harm questionnaire online:

> . . . hoping that it might help other people. It was also good, because it made me think about it.

That same day she did not take her medication (an anti-psychotic) and took alcohol to make herself feel better, after she was upset by reading her old section reports. She wrote:

> They upset me a bit. It made me see how I used to be and how close I keep getting to going back to being like that.

The therapists in the unit, as stated before, drew on psychoanalytic understanding, which is based more on patterns manifest in therapy (particularly in the transference) rather than in observable behaviours. Jenkyns (1996; also discussed in Chapter 1) is close to the original object relations interpretation, when she discusses how the concepts of projection and introjection are particularly relevant to the therapeutic effectiveness of role work. She emphasises that object relations imply a relationship with another. When this is unintegrated, it means relating to part-objects, which are in conflict with each other. Often, through splitting, bad experiences – especially the aggression felt in response to those experiences – are projected onto the other in the relationship. In Sally's case, the aggression was turned very much against herself and others were (un)wittingly engaged in this process.

In Chapter 3, I discussed relevant dramatherapy studies evaluated as part of the systematic review. The model of working in this case is close to Brem (2002) and Stamp (1998), while being linked to an understanding of 'acting out' formulated in relation to clients with eating disorders (Dokter 1994). The distancing process of the arts is related to expression through symbol and metaphor. The symbolisation can be difficult for BPD clients, due to an underdeveloped capacity to sublimate (Kernberg 1975). Sublimation is understood as the capacity to deal with frustration by the use of constructive or symbolic activities. Schwartz-Salant (1989) says that the possibility of play is usually absent for the BPD client, as they cannot experience the creativity of the transitional play space while in a state of confusion. He also emphasises the importance for the therapist not to use interpretation as a defence: the therapist may fill the emotional void with action. In a verbal context, this may mean using commentary to fill the space rather than undergo the experience of absence. A dramatherapist may fill this experience of absence by introducing dramatic structures to act on the anxiety of (not) being. It may be that a dramatherapist feels the need to justify their role in advocating action as part of a strongly held belief in the transformative nature of action, which could be defensively held/used in the therapeutic relationship.

Schwartz-Salant (1989) argues that the therapist's defensive action can collude with the borderline client's impulsiveness. Lavender and Sobelman (1995) identify three possible destructive ways of using the movement process in group dance movement therapy. They include a direct discharge through action (no symbolisation), stereotyped movement (repetitive, monotonous) and wish-fulfillment dances (stylised and emotionally detached portraits of romanticised human relationships). Lavender and Sobelman do not mention the possibility of eroticised acting out, or the denial of relationship through the arts activities (Levens 1995). These arts therapists stress the transformative possibility within the arts, but also advocate a suspension of action where necessary. This connects with Schwartz-Salant's advocacy for allowing oneself to be, whilst signposting that the client may experience either an imaginative lacunae or a torrential flow of imagery and fantasies which void experiencing feelings. The latter seems aptly illustrated by one of Sally's poems, entitled *Brain Activity*:

Thoughts racing
Emotions buzzing
So much
BRAIN ACTIVITY
I need a spray
To cover it up
All this
BRAIN ACTIVITY
I need some pills
To eventually rest
Stop this
BRAIN ACTIVITY

Case study

This case study concerns Sally's first 8 months of a two-and-a-half year treatment. She was on probationary discharge from a secure unit for the first 6 months, with a condition of daily attendance if she was not to be returned there. She and Kate joined the existing client group of Belle, Carol and Ted (Jack, Lia and Nathan joined several months later). All attended the day treatment programme of psychological therapy groups.

As well as her BPD diagnosis, Sally was diagnosed with self-harming and adjustment disorder. The unit identified no other stressors in this early stage of her treatment, which was still considered to be an extended assessment period while in transition from the secure inpatient unit. Her previous treatment was drug treatment, as well as receiving in- and outpatient child and adolescent psychiatric treatment.

In the researcher's interview with her, Sally said she attended the unit because she had nowhere else to go and needed to do something during the day. She also needed to get things off her chest.

> I needed something after hospital, having been there so long. I needed a step that was in between hospital and the outside world. I couldn't just leave and go to college or a job. I just can't cope. I want to kill myself. Now being in a rational state I can see that people do not want me to do it, but sometimes I get into a state where I think they all want to do it as well, so there is nothing to stop me. When I am in one state of mind, I cannot remember being in another one. When I am happy I cannot remember being sad or vice versa. I can remember what it was like, but not imagine that I will ever go back to that.

From her previous treatments, she felt the antidepressants and cognitive behaviour therapy had helped. People physically stopping her from harming herself were part of that help. When discussing her experience in the arts therapies groups, she felt it was a way of letting people 'sort of' know what she was feeling. She considered that it was sometimes harder to create an image than to say it.

This was in contrast with the staff team's view that the arts therapies were a less threatening way for clients to relate to others, as well as connecting with their own emotional life. Within the arts therapies groups, they observed that Sally was able to get some of her frustration and self-hatred out more powerfully in movement than in image making. The art therapist affirmed that she felt that Sally was able to use the art to illustrate some of the dramatic feelings she had about herself. Sally mentions in her post-DMT/Dramatherapy questionnaires that she found the 'kicking of a ball to express feeling' helpful. Occasionally a structure sparked off negative associations, for example she found the relaxation unhelpful. She imagined herself 'in a field, which brought back bad memories'. In the health diary she mentioned that playing felt good at the time, but later she felt guilty about having fun. When asked what she expected from the treatment, she focused on wanting to stop cutting and killing herself, and that she needed to 'learn to cope with people'.

The first 8 months in the unit centred around whether Sally would be able to feel part of the client group and engage with the treatment or not. It was a struggle for her and the rest of the group. Her completion of evaluation questionnaires fluctuated, as did her attendance in the focus groups. She seemed to be trying to find her feet both in the unit and in the research. She said in the research focus group that walking around made her feel able to connect to people somewhat. She also said that she was not sure what the arts therapies groups were about. She had wondered whether to join in or not, but was glad in retrospect that she did not join in much.

Two months later there was a significant shift in engagement with three of the clients, when Sally opened up about the conflict she was feeling. She said that she felt 'thick, as she could not get her drawing right' in the art therapy afternoon group and worried about Jack and Lia feeling bad when they did not participate and absented themselves. In the morning DMT/dramatherapy group she connected to Kate. She commented that kicking the ball let out some feelings and said she really enjoyed going out for a walk and playing with Kate. The dramatherapist and dance movement therapist were placed in a dilemma when Sally and Kate requested to go for a walk in therapy group time, as there were only the two of them present and the sun was shining. Sally and Kate splashed in the children's pool and discussed the fact that they had felt unselfconscious and 'not bothered about people seeing my scars' (they had rolled up their sleeves and trousers/skirt and exposed more skin than was normally visible). Following this outing, Sally wrote the following poem in her diary:

Sun
　　Beating down on me
　　Keeping me alive
　　Changing my skin
　　In a sociably acceptable way
　　A way I don't have to hide
　　Now, but maybe only for today
　　Maybe I
　　Won't have to
　　Change my skin

This connection with Kate was brought to an abrupt end when Kate suddenly left the unit. She had been working towards an ending, but left earlier than planned. Sally did not complete a questionnaire, nor did she attend the focus group. The staff focus group commented that Kate not coming back to say goodbye might have been upsetting to Sally. In her questionnaire she said she 'felt crap' and saw herself as unhelpful. The staff group was concerned that her self-harming seemed to be escalating. The summer break was due to start. In her diary Sally wrote that in getting closer to others she was more worried for them. She found it hard to talk honestly to people and that her wanting to cut herself increased. She wrote that she was 'trying to block things out and act happy' and was 'Making plans to cut later on'. A poem expressed how she felt in relation to the cutting:

Cut,
Deep,
Watch it
Weep.

Cut,
A gash,
Watch myself
Slash

Cut,
The flesh
Wipe out the scars
And start afresh.

After Kate's leaving, Sally continued to build relationships with other group members. Soon afterwards, Belle was admitted to hospital after a serious overdose. Sally was upset and sat out in the drama and movement group. Sally said that, 'all the groups felt crap at the moment' and complained that the art therapist 'had been rude'. My participant observation notes explained the 'rudeness' in that the therapist commented on the silence and asked Sally about her image. Sally's questionnaire seemed to indicate being upset at having been asked, although she commented that other clients, who would not discuss their images, were felt to be unhelpful. During the next few weeks she was frequently absent, showing further ambivalence. Sally said she could not see the point of 'all this wobbling up and down' and did not want to comment on her absence. The staff focus group expressed frustration about her 'dramatic absence' and thought it might be related to the fact that she was coming up towards the end of her probationary period in the unit.

Soon after this Sally hit a crisis period. She walked out of the drama-therapy group, threatening to throw herself in front of a train. The group followed her half-way to the railway line, where they persuaded her to return to the unit. Following this incident she created a red image stating 'HELP'. The staff focus group wondered whether the crisis was a response to being included in the group.

The next week Sally arrived late and stayed outside the DMT/ dramatherapy group waiting. She had not asked to come in and said she found it hard to ask for help. She articulated ambivalence about staff questions. On the one hand she felt that they were intrusive; on the other hand she found it hard to ask for help. She wanted the staff to respect her privacy. Sally commented that everything felt unhelpful. The following week Sally participated in the group and said she was pleased with the shortening of the DMT/dramatherapy group by 15 minutes. She felt it was good 'considering how I hate it. Sometimes I get this burst of energy; I might now not join in again for a month'. She also said that joining in the movement stopped her from walking out. She said in the questionnaire that she enjoyed the relaxation this time, but the structure where clients walked behind each other made her 'feel paranoid'.

Her engagement with the therapists became both closer and more openly conflictual in the next phase. Unit staff changes were announced. Sally was upset about this in the sessions. She was late and angry, but did not want to discuss reasons. Later she said she had planned to be absent today, woke up wanting to go, but was then late. The next week Sally felt the session was frustrating. She said in the focus group that the dance movement therapist was 'twisting' the clients' words. Sally identified with the other clients; she left the session, then returned and left early with all the other clients.

The following week the clients negotiated that the drama and movement therapy group be used for talking. They said they wanted to talk, because there was so much staff turnover. They felt that there was no space for their concerns (the dance movement therapist announced that there would be a 4-week break over December, as she was on annual leave). Sally said it was good to be able to talk and that the session could be adapted.

As the researcher was soon leaving the unit, Sally asked her in the session whether she really needed to leave and cried when the response was affirmative. The clients commented on the researcher's leaving and discussed where she fitted in the hierarchy. Sally said, 'She is one up from us, but one down from the staff'. It was interesting that this in-between position seemed to evoke the notion of being an alien/alienation. The clients explored the 'foreign' identity of the art therapist, the researcher and a group member (Dokter 2005/2006). Sally seemed to be able to connect to this belonging/not belonging dynamic. She was able to say goodbye, found it a good experience and connected with the other group members by

Figure 6.3. Sally's self-portrait 2

90

asking to do a group painting in the researcher's final art therapy session (in contrast to not being able to say goodbye to Kate and struggling to connect to the other clients 6 months earlier).

Case discussion

Sally's case study highlights areas of concern for arts therapists working with adolescent clients, as well as with those diagnosed with borderline personality disorder. The importance of group therapy for adolescents is discussed, but with a proviso that potential destructiveness can be transmitted between clients. Clients themselves indicated the need for longer-term therapy (Winter et al. 2009), whilst randomised control trials (RTCs) indicate the potential usefulness of brief therapy (Hawton et al. 1999). A review of arts therapy evidence (Smeijsters and van Cleven 2006) focusing on anger and aggression can produce transformative effects potentially facilitating mentalisation. There is a very high attrition rate of BPD and adolescent self-harming clients in psychological therapy and other interventions. The continued engagement of a client such as Sally in an ongoing process of personal change is a positive sign that arts therapies groups can be effective. Cases such as hers do not lend themselves to RCTs. Individual replication of case studies should be considered as evidence for the higher chronicity of cases arts therapists tend to work with. However, this does not mean that Sally does not highlight shortcomings and pitfalls in arts therapeutic treatment.

Her constant switching between engagement and breaking off contact, between attachment and separation, highlights the longer-term work of learning to build a therapeutic alliance. More trusting relationships with peers and therapists need time to develop, so that grieving can become a part of relating. Ainsworth (Fonagy et al. 2002) has highlighted different styles of attachment in her adult attachment interview, which indicate useful lessons for adolescent, potentially also older, BPD clients. The normal developmental stage in adolescence of working towards individuation, learning to integrate conflicted aspects of the self, can be seen in Sally as well as her more chaotic attachment style and rapidly fluctuating mood states. Rice and Benson (2005) note that adequate grief and mourning are crucial for alleviating destructiveness, as they reduce projections. In the first loss of Kate, Sally had just started to attach herself and Kate's abrupt leaving without saying goodbye exacerbated Sally's difficulties, as shown in increased self-harm. Belle's suicide attempt further added to Sally's hopelessness, which was experienced by the other group members and therapists. It resulted in a staff–client split, where the clients projected their anger at the therapists' perceived uselessness by not attending the sessions and walking out to visit and support Belle. The concept of destructive transmission could be used to understand Sally's subsequent acting out, walking out of the group to the railway line, threatening to kill herself.

The staff team saw her behaviour more as an expression of her ambivalence about being in relationships. This would be consistent with both their medical and psychodynamic understanding, namely the diagnostic criteria of BPD, as well as Kohut's theory about the need for a self-object, as used by Lavender and Sobelman (1995). The latter identify concrete movement as one of the stereotypical characteristics of BPD clients in dance movement therapy (DMT), seeing the lack of symbolisation as purely destructive. Their understanding about the symbolic is linked to that of other arts therapists who see the healing distancing process of the arts as related to expression through symbol and metaphor. I wonder whether this idea needs to be considered in more detail when working with destructiveness in adolescents. Maybe moving from concrete to symbolic is a necessary developmental stage, not just at school age (following Piaget 1983), but also in the next developmental stage. Moving from concrete to symbolic may be a necessary stage of development for an adolescent coming to terms with the reality of destructiveness in oneself and life in general (Winnicott 1967, Guggenbuhl-Craig 1971, Frankl 1998). Moving from concrete to symbolic might mean integrating destructiveness and pain whilst moving from the schizoid to the depressive position (Klein 1946). Maggie McAlister (Chapter 11) also looks at the development of symbolism in psychotic clients.

In dramatherapy, the developmental model enables an assessment/ intervention strategy via embodiment to projective to role play (Jennings et al. 1994). This may enable a development along necessary lines, rather than a split between image making and embodiment which Sally experienced between DMT/dramatherapy and art therapy groups. I wonder whether different levels of play and concrete embodiment may be a precursor of symbolic embodiment, thus capable of transformation/development rather than only a destructive facet. The 'kicking the ball to let off steam' could become transformed in the symbolic movement of moving through a meadow.

However, a focus on the arts mode can exclude the interpersonal element of the arts therapies transference triangle (Jones 2005). The BACP systematic review (Winter et al. 2009) showed the crucial importance of the therapeutic alliance when working with self-harming clients. Sally's case study shows the difficulty in doing so through testing, splitting and breaking of boundaries. I wonder whether breaking the boundary of space, by going for a walk with Kate instead of maintaining the boundary of the therapy session, with both therapists accompanying the clients, was a parallel to the breaking of boundaries by the group – the first time when the clients visited Belle in hospital during session time and secondly when Sally walked out of therapy to the railway line. Was this therapist collusion in breaking boundaries a first step towards more destructive acting out of hopelessness and helplessness? On the other hand, the paradoxical nature of the (lack of) intervention meant that Sally and Kate could allow themselves to play outside the therapy session, where they had continuously struggled to play within the expected boundary. They risked showing their 'true' scarred skin, rather than feeling they had to hide their 'true' selves. Only later in treatment, when Sally could engage more with fellow clients and therapist, could she use the arts therapies groups as a healing setting for play to connect with herself through relaxation in the DMT/dramatherapy session and with others through a group painting in art therapy.

I wonder whether the ability to establish relationships with peers was a crucial developmental step for Sally to establish relationships with therapists. As she had been in a secure setting, staff were experienced as controllers who withheld what you needed or 'twisted' your words and/or images in their interpretations. Being able to ask to 'play' in a way of her choosing, be it talking or painting, was another crucial step for Sally in feeling that the therapy space or the relationship could be influenced by her, become truly interpersonal, rather than rejecting or inviting or avoiding control.

Arts therapists, in their choice of medium and structure, may be more likely to be experienced as controlling, and become the 'overactive' therapist who fills the void with commentary or action (Schwartz-Salant 1989).

Conclusion

Summarising the benefits and pitfalls of dramatherapy group work input to young people with BPD, arising from this case study:

Potential benefits:
- Relationships with peers as support/attachment to counter-balance the possibility of destructive transmission.
- Length of therapy. Clients themselves indicated the need for longer-term therapy (Winter et al. 2009), whilst randomised control trials indicate the potential usefulness of brief therapy (Hawton et al. 1999). Attachment styles need to be considered (see below).
- A review of arts therapy evidence indicates that the potential focus on anger and aggression as destructive processes can produce transformative effects (Smeijsters and van Cleven 2006), with a potential link to facilitating mentalization processes.
- High attrition rates. The continued engagement of a client such as Sally in an ongoing process of personal change is a positive sign that this type of group therapy can be effective. Cases such as hers do not lend themselves to RCTs. Individual replication of case studies should be

considered as evidence for the higher chronicity of cases dramatherapists tend to work with.

- Attachment and developmental issues to consider. Sally's constant switching between engagement and breaking off contact, between attachment and separation, highlights the longer-term work of learning to build a therapeutic alliance. More trusting relationships with peers and therapists need time to develop, so that grieving (rather than destructive acting out) can become a part of relating.

Therapist adjustment may be needed in:
- Symbolisation: can different levels of play and concrete embodiment be a precursor of symbolic embodiment?
- Focus on interpersonal aspects as well as arts mode to develop therapeutic alliance.
- The ability to establish relationships with peers may be a crucial developmental step in establishing relationships with therapists.
- Directive/non-directive therapist orientation should be adjusted to client need; issues of control to be considered in the counter-transference.
- Therapist to be aware of the possibility that moving into action to fill the void can be destructive.

7

SELF-HARM IN CLIENTS WITH LEARNING DISABILITIES: DRAMATHERAPISTS' PERCEPTIONS AND METHODOLOGY

Jane Jackson

Brief overview of chapter

This chapter begins by outlining the research methodology and context for the study of self-harm in clients with severe to profound learning disabilities. After a definition of the main concepts and an overview of literature, the findings are presented: What meaning do dramatherapists give to self-harm? What interventions do they use? What are the outcomes? A case study illustrates the practice and the ethics of the interventions are considered. The chapter concludes by reviewing and evaluating the findings and how and/or whether they can be generalised for other client groups.

Introduction

Methodology

The following is based on a qualitative research project. The research question was, 'Is self-injurious behaviour a form of communication by adults with severe to profound learning disabilities, and can interventions be made within dramatherapy to support those who self-injure?'. I undertook semi-structured interviews with dramatherapists (the research participants) working at the same institution, to discover whether self-harm was a communicative act and what interventions were used. Information was collated to record occurrences in the therapeutic space (interventions and interpretations). This information was then clustered into recurring themes that emerged through the analysis of the data.

Research participants

In the UK context of dramatherapy provision, 23.6% of dramatherapists work with the learning disability population (Karkou and Sanderson 2006).

The seven research participants in this study all worked with this client group, working for the same National Health Service (NHS) Primary Care Trust. They were also homogeneous in their training background. One trained at Kingsway Princeton College, which became the Sesame Institute, the remainder at Sesame. Many Sesame practitioners call themselves drama and movement therapists – Sesame training holds these two elements at its core (Karkou and Sanderson 2006). Perhaps Sesame's oblique approach is more suitable for this client group, where difficulties can be 'expressed through metaphor and symbol without the need for verbal confrontation and exposure' (Karkou and Sanderson 2006: 223).

When comparing the sample data of research participants with full membership of the British Association of Dramatherapists (BADth 2008), the research participants included more male than female therapists. Their ethnic self-definition was 57% white British, 28% white other and 15% mixed race. They had an average age of 42.6 years, with 85% in the 41–50 age bracket. As a group, they had an average of 12.3 years post-qualifying experience (range 3–23 years).

However, the research participants' comments on individual dramatherapy orientation and ways of working were varied and heterogeneous. Despite similar experiences in formative training and methods of approach, they had some differing views on the cause and meaning of self-harm and type of intervention, and each developed their own working style, based on their own self, their influences and interests beyond dramatherapy. Interventions were based on working creatively with a client for the purposes of healing and growth – the ethos of dramatherapy (BADth 2009). In the resulting practice-based evidence, dramatherapists are not identified and client names have been changed to maintain confidentiality.

Introduction to the client group and setting

The clients are diagnosed as having severe to profound learning disabilities, and are mainly non-verbal. Some also have dual diagnoses with mental illness and many have physical disabilities, sensory impairments and self-harm. The definitions used are:

1. *Severe to profound learning disability*. The British Government Department of Health's White Paper *Valuing People* defines learning disability as including the presence of:

- A significantly reduced ability to understand new or complex information, to learn new skills (impaired intelligence), with;
- A reduced ability to cope independently (impaired social functioning);

- Which started before adulthood, with a lasting effect on development.

(Department of Health 2001: 14)

Those with severe and profound learning disabilities come under the heading 'People with Additional and Complex Needs' (Department of Health 2001: 100) who 'often have other associated health problems, such as physical disabilities, sensory impairments and epilepsy' (Department of Health 2001: 100) and 'may have difficulty communicating their needs and wishes' (Department of Health 2001: 101).

2. *Self-harm/self-injurious behaviour.* I have chosen the term 'self-harm' over that more frequently used in this client group, 'self-injurious behaviour'. Self-injurious behaviour often comes under the umbrella of challenging behaviour, and is described as:

Any behaviour, initiated by the individual, which directly results in physical harm to that individual. Physical harm (includes) bruising, lacerations, bleeding, bone fractures and breakages, and other tissue damage.

(Murphy and Wilson 1985, cited in Murphy 2003: 1)

The terminology evolved over the years from '*Problem* behaviour in people with severe learning disabilities' (my italics; Zarkowska and Clements 1988) to 'People with learning disabilities who have challenging behaviour' (Mansell 1993: 3). Mansell gives a more appropriate definition in the revised report: people whose behaviour 'presents a challenge to services' (Mansell 2007: 5).

Setting

The NHS setting was a long-term residential institution. On site were medical and therapeutic departments and opportunities for social activities. Most of the residents had lived there since childhood, with the majority in the age range 40–60 years. My research coincided with the institution's slow closure. The UK government legislated the closure of these sites by April 2004, although its reasons were ambiguous: 'research has raised significant concerns about the quality of life enjoyed by people living in NHS residential campuses' (Department of Health 2001: 75). The date for closing this institution had been delayed. The ongoing closure meant huge changes for many clients – some moved into local or more distant community homes. As homes within the site closed, other clients were relocated within the institution, perhaps more than once. Statistics show that self-harm is higher for this client group when they live within institutions than in the community. The prevalence of non-institutional self-harm is 4–10% (Murphy and Wilson 1985; Qureshi 1993, 1994; Halliday and Mackrell 1998); this increases to 8–15% within institutions (Murphy 2003; Wolverson 2006; Oliver and Head 1990). This could be due to greater severity of the learning disability in such settings, but other factors relating to the dynamics of the institution and the experience of institutionalisation may play a role.

Dramatherapy within this setting was initiated by a dramatherapy charity, and remained in place for 23 years. Following referral, a drama-therapist met with the client to make a detailed assessment. Clients then began a series of eight to twelve sessions. If dramatherapy was considered a suitable medium, they would continue. The institution's policy was that all residents would receive at least one weekly creative therapy session. Dramatherapy sessions generally consisted of group work for an hour each week, with one-to-one support for each client (e.g. three dramatherapists and three clients in one group). A dramatherapist worked with specific individuals each week, within the same group setting. Continuation of an individual's dramatherapy depended on various factors, but the intention was for long-term work.

Evaluation of clinical work focused on an individual client's responses and the group as a whole. Evaluation methods were peer supervision, external clinical supervision, 6-monthly review days, feedback from other staff members and through report writing and attendance at client meetings. These less formal evaluation methods are frequently used by dramathera-pists, as shown in a BADth survey, where client observation (20%) and self-evaluation devised by the practitioner (27%) are common (Winn 2008). Dramatherapy aims were to provide a safe place for clients to explore their emotional needs and to support their mental health. The sessions focused on building self-esteem, improving social interaction, developing communica-tion and self-expression, building relationships and having fun. Working with self-harm was part of the work, but not the main focus.

Main clinical themes and frameworks

Psychotherapy is relatively new to this client group. Emerson et al. (1994: 10) wrote that people are 'unlikely to receive specific psychological help for their challenging behaviour'. Over a decade later, Mansell (2007: 8) writes, 'psychological treatment for challenging behaviour remains difficult to get'. In London, psychotherapy services for adults with learning disabilities have been offered at Respond since 1991 and the Tavistock Clinic since 1995. Some of this work has been published (Simpson and Miller 2004; Cottis 2009) but little has focused specifically on self-harm.

Therapy offers 'the best chance of unearthing some of the reasons behind the self-harming behaviour' (Jones et al. 2004: 492) but it is uncertain what orientation this therapy should take. Cognitive-behavioural and psychodynamic orientations are evaluated as limited, but showing 'evidence that individuals make improvements' (Beail, in Twist and Montgomery 2005: 354).

In arts therapies research, the efficacy of music therapy in relation to self-harm found no reduction of self-harm in four case studies (Lawes and Woodcock 1995). Wigram (1993: 274) suggests the use of 'low-frequency sound and sedative music' to reduce self-harm, whilst Warner (2007) writes that in accepting challenging behaviour as communication, there can be a musical response in therapy 'by improvising in an empathic manner, possibly using similar sounds and body postures' that 'allows the client to experience an acknowledgement of their feelings and communications' (Warner 2007: 49).

Dramatherapists such as Anna Chesner (1994, 1995), Jo James (1996a and 1996b) and Noëlle Blackman (2003, 2008) are authors on learning disability, but do not focus on self-harm, whilst dramatherapy case study research in the area of self-harm focuses on people without a learning disability. Methods documented are through physically connecting with the body in a creative rather than destructive manner (Andersen-Warren and Grainger 2000) or by using 'creative activity as a substitute for self-harm' (Brem 2002: 21). This offers containment and a way of projecting experiences and feelings onto or into the creative activity or object (Brem 2002). Non-arts therapies authors also make connections to using metaphor in therapy, or look at the symbolic meaning of self-harm (Collins 1996; Gardner 2001). However, in dramatherapy there is a gap in the literature regarding this client group and self-harm.

Dramatherapists and self-harm: aetiology and interventions

This section discusses how dramatherapists understand the cause of self-harm and how this connects to the meanings they ascribe to the behaviours and the ways of intervening they have developed. The central importance of the therapeutic relationship is illustrated with a vignette about Ruth later in the chapter.

Aetiology and meaning of self-harm

The impact of the learning disability on the propensity towards self-harm was considered. One dramatherapist felt that 'limited capacity for thought can often result in acting out and action occurs in the space where ideally thoughts would emerge' (all quotations, unless otherwise attributed, are from interview data). The inability to communicate verbally was another suggested reason. One dramatherapist spoke of how movement and action could be a way of non-verbally communicating something that has happened, whilst another considered self-harm as self-expression. Others thought about the frustration of understanding the speech of others whilst being unable to speak.

According to many of the dramatherapists, the institution played a part in the reasons that people engaged in self-harm, with one dramatherapist describing that 'a large institution has been here for 100 years, enormous wards, a nursing culture, a medical model of illness, a behavioural approach where people are not heard'. Another felt it was 'a huge indictment on this place' that her client self-harmed so much, whilst another's assessment of the impact on his client was that 'the environment's failed her, challenged her and let her down'.

Several dramatherapists spoke of how self-harm was perceived and responded to by residential care staff, where self-harm was sometimes seen as behaving badly or attention seeking. Staff had ignored or commented with insensitivity towards expressions of 'negative' emotions. The institutionalised culture, linked with the outdated idea of challenging behaviour, meant that there was distinct challenge for dramatherapists in focusing on self-harm as a form of communication.

Dramatherapists considered that there was communication within self-harm, summed up by one: 'Any action that happens is never something that just happens, it always has intention and communication behind it'. Self-harm was also called 'a very valuable communication tool'. An example of self-harm being used as direct communication was cited: 'she did it [self-harmed], she communicated something, somebody reacted and then she responded and she stopped the behaviour'.

The complexity of communication was revealed by one dramatherapist, who felt that self-harm was being used to 'communicate their feeling, their request, their thoughts, their hurt'; or, in the words of another, 'creating *outside* a sense of what that person might feel about themselves *inside*'. All the dramatherapists gave many examples of a range of feelings they felt were being shared through the self-harm: frustration; boredom; anxiety; apprehension; dehumanisation; low self-esteem; loneliness; lack of relationship; not feeling good enough; rejection; anger; uncertainty; lack of confidence; difficult thoughts; insecurity; lack of trust; fear; shyness; distress; rage; self-loathing; guilt; safety; worthlessness; uselessness; isolation; depression; deep chronic distress; sadness; self-hating; feeling unsafe; excitement; confusion; physical pain. All these were described in the context of specific work with specific clients. Two dramatherapists identified lack of sexual intimacy as a possible reason for self-harm. One identified it as frustration, whilst another considered that some clients 'don't appropriately know how to get sexual enjoyment'. Three dramatherapists mentioned past abuse or trauma as a possible precipitant. One gave general comments and listed the types of abuse as 'physical, emotional, sometimes sexual':

> I do believe that in many cases it [self-harm] stems from abuse in a variety of forms, often originating in formative years and being then continued and reinforced through adulthood.

One dramatherapist gave as evidence of suspected sexual abuse how the client was often inappropriately physically close to the therapist, and focused on oral sensations of mouth and fingers. Another evidenced possible trauma by the way the client was fearful and repeated sentences.

In terms of what the client might be consciously or unconsciously asking for, there were many suggestions, based on specific clients. The needs were: to be made safe; to be seen; to be acknowledged; to be prevented from self-harming; reassurance; affirmation; space; contact; being witnessed when in pain; meeting; engaging; being listened to.

The therapeutic relationship and offering interventions

The core of the work was the development of a trusting therapeutic relationship, so that clients felt enabled to take supported risks by responding to the interventions offered. The benefits of working long-term are of particular importance for this client group, who may have experienced many fractured attachments. Blackman states that 'it can take some time for long-term defences to come down in order that deeper work can take place' (Blackman 2008: 189). Many of the dramatherapists worked intuitively in their response to self-harm and were flexible in offering an intervention that depended on their understanding of the communication. This is often through transference or counter-transference feelings experienced by the dramatherapist, which can then influence the dramatherapist's response and intervention. Sinason (1992) describes the value of this:

> I will know from my own counter-transference feelings whether the blow was aggressive, hopeful; whether it was to knock something bad out or something good in.
>
> (Sinason 1992: 114)

An example of this unconscious communication was:

> . . . maybe I was sitting behind her, *maybe* she was *just* giving me her weight, maybe she was just beginning to relax, and it would always be the moment that I considered in my mind that we were together and OK, *that* would be when she would hit herself.

The interpretation given was that there was something:

101

. . . inter-psychic between the two of us because it would be about, *(sigh)* OK we're all, *(explosive sound)* and I felt it was communicating 'No. . . . we're not as together as you think we are, and can I remind you that it is not possible for me to be at peace and relaxed with an other'.

Interventions offered and rationale

The dramatherapists spoke of the interventions they offered and their aim for the client in that moment. There was the acknowledgement from some that, at times, interventions were trial and error. I have categorised the interventions and their rationales into behavioural, creative and dramatherapeutic:

(A) *Behavioural interventions: ignoring, physical prevention and distraction*
- *Ignoring.* Doing nothing in response to self-harm had two rationales:
    1. The hope that by ignoring the action the client would not do it again.
    2. A silent acknowledgement that self-harm is the client's choice.
- *Physical prevention.* Physically intervening had two rationales:
    1. To prevent further damage to the client, ensuring the client knew this was out of concern, not punitive.
    2. To protect the therapist, as witnessing the self-harm had become unbearable.

Two dramatherapists stated that physical prevention often had the opposite effect – the self-harm continued, or the feeling behind the self-harm increased. Another dramatherapist never used this intervention, because the client would not feel heard, or might consider that the therapist was not taking the emotion seriously.
- *Distraction.* Using objects or instruments had two rationales:
    1. Shifting focus from self-harm by offering an alternative outlet for self-expression.
    2. Building up confidence through development of another skill.

(B) *Creative interventions: sound and verbal*
- *Sound.* Sound interventions used voice or music as an alternative to self-harm:
    1. Mirroring and amplifying a client's vocals, so feelings were not built up internally but released outwards.

2. Playing recorded music; using similar music to work with client feeling as a safe container or as a release, or conflicting music to shift the mood.

- *Verbal.* Verbal interventions had several rationales:
  1. To let the client know that their self-harm was being witnessed, and to wonder aloud why this might be occurring.
  2. To give the client contact with what was happening in the moment, as s/he may be dissociating from the self-harm.
  3. To help the client make connections by providing a voice for the non-verbal communication, and suggest interpretations of what the client might be saying.
  4. There was also a suggested verbal acknowledgement that although the client might be able to use alternatives to self-harm in dramatherapy sessions, they might still need to self-harm elsewhere.

(C) *Dramatherapy interventions: symbolic, posture, touch and physical*

- *Symbolic.* The rationale was to make connections through symbol or imagery. An example was given of a client who often knocked over or threw chairs. The dramatherapist linked this with the chair symbolising authority, and the client seemed to be throwing that authority overboard.
- *Posture.* Offering an alternative posture to that of the client. For example, if the client was crouched over, the therapist's posture would be open and stretched out. There were two rationales for this:
  1. To show a different way of being – that one could give space to the whole body.
  2. To give the client a sense of relaxation through the therapist's body.
- *Touch.* I make a distinction between touch and physical interventions, the former using touch with the hands, as opposed to the potential to use the body more fully in a physical intervention. There were two rationales for the use of touch with hands:
  1. A dramatherapist gives gentle but firm hand contact to the head of the client, to soothe and calm, and to ground the client.
  2. If a client has hit his own head, the dramatherapist will put their own hand very gently on the site of injury, to give him the opposite sensation of what he's giving himself.
- *Physical.* There were two rationales for physical interventions:
  1. To explore relationship, as in the vignette of Ruth below.

2. To meet the client's energy. An example was given of working around kicking against containment. The drama-therapist put their arms around the client, who then pushed against that container. The energy had a fighting quality to it, where the client responded like with like.

Case vignette: dramatherapy with Ruth

The work with Ruth is an example of how the action of self-harm can be transformed into something healthier. Ruth worked in a dramatherapy group with one-to-one therapist support for each client, for over 20 years. When one dramatherapist met her 22 years previously, Ruth frequently banged her head against walls, her wheelchair or with her fist. If on the floor, Ruth would crash backwards to bang her head on the floor. She wore a protective leather helmet. In dramatherapy, Ruth scooted around the floor on her bottom, and one of the dramatherapists would constantly follow to ensure that if Ruth crashed backwards, the therapist was in place to prevent her head hitting the floor. Over time, the work developed as a mixture of physical and symbolic interventions, where the dramatherapists helped Ruth to explore relationship by encouraging her to physically find her way through, around or over human obstacles:

> . . . of being helped, of being kind of against relationships, of through relationships, of over, of together and separateness, and I think using that . . . as a metaphor for relationships with people, that sometimes you clash, sometimes you need separate space, sometimes you get tangled up together, sometimes one's helping the other . . . sometimes it's funny, sometimes it's a bit scary, but . . . it doesn't mean that we then separate completely, but that we maintain that thread.

Ruth began to have:

> . . . reflective times of smiling and just changing her sounds from 'AAHH' to 'du du du du du du du' sounds to her then, in those separate times . . . moving towards me after she'd had her time to think, rather than me moving towards her.

Eventually:

> . . . instead of banging her head she transferred that, filling the space with different kinds of activities, and she transferred the going to the edge/taking risks to try making/taking risks in her relationship with me.

Her previous movement of leaning back and smacking her head on the floor was transformed into leaning back and stopping. Ruth began to wear her helmet less, and eventually it was no longer needed. It was felt that the helmet's removal:

> . . . opened her up again into relationship in a way; that something of the un-masking . . . not having to be protected, but being able to be herself . . . it felt like she could take much better, greater responsibility for herself, it felt life-changing.

Through the dramatherapy work, Ruth developed:

> . . . a quality of life, and we had that . . . specifically fed back to us that it was very specifically dramatherapy . . . that had made this change in her life.

This work with Ruth highlights the importance of working long-term with this client group and how with time, patience, sensitivity and taking risks, real change can occur.

> Change in therapy with people with a learning disability can be small and take time. Although it is possible that these results could be argued as insignificant in statistical terms, we know from our positions as therapists that such changes are not insignificant to the clients themselves or to those around them.
>
> (Pounsett et al. 2006: 95)

Observations, reflections and discussions

Conclusions from clinical practice

The research question focused on discovering whether there was communication behind self-harm in this client group. The dramatherapists all believed this to be the case and suggested an array of meanings and feelings behind the action. They acknowledged that a client might self-harm for different reasons at different moments, depending on the individual, the situation in the session, the different relationships within the session and the client's life situation. This reveals an approach that appreciates emotional expression through self-harm, taking into account the person as a whole, and links in with the writings of Lovell (2007) and Jones et al. (2004). The holistic view is something that may have been ignored nationally until the publication of the *Valuing People* White Paper (Department of Health 2001). Some of the institutional practices and attitudes witnessed towards clients who self-harmed were outmoded. Increased links between dramatherapists and other staff may have enabled more of a shift in attitude and consistency of care and support. The findings reveal a variety of interventions, the reasons for their choice, and some of the outcomes. The dramatherapists are often clear in offering a specific intervention at a specific time with a specific client. The therapeutic relationship is the stable base from which drama-therapeutic interventions are offered.

Evaluation, areas for further research and generality

Ruth's response to the dramatherapeutic interventions had a positive outcome. For some clients there was also a reduction in self-harm, whilst in others an increase was noted, which was often around the changes in their lives. For one client for whom it had recently been an especially turbulent time, the amount and severity of her self-harm had increased substantially, and it was felt that 'sometimes hitting herself is *better* than hitting the drum because otherwise . . . she would have moved onto the drum, and she would not have hit herself again'.

The research analysis therefore suggested that changes in self-harm often depended on life circumstances, and it is difficult to make any arguments for whether dramatherapeutic interventions supported those people. However, as this was practice-based evidence on gathering impressions of possible meaning and ways to work with people who self-harm, the changes taking place at the time of the research would have no reason to alter the research findings. Many clients who self-harmed had done so for many years. To offer an alternative release of that energy was difficult for some clients to attempt or assimilate, so the interventions offered were not always accepted by the client. This research can be used by a multidisciplinary team to provide wider consideration to the possibilities of meaning of self-harm, and the variety of ways that a person can be supported when self-harming. The research may be transferable to other client groups, regard-less of the level of ability or disability of the client who self-harms. The creative interventions suggested could be offered as a means of emotional expression for those whose self-harm might be deemed as more usual (such as smoking or excessive alcohol consumption).

Ethical considerations

There are some considerations to be made regarding the ethics of drama-therapeutic interventions offered. The interventions of ignoring or physic-ally preventing self-harm are contentious for opposite reasons, but both relate to choice and autonomy. If a therapist ignores self-harm, seeing it as the ultimate right of the client, are they maintaining a safe therapeutic environment? However, if a therapist intervenes to prevent a client from harming themselves, which may seem appropriate to prevent further damage, this takes away client choice. With interventions involving touch, some may seem ethically unsound. The two issues here are consent and touch. With consent, BADth states that 'the client must understand the nature of dramatherapy and the relevance of the art form to therapy' (BADth 2005). This understanding is developed with this client group over time through the therapeutic relationship. With touch, BADth states that 'the nature and purpose of touch must be explained and informed consent sought prior to any physical contact is initiated' [sic] (BADth 2005). Within the therapeutic relationship, the dramatherapist will ascertain how a particular client makes their wishes known, and will act on these. In the research context, the work occurred in group sessions, where other clients and therapists were present. It was therefore witnessed, protecting both client and therapist.

Summary of key findings

Self-harm in this client group has not been taken as seriously as self-harm within the general population. Traditional understandings of self-harm have not incorporated notions that it is an emotional response to past trauma or present stress. It has often been seen simply as something that this client group does, and perceived as challenging. When self-harm is acknowledged, focused on and worked with in a therapeutic setting, the client is given possibilities to expand their communication, and process more difficult feelings, in a healthier expressive form. Dramatherapeutic interventions take many forms and there are a variety of rationales for choosing the appropriate intervention, based on what is the considered need of the client in that moment. The development of a positive, stable and trusting therapeutic relationship is paramount. Ethical considerations around choice, consent and touch need to be considered. Communication with all those involved in the client's life could lead to consistency of input and the integration of the work in the therapy space throughout the life of the client.

8

DRAMATHERAPY AND ADDICTION: LEARNING TO LIVE WITH DESTRUCTIVENESS

Lia Zografou

Brief overview of chapter

This chapter will draw upon my research with members of Narcotics Anonymous (NA) to elucidate aspects of the author's dramatherapy practice which were affected by notions of destructiveness, both in process and content. Working with addicted populations is challenging at the best of times. Introducing a creative approach to people who have firmly established cognitive constructs about self, world and addiction can often feel like a never-ending struggle on the road to nowhere, under the constant threat of clients relapsing. The fundamental concepts of NA are crucial in comprehending this client group's notions of destructiveness in both behavioural and intrapersonal terms. I will present examples of insights gained from my experience as both a practitioner and a researcher, stressing that the dialogue between practice and research can improve both and offer useful tools in tackling destructiveness in the process of therapy with addicted clients.

Introduction to setting and client group

The research was conducted with four members of Narcotics Anonymous in Greece. For a more detailed discussion, please refer to an earlier published version of this project (Zografou 2007). The focus of this chapter is a 10-week dramatherapy group, held in my private practice. The aim was to assess the compatibility of dramatherapy with the 12-step philosophy and ascertain whether dramatherapy could affect change to the attitudes of NA members on their addiction and recovery. The client group, two men and two women, were members of NA for differing amounts of time, ranging from 9 months to almost 11 years, and had been addicted to various substances, heroin being common among them. All clients' names have been changed to preserve their anonymity. Semi-structured interviews were conducted before and after the group whereby questions pertaining to beliefs and attitudes about addiction and recovery were asked and art work (drawings, masks, written scripts) produced during the 10-week group were examined by the clients themselves during the post-group interview. The findings were processed and analysed according to Moustakas' phenomenological method, namely collecting significant statements around thematic clusters and engaging with them through bracketing to extrapolate individual and collective textural and structural descriptions which reveal essential meanings of the clients' experience (Moustakas 1994). I discuss the rationale and methodology as well as the dramatherapeutic model I employed in more detail below.

Definitions of addiction – the NA approach

Drug addiction is a 'veritable semantic minefield' without a unifying theory to contain its vast complexities, yet full of descriptive terms such as 'drug addict' or 'alcoholic' to refer to certain people who habitually consume psychoactive substances (Glass 1991).

Definitions of recovery vary among theoretical approaches and treatment styles. In broad terms, we could say that all clinicians and clients agree that recovery involves sustained management of the addictive disorder, abstinence from addictive behaviour and improved biophysical, social and spiritual well-being (Rasmussen 2000).

Unique among addiction theories is the view upheld by the Anonymous self-support groups: according to Alcoholics Anonymous (AA), the very first of its kind and precursor to Narcotics Anonymous (NA), alcoholism (and by extension any other addictive disorder) is a progressive and incurable disease of the spirit, originating in fundamentally flawed perceptions of self, power and control over oneself, of which drug abuse is only one of multiple manifestations – 'Once an alcoholic, always an alcoholic' (Alcoholics Anonymous 2001). What is implied in this deceptively simple adage is that the destructive impulses and characteristics which propelled the individual to engage in addictive behaviour in the first place can never be eradicated by abstinence, only regulated. The fellowship member comes to understand his/her core being as someone who operates in the world in a dysfunctional, immature mode in all aspects of his/her daily existence. The disease will never be cured, even if the person stops drinking or using the drug (Flores 1997). The only thing an addicted person can achieve is to halter the speed of the disease's destructive course and the means to achieve this are the 12 steps of recovery, a structured system of self-renewal – a design for living not just drug-free and sober but with humility and acceptance of one's limitations.

At the heart of this definition of addiction lies a qualification of the alcoholic disease as unique:

An illness of this sort – and we have come to believe it an illness – involves those about us in a way no other human sickness can. If a person has cancer all are sorry for him and no one is angry or hurt. But not so with the alcoholic illness, for with it there goes *annihilation of all the things worthwhile in life. It engulfs all whose lives touch the sufferer's.* It brings misunderstanding, fierce resentment, financial insecurity, disgusted friends and employers, warped lives of blameless children, sad wives and parents – anyone can increase the list.

(Alcoholics Anonymous 2001: 18; my emphasis)

A deeply embedded seed of destructiveness forms the core of the Anonymous fellowships' definition of the addict. The addict is not just like any other human being:

The delusion that we are like other people, or presently may be, has to be smashed . . . We are like men who have lost their legs; they never grow new ones.

(Alcoholics Anonymous 2001: 30)

The addict is regarded as both destroyed and destroyer, irrevocably damaged and certain to be damaging (to self and others) unless he or she surrenders first to the annihilating power of the disease (Step 1) and subsequently to the reparative benevolence of a Higher Power as he or she believes it to be (Step 2).

Upon acceptance of their status as addicts, members of the Anonymous fellowships embark on a rigorous regime of self-restructuring which is never-ending: 'Recovery is a journey, not a destination. Many people describe themselves as 'recovering' but not 'recovered' (Rasmussen 2000: 142).

To many the Anonymous fellowships' approach appears rigid and has been widely criticised. The main points of contention are that NA is hostile to other types of therapeutic approaches and that its overt spiritual orientation alienates help-seekers who do not necessarily espouse its suggested definitions of addiction (Larkin and Griffiths 2002). However, as a treatment approach, Narcotics Anonymous is highly successful (Flores 1997; Roth and Fonagy 2004) and most practitioners in the field of addiction will be compelled to work within its conceptual frameworks (Fisher and Cooper 1990).

Extending the discussion in my previous publication (Zografou 2007) will address some particularly thorny issues that arose from the encounter between a creative method of therapy and the NA philosophy, which pertain to the exploration of destructiveness as a force to contend with during therapy and research. I hope that this chapter will provide support, encouragement and creative ideas to dramatherapists facing similar problems, both as practitioners and researchers.

Dramatherapy and destructiveness

The dramatherapy model used during the group intervention was the Hero's Journey, based on the tradition of the mono-myth (Campbell 1993) as adapted by Paul Rebillot (1993) and Steve Mitchell (1996). I chose this model because of the particular nature of this client group who are engaged in a systematic encounter of past and future aspects of their identity, their old destructive self and new, healthier modes of being. As Campbell (1993) explains, the hero in the mono-myth receives a call to adventure which takes him away from familiar territory (habit, tradition) into a liminal space of supernatural wonder where he has to face unpredictable challenges against powerful enemies, from which he emerges victorious and transformed.

In this dramatherapeutic model the ritual encounters with the 'Demon of Resistance' (Rebillot 1993) provide the container wherein numerous different forces within the person are released. Destructive tendencies, nihilism, hostility and despondency engage in battle with hope, imagination, desire and optimism. As Mitchell (1996) explains, the clients create heroic characters that possess the resilience to take on the subversive, oppositional forces exemplified in the 'Demon of Resistance', whose aim is to undermine the whole project of self-renewal and discovery. I regard this model as ideal for populations struggling with destructiveness, because it not only honours and contains destructiveness using dramatic language but also allows for the investigation of differing degrees and stages of resistance in the therapeutic process.

In this group the meeting between heroic (constructive, transformative, health promoting) and demonic (destructive, apathetic, resistant) aspects of self, as encouraged by the 'Hero's Journey' (Rebillot 1993), proved challenging and revealed a host of resistances which the interviews were not able to capture. The dramatherapy setting served as a catalyst for personal disclosure and the findings support that even though perceptions of addiction remained unchanged, dramatherapy contributed to change in perceptions of recovery by enhancing creativity and encouraging playful collaboration and intimacy (Zografou 2007).

Destructiveness in the process – phenomenology as a tool

The first and most serious challenge I faced as both practitioner and phenomenological researcher was to abandon my own preconceived notions about NA and its definition. The ability to engage with a phenomenon with one's perception, unencumbered by previous knowledge, is the *sine qua non* of phenomenological inquiry. This freedom from assumptions and expectations was called *Epoche* by Husserl and explained by Clark Moustakas as the way to 'look with care, to see what is really there, and to stay away from everyday habits of knowing things, people, and events'

(Moustakas 1994: 85). When the phenomenological method is applied to therapy, suspension of prior knowledge, otherwise known as *bracketing*, is never complete (Spinelli 1989). Spinelli regards bracketing as the main therapeutic task. He advocates a stance that is based on empathy, neutrality and descriptive questioning to examine the *how* of the experience and not seek any possible underlying causes, so that clients 'recognize the elastic nature of their experience and, thereby, reacknowledge their role as active interpreters of, rather than passive reactors to, the "givens" of life' (Spinelli 1989: 131). He explains that 'feeling powerless, often expressing a deep self-hatred and loathing, such individuals want to be told what to do, who to be, how to change for the better, what technique they need to be taught in order to improve a particular aspect of their lives' (Spinelli 1989: 132). The task is therefore to be an 'attendant' and a facilitator of self-exploration, rather than a directive authority on what is right.

Given the nature of this particular client group, such a goal initially resembled an unrealistic quest. The interviews were structured in such a way that participants would talk freely and openly about their personal experience of addiction. They all, however, declared their strong devotion to NA tenets and, as was to be expected, all at times referred to their experience using popular phraseology from the NA vocabulary.

One participant's self-description was: 'I am an addictive personality, which means, that even without drugs, there's always this trait that . . . needs some special treatment, which is happening now and things are going well. But in the past I thought my problem was heroin'. All regarded NA, the steps and the community of fellow addicts as the most important aspects of their lives in recovery. 'The members are valuable to me because I trust them . . . and they are very valuable to me because I can say anything and there is total understanding'.

Soon after the initial interviews, the researcher in me felt doubtful and despondent. I often thought, has the NA language contaminated these people and therefore rendered them unable to speak for themselves in an original way? What is the point in interviewing persons who have espoused and internalised a philosophy of life so single-mindedly? I struggled to find the personal meaning behind the repetitive, clichéd answers.

As a therapist I seriously questioned whether dramatherapy would have any impact at all on clients who were already so set in their self-perceptions and so ready to describe themselves in such firmly established, prescribed terms. Would there be room for new insight and new self-awareness? How could new knowledge pass through the mesh of cognitive filters that the strongly held NA beliefs had established in the clients' minds? Had the NA philosophy destroyed all possibility of creative and transformative self-exploration through dramatherapy?

Despite my apprehensions, the experience of group dramatherapy proved very instructive and reassuring. Bypassing conscious control, the process of creating, meeting and confronting the characters of the Hero and the Demon of Resistance revealed intrapersonal tensions which the interviews had not, and quite possibly could not, have brought to light. Iris and Philip both discovered aspects of themselves they had not addressed before: Philip faced his rage and fear of exposure when he embodied his Hero and let out a loud war cry during his battle with the Demon (Zografou 2007). Iris admitted and modified her perfectionism when she created an impossibly perfect Hero. Her scripted dialogue between her Hero AIX and her Demon BRR illustrates this:

BRR: Stop Aix! I said Stop!

AIX: Stop? Why? I can't. I have work to do in the world. People are suffering: poverty, hunger, illnesses, wars, evil.

BRR: You have to stop, though. You ought to see me and hear me out. I am here. I am always here. Don't pretend I don't exist. You know very well I have the power to stop you on your tracks. You can't live without seeing me too. Without giving to me some of the love you have.

AIX: But everytime I tried you pushed me away. You harmed me.

BRR: That's my nature. I am sick, I am telling you. I am made this way. And you made me. Because otherwise there would not be balance. The perfect would not exist.

AIX: But the perfect does exist.

BRR: Not in the real world that I live and you live in. That we both live in.

This dialogue, scripted in the ninth session, was a far cry from the pristine, aloof, passionless Hero that Iris had originally created in the third session. It was beyond the scope of my project to ascertain to what this change could be attributed. However, it is worth noting that this new inner position did manifest within the group and found apposite expression in the dramatised struggle.

Interestingly, Iris did not attribute much importance to dramatherapy as a helper in her recovery during her second interview. She felt she had:

> . . . exorcised the greatest part of the past through the steps. So the work we did here was too light for me, it didn't help me, didn't move me forward substantially. There were some pleasant moments that also worked therapeutically on some themes but no essential changes. I mean, I've sorted out the heavy stuff, I know who I am . . .

The challenge for the practitioner is to listen to a comment on the therapy and bracket her own desire to be affirmed. Like a person wearing bifocals, I had to remain flexible, shifting from a close-up to a more distanced view, yet focused, always querying what was addressed to the practitioner and what to the researcher, where the useful message lay and how it could best be used for therapy and research alike. Exercising my perceptual muscles this way protected me from feeling victimised and annihilated by NA philosophy as a practitioner on the one hand, and prompted me to keep a fresh, open-minded attitude as a researcher on the other. It would have been too tempting to see the research as a binary conflict and become divided internally into 'good therapist/bad researcher' or 'good researcher/bad therapist'. This certainly could have been compounded by the multiple polarisations which were prevalent in this project. The clients embodied the polarised perceptions of the self as 'user' and 'sober', in active use and in recovery, in need and in control, experiencing life before NA and life after NA. In such a project, the most obvious polarity was between the Hero and the Demon, carrying with it the danger of intensifying the Manichean split between good and bad, light and shadow, thus oversimplifying the struggle to recover from self-destruction and engage fully with life.

The researching attitude facilitated a shift in the manner in which I approached my therapeutic practice. After my initial reaction, I chose not to judge the fact that the NA members possessed a particular vocabulary, which to me initially appeared 'destructive' of any creativity in therapy and the therapeutics of creativity by extension. I could appreciate that this cognitive rigidity was integral to their recovery process and that their lives depended on it.

The task then became for me to respect the clients' anonymity as 'addicted Everyman', yet honour their unique individuality in the true spirit of phenomenologically informed therapy. Thus, I could appreciate the contributions of the creative methods used in therapy and formulate questions about the clients' creative work. I could allow myself to notice key moments in their therapeutic process when change did occur, and was freed from my own Demon of Resistance, namely my fear of comparing unfavourably to the 12-step programme.

I also appreciated that bracketing is more than simply a technique or a mental attitude. It has to be an embodied disposition towards unknowing. In other words, the therapist and the phenomenological researcher have to embody fully the role of an ignoramus, an innocent, and go on their own Hero's Journey of facing personal and professional resistances, embracing the unknown and arriving at a new state of being with openness and curiosity. I cannot with any certainty say whether the internal shift enabled me to trust the dramatherapeutic process or vice versa. I do know that both occurred almost concurrently and complemented each other.

Through this process of self-examination and bracketing I became acutely aware of my own tacit assumptions and expectations about the goals of therapy. Of course, the ultimate goal is recovery, but when working with NA members any deviation from the accepted definition will only promote confusion and conflict between clients and therapist. To my NA clients, the struggle between Hero and Demon could never be conclusive, as their self-view implies a continuous confrontation with their destructive elements. It is perhaps no coincidence that this group got 'stuck' at the first ordeal and were unable to complete the journey. There was nothing to prevent the group from exploring the mono-myth 'just for today', flexibly adapting it to the core NA belief that the struggle is constantly renewed (Zografou 2007). The 'Hero's Journey' allows for the struggle to be structured flexibly and can be repeated as often or at whichever pace is appropriate to the client group. However, it would have been interesting to see how a longer time frame would have affected the clients' ability to complete the cycle and what modifications to the approach would have been required.

Process in metaphor – drama as a tool

There is a distinct lack of findings on group processes such as resistance or analysis of transference and counter-transference in therapy with addicted clients. Such phenomena are all too frequent but rarely examined (Flores 1997). Flores advocates that resistance, the unconscious withholding of emotional material that seems threatening or potentially harmful to the client, or the tendency to avoid presenting any material potentially meaningful to the therapist, must be seen as a creative stage in the therapeutic process and not be pathologised (Flores 1997: 465). Instead, he stresses that it should take priority over everything else. Furthermore, transference and counter-transference issues in group work with addicts also merit careful analysis 'because of the intense hostility, anger, disrespect and distrust these patients commonly provoke in others' (Flores 1997: 457). Yalom (1995) and Cox (1988) also highlight the group's dependency, desire for control and unrealistic expectations from the leader as common and natural processes in group therapy.

This dramatherapy group was rife with resistance, which most frequently took the form of split disclosures (one thing said to the researcher and the opposite to the therapist, as discussed above), split loyalties (as will be discussed below) and immobilisation or 'stuckness' under the threat of relapse. The following episode illustrates the potentially destructive force of resistance.

In a moment of one client's crisis, the therapy room suddenly filled with fear, mistrust, guilt and the desire to escape, another reflection of the familiar dynamics of drug use. Again, bracketing provided the necessary tool for handling the crisis. Remaining suspended, neither continuing with the scheduled tasks nor becoming reactive to the intense emotionality of the situation, allowed me and the group the space and time to contain this powerful resistance. The crisis started when Anna, the youngest NA member of the group, threatened that she was on the verge of using again. Anna had been clean only 9 months at the beginning of the research project and was still grappling with Step 1 (the admission that she was powerless over her addiction). Unlike the other group members, she, as was to be expected, was still very vulnerable to the destructive pull of drugs.

In session six, upon drawing the face of her Demon of Resistance, Satanious, Anna was overwhelmed by feelings of inadequacy, despondency and the desire to shoot heroin again. She was almost entirely defeated by the familiar power of Satanious, a creature who constantly judged, denigrated her and mocked her efforts to turn her life around. When faced with the threat of relapse within a rehabilitation setting, the therapist is somewhat protected and supported by other professionals who can share the burden and monitor the client. During this project, however, there was no such setting to contain the potentially splintering forces of such a threat. I was conducting the project independently and in my own premises. Destruction loomed large for Anna, the rest of the group and potentially for the project itself. At this moment I appreciated the power of the fellowship and employed the phraseology of NA myself in order to ensure Anna could understand me, make constructive use of her fellow NA members and her sponsor and contain this crisis. It was at that moment that I queried most seriously how dramatherapy could support Anna's precarious recovery.

As a therapist I felt shaken. As a researcher I noted that the creation of a Demon of Resistance can be overwhelming to someone who has not yet fully accepted their helpless status as an addict (Step 1). Once this has been established, as was the case with the other, more advanced NA members, the creation of the Demon was decidedly easier, at least as a process. Conversely, if the Demon is handled with caution and sensitivity and is introduced at an appropriate pace, the experience can be a powerful adjunct and auxiliary to Step 1. In Anna's case, the crisis showed her how truly powerless she was in front of her addiction. She came back the following week to complete the confrontation with her Demon Satanious (SAT):

SAT: Well, we meet. I caught you!

AG: I came to meet you! So, what do you finally want? And what right do you have to want anything and how can you bother me? You're denying me my freedom, my breath. You deny me my life.

SAT: Why don't you go fuck yourself? Ridiculous little girl, you're just play acting! All charm and sweet airs. Stay a while. Look at who you are, see how others see you.

AG: Who are you to set boundaries, who are you to tame, who are you to guard, who are you to imprison me?

SAT: I am your conscience, which you buried a long time ago, living this way, and can't watch you hurt and waste yourself like this. I want what's best for you, really. I want you to become a person.

AG: You mean (*looks at him cautiously*) you will help me or sentence me to life imprisonment (*remembers the weight in her soul when he sometimes takes over. The description of the landscape where he keeps her has no colour. It's miserable and dark. The soul is captive. She remembers and . . . does not allow it*). Okay, mistake, but . . . I won't let you take me to that place again.

Anna's improvised dialogue clearly contains a process of self-reflection and decision making that is marked by conscious and deliberate self-control. Anna doesn't simply react; she remembers and, within parentheses in the text, she actively decides not to allow the repetition of Satanious' abuse. She takes a firm stance against him and resolves not to expose herself to harm again. This experience stayed with Anna and marked a shift towards more self-regulation and self-protection. During her last interview, when asked about what she appreciated about dramatherapy, Anna said:

> But what stuck with me most is that I don't need to be very open to everybody, even in a group. When I thought I was obliged to be. And maybe tomorrow I will be part of a group I have chosen and the people will have chosen me and I will feel very okay with that, and I will feel trust. And this, yes, helped me.

Anna was eventually able to contain her destructive impulses in the character of her Demon and allow her newly emerging healthy qualities to find location and expression in her Heroine.

Clinical practice and addiction: the way of least resistance – faith, hope and destructiveness

Staying with resistance as it appeared (Flores 1997), I called for what Yalom calls a 'process check-up' (Yalom 1995: 352). Just as I was handling Anna's threat of relapse, Philip began to attack me verbally about being too directive towards Anna. The group split. Two were openly hostile towards me, and two supported me. Tempers calmed eventually and Philip tried to make amends. Talking openly about the process furthered my thinking as both researcher and therapist. During the final dramatherapy session I thanked the group and mentioned how much I was enjoying working with them. Suddenly one member shouted: 'We have addicted you to us!' followed by laughter from everyone. Murray Cox (1988) and Flores (1997) caution therapists to watch for such spontaneous disclosures of intent. Was this client voicing a deeper unconscious desire on behalf of the whole group? Had I been manipulated? At times the clients complained, 'What's this kind of work, this dramatherapy, got to do with addiction?' When I checked my own feelings in response to that challenge, however, I realised that the work indeed had everything to do with addiction. My own countertransference at that moment spoke volumes: I felt angry, indignant, unjustly used, tricked, insecure, terribly lonely. All these were feelings the study revealed as the most powerful aspects of an addict's experience (Zografou 2007), which she or he would then try to numb with drugs. Could this have been the final parting gift the participants offered the practitioner? Did they transform their painful feelings of inadequacy, fear and discomfort during the confrontation between Hero and Demon into violent feelings towards the therapist who makes them suffer? Did they 'use' the therapist in this instance to contain the painful feelings? And could this have been the motivation behind some participants' denial to acknowledge any substantial help from the group during the second interview? Even though the scope of the project was too limited to address these questions, I felt that as a therapist I had received valuable stimulation for further thinking on how to meet such clients in the future.

Conclusions from clinical practice

The most valuable tools to cope with destructiveness that I discovered in this project were: being attentive to one's countertransference; reflecting constantly between process and content; bracketing assumptions and prior knowledge; trusting the dramatic ritual as a container and catalyst in moments of immobility and cognitive stagnation (Grainger 1990); and flexibly moving beyond polarised thinking by attending to clients' constructs and matching their expressions in the here-and-now to those in the play/liminal space. Addicted clients are struggling to maintain their resilience in the face of imminent relapse. Equally, the therapist to addicted clients is also struggling to maintain her own resilience. Faith and hope are the first casualties of destructive resistance if it is only seen as a foe and not as a disguised friend. Resistance was an invaluable source of new knowledge and tremendous psychic mobilisation for both clients and therapist.

Evaluation and areas for further research

A project of this scale and scope inevitably asked more questions than provided answers. It most evidently highlighted the need for more detailed exploration of the use of ritual in dramatherapy and the effectiveness of the ritual theatre form as a container of destructiveness. Initial findings from this very small sample indicate and support the beneficial effect of dramatisation and dramatic play in improving addicts' spontaneity and ability to self-disclose and self-regulate. Further systematic and critical research on assessment and therapeutic process in dramatherapy (analysis of resistance and transference/counter-transference phenomena), with larger population samples, would better inform on the adaptability of this or any other creative method with recovering addicts and assist in tailoring appropriate interventions.

9

ON BONDAGE AND LIBERTY:
THE ART OF THE POSSIBLE IN
MEDIUM-SECURE SETTINGS

Henri Seebohm

Brief overview of chapter

This chapter uses three clinical vignettes to explore the concept of the dramatherapist or the artistic medium being taken or held 'hostage' in the therapy space within a forensic psychiatric setting, when working with individuals who have highly complex pathologies. The vignettes are all anonymised accounts used to illustrate this particular interpersonal dynamic. Details of identity and context have been changed in order to preserve confidentiality. They are interwoven with theory drawn from the psycho-dynamic tradition. Particular focus is given to ideas of captivity, security and engagement with the medium and with the therapeutic relationship. The chapter demonstrates that even when the dramatic medium and/or the therapeutic relationship is 'under attack', it is still possible to keep creative possibility alive.

Introduction

This examination of destructiveness within the medium of dramatherapy has primarily been motivated from my experience of working as a female dramatherapist in a forensic psychiatric setting. I work with male patients both individually and in groups, with diagnoses of paranoid schizophrenia, schizo-affective disorder and borderline personality disorder, who have all committed serious offences and have been sectioned under the 1983 Mental Health Act. Patients are referred to dramatherapy by the clinical team as part of their rehabilitation treatment and often in order to develop insight into both their offending behaviour and their mental illness, as well as to develop capacity for social, reflective and interpersonal skills.

Whilst dramatherapy has facilitated many creative possibilities of change in the patients' experience of rehabilitation, a recurring theme in the clinical work of a forensic set-up is a form of 'defendedness', which can be seen as resistance to, or an attempt to destroy, the possibility of utilising a creative

120

space – the dramatherapy process. I have observed, where patients have particularly complex pathologies, that my experience of such destructiveness has left me feeling like the therapist–hostage in captivity, and at other times I felt cast in the role of captor–perpetrator, carrying their sense that I have the potential to destroy them. This dynamic is further intensified in individual work, where there is not a co-working relationship for the therapist and the nature of the dyad is inescapable.

As a dramatherapist, my concern is for what is being represented from the internal world of the patient within the external world (Gruen 2007) and how the artistic medium can contain and help to bridge this experience in such a way that creates greater insight and awareness of self and will reduce the risk of relapse and recidivism. The challenge here is when destructiveness is systematically enacted upon the artistic medium, and what such an enactment does to the dramatherapist's capacity to think about what is happening.

In the forensic dramatherapy space, we regularly see many defensive manoeuvres being played out. The apparently mindless and repetitive need to assert rigid control of the medium and/or the therapist can be seen as symptomatic of the defensive organisation of the patient's internal world. Such primitive defensive organisation may be expressed in a variety of destructive ways – the 'mindless' logic being 'the best form of defence is attack'. The dramatherapist has to find a way of respecting, understanding and harnessing the destructive attacks so that annihilation is *not* the end result for patient, therapist or the medium.

The invitation to engage in dramatic play may be rejected, resisted, ridiculed and crushed: which may be experienced by the therapist as the patient breaking, entering and diverting the therapist's capacity to think. On a more extreme level, such responses may be experienced as sadistic aggression towards the medium and/or the dramatherapist, in the form of violent and/or sexualised impulses, both of which serve to control the other. Finally the space can become a theatre of war for the patient, both terrorised and terrorising, sometimes leaving the therapist holding the shattered pieces of debris, as in the aftermath of war. This may echo the patient's own life experience, which has left them struggling to hold together the debris of their own history.

In thinking about inpatient treatment, Skogstad suggests: 'a requirement of the treatment of . . . patients is to help them become "thinkers and feelers" instead of "actor" (Masterson 1972)' (Skogstad 2004: 2). Although the dramatherapist recognises that the 'actor' here refers to the individual lacking in impulse control and insight, whose 'acting out' may well be destructive, the dramatherapeutic approach to treatment might be that the very process of 'acting' in a contained environment can provide the dramatic distance and the reframing of experience that may help them become 'thinking, feeling, actors' in their own narrative.

Forensic psychodynamic psychotherapy emphasises the criminal act as an important focus within this narrative, as the offence can 'tell us much about aspects of the internal (mental) world of the perpetrator' (Cordess and Hyatt Williams 1996: 19). As McAlister (2002: 357) explains, 'the offence itself . . . can be seen as an enactment, or a wish to evacuate through action, intolerable states of mind such as paranoia and violent phantasies'.

Wheldon suggests that the action of the offence shows an inability to think and a shut down which becomes evident in certain areas of psychopathology, for example the psychosis in the offender with schizophrenia, the perversion in a sex offender. Like Skogstad, she suggests that the therapeutic endeavour is to help the patient to think; however, she points out that:

> . . . at times the patient's tendency to make sadistic attacks on his own capacity for thought and reflection is projected and directed against the therapist's capacity to think and reflect, and it is then that the therapist feels confused, numbed and unable to make any useful interpretations.
>
> (Skogstad 1997: 15)

The following vignettes draw upon some of my own experiences in the clinical space in order to consider what choices are left for the dramatherapist when working with the dynamic of being held captive or hostage in the space. It is worth noting that all three patients felt unable to join a dramatherapy group due to the exposing nature of being in a group and the difficulties that they experience in maintaining relationships with others.

Vignette One

One of my earliest experiences as a dramatherapist was working in a community mental health centre and seeing individual outpatients. One patient in particular was referred by his GP for problems with anger. I agreed to see him weekly with the aim of helping him to cope with his anger, which seemed to be having a detrimental impact on his relationships. What I experienced was that he would treat the session as a kind of confession for all the violence that he had just subjected his partner to, whereupon he would leave, unburdened and cleansed. He would then not turn up for weeks, only to return following another violent incident. I also discovered that he would only turn up when his partner had offered to drive him to the appointment, which he only accepted following an outburst of violence. During the sessions I felt bullied into being an 'ear' for his guilt; however, I was not allowed to have a 'mind' or a 'mouth' and any attempt to reflect on my experience was silenced, so that I was left feeling as though I too had been stamped on, like his partner. In the counter-transference, I felt constricted by an unspoken threat that if I said anything that might be challenging, he might walk out and make me responsible for anything he might do as a result.

Just as the client's partner was given the responsibility for causing his vicious attacks by provoking him ('she pushed me', 'she made me do it'), I was given the responsibility for being the mediator for his guilt. Having evacuated his intolerable feelings into his partner and their property, through physical violence, his need to defend against knowing the damage that this caused created a parallel evacuation into the therapist by attempting to omnipotently control what was allowed and not allowed to be said.

Although this client was not a forensic patient, there was a sense that he had just come from the scene of a crime, which could potentially be re-enacted at any moment. My sense of being held hostage was also in response to the contents of his 'confession', which was letting me know that he was a dangerous man who, when aroused, was unable to contain his feelings. The unpredictability of his violence and therefore his attendance meant that my ability to provide a sense of containment for him was severely restricted. On the other hand, if he were to experience a sense of containment by me, potential feelings of dependency would threaten his ability to omnipotently control his objects, and so the vicious cycle of the 'core complex' is re-enacted. (Glasser 1979) (see Vignette Three). It may be worth noting that this individual was seen within a community setting without the extra layer of physical security that a locked forensic setting provides. The addition of an external holding environment may have enabled him to engage therapeutically.

Vignette Two

Bill, a white man in his late 50s, had a diagnosis of paranoid schizophrenia and a long psychiatric forensic history, having spent more than two-thirds of his life incarcerated. His criminal behaviour went back to pre-adolescent times and his main activity was burglary. He was referred for individual dramatherapy as part of a multidisciplinary treatment, which included other professional interventions. However, after the first year, he voluntarily stopped attending any other sessions and 'sacked' the psychologist. I was then left in the position of being the only member of the team able to give regular feedback on his therapeutic progress. At first, Bill always referred to me by the name of his previous prison visitor. This took about 2 years to shake off and the next role that I was assigned was to replace his daughter, who neglected to visit him. He consistently resisted engaging with the medium, as he believed that 'acting' was not real and he was not interested in being 'fake'. This reflected an aspect of his psychosis, in that he was very concrete in his thinking and his ability to symbolise was limited.

However, he would also divulge elaborate descriptions of a parallel dimension to the physical world – a spiritual realm of territory-warring warriors amongst whom he was a leading protagonist.

The sessions with Bill involved his recounting of both his real-life history, which included his criminal life in the 'underworld' (his term), his sexual relationships with women and his experience of incarceration; and his parallel world where he was a spiritual warrior controlling international military manoeuvres. My experience of this, as with the client above, was that I was being held captive to his outpourings. Both his refusal to use the medium and his need to position me as the listener to his stories, in a supportive, unchallenging role, rather like a coffee morning with the prison visitor, or the idealising daughter, rendered me feeling impotent and disempowered. In the counter-transference, despite the dramatic tales of sex, violence and criminal life, I found myself frequently feeling tired and at times having to literally pinch myself to remain awake.

Supervision helped me to understand that my somatised exhaustion/ dissociation was perhaps my own defence against being controlled by Bill. It is interesting that from pre-adolescence, Bill was breaking and entering to take possession of something that he felt deprived of. Winnicott et al. (1984) talk about the delinquent's action being a desire to retrieve something lost, so that the external world may provide it. My experience with Bill was that his incarceration was the only way in which he was able to find the containment that he was originally deprived of. As a therapist, I also felt that my dissociation was my defence not only against being controlled, but also against the action of Bill breaking, entering and stealing part of me – the thinking, creative part of me, leaving the space deprived of the medium and ensuring that he was the story-teller and I remained the object of his fantasies. Another possibility was that I actually felt positioned in an inescapable incarceration by him, as I remained the only professional that he was willing to see within his care-plan, thus ensuring that he was not deprived of me.

There are numerous accounts of therapists struggling with the transference and counter-transference in working with psychotic patients, and what is interesting is that much of the identified material stems from the (pre-Oedipal) dyadic relationship with the mother, which is manifested when the patient wishes to have omnipotent control or possession of the therapist/mother. Doctor (1999) suggests that sexualised or eroticised transference is one in which psychotic processes reside, and there is little or no capacity to tolerate the therapist as a separate entity. Glasser stresses the importance of bringing in the third presence, moving from the dyad to the triad (Oedipal configuration). He says that:

> . . . what offers a solution to those found by the pervert and the
> psychotic is . . . the presence of the father. With the father present,

the infant can seek a solution to the core complex's 'irreconcilable conflict of opposites' by turning to the father as an alternative object.

(Glasser 1985: 409)

Of course, Glasser's assertion begs the question of what happens when the father proves not to be a healthy, adaptive, available 'alternative object', but is indeed a distorting, toxic perpetrator. If the third presence generates anxiety, then the possibility of reconciling the 'irrenconcilability of opposites' becomes hopeless. This may equally manifest within the therapeutic relationship, where the art form becomes the third presence, seen by the patient as a threatening object, offering no solution to what is intolerable.

For the psychotic patient who wishes to possess or control the therapist, the presence of anything else may be experienced as threat and will be accordingly attacked. This includes the space in the therapist's mind to think and make links (Bion 1959). When working with schizophrenic patients, where fantasy and reality can either merge or become polarised through concrete thinking, the 'creative space' of the dramatherapist could, potentially, be another target for an attack.

To transform the potential attack on the 'creative space', the drama-therapist has to foster a sense of collaboration and offer a creative inter-vention that is tolerable to the patient. A break-through occurred in the work with Bill, when I offered the medium of film as an alternative to embodiment. The repositioning of client and therapist to side-by-side, rather than facing one another, opened up the third physical space for the medium, the DVD player. This repositioning of the triad provided enough dramatic distance for Bill to work with the medium, which could also be safely controlled by the push of a button.

After 6 years of dramatherapy as part of his rehabilitation treatment, Bill was granted a conditional discharge by the Ministry of Justice, from medium security to a low-secure community setting. He had internalised some sense of containment and security where he no longer needed to take others hostage or be captive in order to tolerate his own feelings and existential fears. His residual psychosis continued to provide him with enough of a refuge to survive the transition from bondage to greater liberty.

Vignette Three

Carl, a black British man in his early 40s, had a diagnosis of schizo-affective disorder and a turbulent history of incarcerations within psy-chiatric and criminal justice institutions. His offending behaviour was burglary, usually in drug-induced states of psychosis. He was referred to individual dramatherapy by the multidisciplinary team as part of his treatment and rehabilitation. He was regarded as one of the more difficult patients on the ward, as his behaviour was unpredictable. At times he would be friendly and sociable, or he would bully other patients and push boundaries with female staff. At other times he would withdraw and spend long periods in his room. The team hoped that the dramatherapy would help Carl to mediate and contain his feelings, with the aim of gaining insight into his mental illness and offending behaviour. In forensic work, there is always an element of assessing risk, of both relapse and recidivism.

Being in the space with Carl proved to be challenging in many ways. At first I experienced him to have a very sensory relationship with the medium. He would pick up and put down small objects/toys on the shelves, he would build Lego towers and cars and then soon after they would be destroyed. The space was reminiscent of a nursery. Jennings' EPR developmental paradigm provided a useful framework to understand how Carl was engaging developmentally with the medium (Jennings et al. 1994).

Carl created a 'nest' of cushions and lay down in it, asking to be covered in fabric. Once this was provided, he wrapped himself up tightly in fabric and moved around like an infant in his cot. This provoked a strong maternal feeling in me; however, this was short-lived. He soon began to eroticise the experience, suggesting that I could lie down with him. This led to him sitting up and suggesting that he could 'give me one in the corner where no one could see', which progressed to him standing and saying: 'Let me fuck you. Go on, you know you want to'. Rather than press the alarm button to call the response team to the room, I remained exactly where I was sitting and asked him to sit down on a chair, after which we discussed the impact and consequence of his communication. In a short space of time, Carl was simultaneously oscillating from the state of infancy to a semblance of adult sexualisation and back again, in such a way that the initial sexual advances had the quality of a young child begging his mother for sweets. However, his perseverance became more aggressive and back in the adult space of sitting on chairs, I suggested that his impulses to sleep or to have sex were ways of avoiding his own feelings of hopelessness and rage. (In supervision, I also wondered if my casual acceptance of his direct sexual advances was a way of avoiding my own feelings of therapeutic impotence.)

A few sessions later, Carl sat down and asked if he could murder me. He then leaned towards me and asked if he could strangle me. In recognising my discomfort, he smiled and reached his hands out towards my neck. 'Go on let me strangle you. Please let me strangle you. I want to strangle you'. This encounter felt sadistic and unrelenting. My very direct experience of fear made me move backwards to avoid contact with him and I communicated clearly that this was unacceptable. At this point, I felt that as well as the potential physical attack, I was also experiencing an emotional and psychological attack, not so much against me as a person but me as a recipient of his projected hopes, desires and dependencies. The previous eroticised encounter had transformed into sadistic aggression in order to try to resolve the overwhelming annihilating experience of intimacy and concomitant dependence that Carl struggled with in relating to another. In order to recover from the destructive act, I was aware that I moved quickly from being hostage of the act to remind him that I was the captor holding the keys and that his behaviour needed containing.

In such defended and destructive ways of relating, Glasser distinguishes between aggression for 'self-preservation' and 'sadistic aggression' and shows how one can become the other. He developed a theory called 'the core complex' (Glasser 1979), where there is an intense longing to merge in a 'blissful union' with another, but this threatens a permanent loss of self through the potential engulfment. This fear of total annihilation brings with it an emotional retreat from the object. However, this 'flight to a safe distance' is experienced as desolate isolation, whose only relief lies in renewing contact with the other. Thereby a vicious cycle is being enacted where intimacy is perceived as annihilating and separateness is perceived as an abandoned state. This primitive functioning clearly parallels the interrelating between infant and mother.

Glasser asserts that the way to solve this cycle and to protect the object from the aggression of the core complex and preserve the relationship:

> . . . is by the widespread use of sexualisation. Aggression is converted into sadism . . . the intention to destroy is converted into a wish to hurt and control. Sexualisation also acts as a binding, organizing force in the internal state of affairs, enabling defensive measures to be more effective and a certain stability to come about.
>
> (Glasser 1979: 289)

Glasser warns that when this process breaks down, '. . . sadism may revert to aggression. Sadism thus shades into sexual crimes, which in turn shade into crimes of violence, the appreciation of the object as a person decreasing in the process' (Glasser 1979: 289).

Temple reminds us that sadism can be an omnipotent defence against psychic pain or loss, so that it is the projection of weakness into another combined with sexual excitement that attempts to avoid any vulnerability. It is thus possible for the therapist 'to become unconsciously the masochistic victim of bullying or sadistic and perverse situation in the therapy' (Temple 1996: 35). The therapist may either feel pushed to be sadistic in response to the patient or accept the role of victim. Temple suggests 'that one of the greatest difficulties [for the therapist] is to intervene in the sado-masochistic relationship between the superego and the patient's self in a way which allows some form of mediation and fairness in this cruel exchange' (Temple 1996: 35).

I frequently experienced that following more meaningful contact, Carl would retreat from me in the space by putting on the radio and blasting out loud music as a means of obliterating my presence and any interventions I may have offered. Such clear enactments of the 'core complex' remind me of Estragon's line in *Waiting for Godot*: 'Don't touch me! Don't question me! Don't speak to me! Stay with me!' (Beckett 1956).

Soon after this period of Carl's attempts to 'merge' or 'obliterate', he was able to locate himself in relation to me through the projective medium in illuminating ways. When looking through some picture cards, he picked out four that he felt were significant. The first image was of a human skeleton, with a large black crow sitting on the bones. He pointed out, 'This is you, picking at my brains'. He then chose an image of a man and a white bird standing facing one another, which he described as: 'The dance of life – that's me and you'. The next image was a stag standing in the road with a juggernaut coming towards it. He said: 'That's me in the road'. When I asked, 'Who was driving the juggernaut?', he replied, 'I don't know, but it's coming towards me'. Finally he chose an image of a bleak and barren landscape with a figure sitting with head in hands. 'This', he said, 'is you, trying to work it all out'.

I was struck by the level of insight and acknowledgement his comments showed, that somewhere in all of the damaged and defended ways of relating, there was a part of him that could recognise that I was there to 'pick his brains', 'dance with him', 'threaten him with intimacy' and also 'think about him', in other words, to hold him in mind.

Despite the level of destructiveness that was manifest in the work, there were also moments of connectedness and hope amongst his expressions of despair and fear. Carl would regularly try to terminate the dramatherapy, then the following week would demand more time or to see me twice a day. Whether or not he engaged with the medium, an important lesson I have learnt from this experience was the necessity to hold the boundaries of time, place and physical proximity, and also at times maintain my presence as a point of stillness around which the dance of life, death and destruction could be enacted.

Along with his consultant psychiatrist, the nurses and social worker, dramatherapy had been the one consistent intervention in his rehabilitation, within which Carl has been able to develop a greater capacity to contain and express himself in ways that had not been possible previously. In his final dramatherapy session, before being discharged into the community, Carl picked out a passage from a children's story book on the shelf and read me part of a story about a boy and the Ice Queen on their final flight in her sleigh before saying goodbye forever. The metaphor was explicit and understood by both therapist and patient. At the end of the session, he said that he would miss me. Carl was leaving the space as an adult, who had learnt to navigate his way through turbulent and at times overwhelming feelings in captivity to create an exit for himself that was both expressive and respectful.

Further reflections

The dramatherapy space had transformed from being a destructive space – a theatre of war – to a 'creative space'. This process can be linked to Winnicott's concept of 'transitional phenomena', which refers to a dimension – the third space, which belongs neither to internal or external reality, and is inextricably linked to play and creativity (Abram 1996: 311). Just as the infant uses 'transitional objects' as ways to separate and symbolise, for dramatherapists, the 'transitional object' can simultaneously be both the 'dramatic medium', to which the patient relates, as well as the 'therapist', to whom the patient relates. Both can become a symbol, which separates the self from others and unites the self with others. Grainger (1992) states that 'drama itself is largely concerned with the experiences of separation and involvement, (or alienation and engulfment) . . . crucial to this process is the combination between structural roles and imaginative freedom which typifies dramatherapy'.

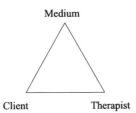

The vignettes show that when the patient is located in a place that feels threatening, they might respond by collapsing the drama or the creative space. However, the dramatherapist may also unwittingly participate in such moments of destructiveness, as described in the following instance.

Carl, the large black man, walks behind me towards the dramatherapy room and mimes that he is shackled and chained to me. On entering the space, he asks, 'What will you have me do, mistress?' I could have collaborated with him and taken up the role of 'mistress' that he was evoking, with a response such as 'Clean up this room!', but instead I said, 'What do you want to do?' The ambiguity of my response diverted us from the dynamic that he was inviting me to explore. Perhaps in my own discomfort of the potent image of the black slave and his white mistress, I had destroyed the potential of that moment to go with the drama. The drama of the black man being led by the white, female, key-holding dramatherapist to her room, in order to 'pick his brains', 'make him dance', 'threaten him with intimacy' and 'work him out'.

In this final image, the destructiveness organised me in such a way that I destroyed the moment by not playing in the medium. Such an image contains a number of associations: the uncomfortable reminder of the cultural legacy of colonialism and apartheid; the captor and the 'bonded' captive; the 'bondage' of the sado-masochist; and finally the paradoxical question of who is rendering whom hostage in the space?

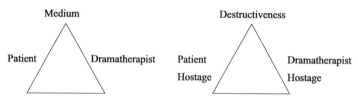

During all three of the vignettes presented, at different moments, the patient, or the therapist or the medium are all held in the position of hostage.

The art of the possible

Working as a dramatherapist, I am all too aware that at the heart of every drama, every dramatic space, every dramatic encounter, there lies conflict, conflict that can be played out in many guises. It can encapsulate Jung's Shadow and persona; Freud's life and death instincts; the ego and super-ego; Klein's splitting and introjection of good and bad breast; Gruen's inward and outward force; Glasser's 'core complex' of self-preservation and sadistic aggression; Winnicott's 'true self' and 'false self'; the sadist and masochist; the leaders of Rosenfeld's (1971) internal mafia gang; Green-wood's (2000) captor and hostage, and the roles of perpetrator and victim. It is the recognition and integration of these poles that bring about psychic change, either in Klein's world of object relations, with the shift from the 'paranoid schizoid' position to the 'depressive position', or in Jung's world of undifferentiated poles of experience, with the integration of the shadow towards individuation.

It is worth acknowledging that we are all on the same continuum of encountering our own destructiveness and it is only in being able to acknowledge, tolerate and perhaps find compassion for our own impulses that we can help others to face their thresholds of resistance, or at least accompany them to be at the threshold. It is through the transference and counter-transference that we have with our clients that we are brought face to face with both the client's destructiveness as well as our own.

This dynamic highlights the importance of drawing on observations around what is happening within each person – the therapist and patient, as well as between them. At any moment, either the therapist or patient might be located in a place that feels threatening, overwhelming, frozen or in the position of hostage in the space. Depending on the intensity of the experience, either the therapist or patient might respond with that primitive defence of destructiveness, by withdrawing from the play space or, alternatively, by collapsing it, demonstrating the cycle of the 'core complex'.

When such moments arise, it would seem that the task of the therapist is to hold the possibility of 'play' in mind, even when the 'play' has been destroyed. As an action organised out of primitive defences expressing the intolerable internal states, destructiveness is an important communication. Even when this means that there is no longer a medium, or total negation of the mind – a feeling of annihilation– the very act of destructiveness is a way of letting someone know about something intolerable, which Winnicott et al. (1984) believed was a request to the external world for help.

Often in the arts therapies, through the triangulation with the medium, something can be mediated that was previously intolerable. When the medium is under attack, there is still the relationship; when the relationship is under attack, there is still the space to think; when the thinking space is under attack, there is simply physical presence; as Estragon says, 'Stay with me' (Beckett 1956).

With the various tools of containment that dramatherapy offers, such as using the mind, body, images, objects and stories, the dramatherapist must be prepared at different times to be cast in all three roles of captor, hostage and bystander, even if these roles are only located in the conscious mind of the therapist. It is only by visiting and playing out these different roles that the actors can be liberated from being perpetually stuck in any one of them. Terry Waite reminds us of such collaboration following his release from Beirut in 1991:

> Freeing hostages is like putting up a stage set, which you do with the captors, agreeing on each piece as you slowly put it together; then you leave an exit through which both the captor and the captive can walk with sincerity and dignity.
>
> www.whatquote.com (seen 2007)

It seems that destructiveness cannot be a phenomenon in isolation, but must have a context in order to be destructive. If the act of destructiveness is the release of something intolerable, the movement of something internal outwards, then it is also an act of potentiality. However, when this act causes harm, how can it be harnessed before it harnesses us? This question can be answered in terms of the dramatherapist finding a way to keep 'play' possible in the therapeutic process as a whole, even though at any particular moment, given very real risk and threat (not just the fantasy), playing and creativity may seem impossible.

By holding on to the potential 'play', whether it will be located in the mind or in the body in space, the dramatherapist can harness destructiveness by holding in mind creative possibilities, thus keeping something alive that may appear destroyed or deadened. This hypothesis of the dramatherapist being able to 'hold something in mind' is concomitant with both other arts therapists as well as the psychodynamic psychoanalytic ideas selected. When this possibility is under threat, in the position of captive the captivated therapist may also have to rely on the mind of the supervisor to help release the therapist–hostage, who in turn may then collaborate with the patient– hostage.

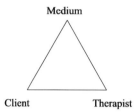

Medium

Client   Therapist

Conclusion

This chapter looks at destructiveness in a dramatherapy space in a forensic psychiatric setting. Destructiveness manifests in such a way that renders the therapist in a position of either hostage or perpetrator, whilst the patient is either captor or captive, respectively. The artistic medium can also be collapsed by such destructiveness, as illustrated in all three clinical vignettes. The dramatherapist has possibilities available to help transform and harness the destructiveness – either by working through the medium or by finding a more collaborative way of relating in the space. This may simply mean staying with the patient and bearing what may feel unbearable for them, in order that they can in turn feel more bearable to themselves. Learning to contain difficult feelings and develop empathy for self and others are important aims for the forensic patient in dramatherapy, so that they will no longer need to evacuate intolerable feelings by acting out (without thinking), thus reducing risk of re-offending and harm to themselves or others.

By using observations from the clinical space and linking them with theoretical ideas, we can consider what choices remain for the dramatherapist when patient and therapist find themselves in what seems like a therapeutic stranglehold in the creative space – to hold on to the art of the possible.

10

SUGAR AND SPICE AND ALL THINGS NICE: A BLACK WOMAN'S ANGER IN A FORENSIC SETTING

Rose Thorn

. . . we have to be the mistress of smiling, masterly at trapeze walking
With feats of balance, being the right amount of small, so as not to unnerve anyone.
And that is where we have to take care
Because we shrink inside
to the size of a bilious ball which turns toxic and acidic
And simmers and rages . . .

(Davis 2010)

Brief overview of chapter

This chapter focuses on a 7-week dramatherapy assessment in a medium-secure unit with Auriel, a black woman in her late thirties who was diagnosed with schizophrenia and whose index offence was arson. I explore the metaphors, stories and roles that emerged both inside the dramatherapy space and within the multidisciplinary team (Stamp 2000). I define the context in which I work the referral process and then follow the chronology of the sessions using clinical vignettes. I analyse my counter-transference and link it to theoretical material. Details have been changed to protect the client's confidentiality; her direct quotes have been put in speech marks.

Introduction

Frameworks of understanding

I have used a case study approach (Grainger 1999; Edwards 1999), using process notes and records from external clinical supervision. Models and theories that underpin this enquiry include: the dramatherapy play–drama continuum (Jones 2007); attachment theory (Adshead 2002); trauma models (Rothschild 2000; Levine 1997); psychodynamic approaches (Bateman and Holmes 1995; Gomez 1996); and feminist theory (hooks 1990; Lorde 1984; Orbach 1998; Welldon 1992).

Setting and client group

The medium-secure unit in which I work has 68 male and 12 female inpatient beds. The arts psychotherapies team (APT) has three drama, two art and three music therapists; each modality has a resourced therapy room. We work across the men's and women's services, facilitating a variety of one-to-one and groups, brief or long-term therapy, depending on the needs of the client and the care pathway agreed by the multidisciplinary team (MDT). The women's service has its own in-house MDT with a leading consultant, psychologists, occupational therapists, a social worker and the nursing team. I contribute to weekly ward rounds and submit a report for the 3-monthly integrated care plan assessment (ICPA).

Racism within forensic settings

The 2008 'Count Me In' census found that 23% of all inpatients belonged to black and minority ethnic (BME) groups; they were more likely to be on medium- or high-secure wards and rates of referral from the criminal justice system were three or more times higher than average.

> . . . controlling people that society sees as 'dangerous' becomes the province of forensic psychiatry. And schizophrenia . . . is the diagnosis that is naturally used to medicalise black protest, despair and anger.
>
> (Fernando et al. 1998: 66)

The legacy of colonialism and slavery has shaped the development of Western forensic psychiatry; institutional racism is present in how BME people are perceived, treated and more often diagnosed with schizophrenia (Littlewood and Lipsedge 1997). An individual's distress cannot be reduced to their 'inner psychic reality' or their 'pathology'; their ethnicity, culture, gender, class and age must also be considered. Understanding what their distress means to them is a process of negotiating meanings rather than fitting the clients into the dominant Eurocentric, white, middle-class norms of 'health' and 'disease' (Kareem and Littlewood 2000).

Blackness in the client–therapist match

> . . . the word 'Black' . . . has social and political meaning both as a chosen and as an ascribed definition of racial and cultural identity.

> Yet it is also . . . limiting, for people are not simply either black or white but . . . complex, multi-layered beings, with a capacity to move between positions.
>
> (Barber and Campbell 1999: 25)

In my experience the word 'black' creates tension in any predominantly white context. I am the only black arts psychotherapist on the APT; I am of mixed heritage (a white and a black parent). Being light-skinned, my experience of racism changes depending on the social context; when in 'white' company it is often assumed that I am white. I receive projections of people's discomfort/racism about not being 'black enough' or looking and sounding 'too white'. Racism can impact deeply on one's sense of self.

'Matching' the ethnicity of the client with the therapist is not necessary (Kareem and Littlewood 2000). Results from a study on African-Americans engaging with psychotherapy revealed that ethnic match appeared to affect the number of treatment sessions attended but not the outcome (Zane et al. 2004). All therapists need to analyse their own issues of identity and address where power has resided historically and is currently played out in society (Dokter 1998).

Originating from slavery, I am aware of the 'privileges' still given to black people with lighter skin. I wondered how Auriel would perceive me in a position of power? I felt an internal and external pressure to engage with Auriel because of an assumed shared experience and responsibility not to pathologise another black woman's experience.

Observations, reflections and discussion

Auriel's referral to the APT

The women's MDT described Auriel's attachment style as 'insecure–avoidant', a tendency to dismiss feelings of need and a diminished capacity for empathy. She had recently attended a 10-week women's dramatherapy group and then withdrew. Clinically obese, Auriel's increasing weight gain fuelled the MDT's anxiety of not knowing how to engage with her; they feared that her isolation was partly due to her being the only black client on the unit. I sensed that there was an assumption from the MDT and APT that she might engage with me because I am black.

Auriel's case history

Auriel was an African-Caribbean woman in her late thirties. Her parents moved to England where she was born, leaving her teenage brother and sister with their maternal grandmother in the Caribbean. Her siblings eventually joined them in a predominantly white rural area of England. Her

135

father had been violent towards her mother; her sister accused him of sexually abusing her and went into care. He left the family home when Auriel was 3; she was very fond of him. Auriel claimed her mother was physically and emotionally abusive towards her.

Auriel said that she had been raped by various male relatives from an early age. She experienced racist bullying at secondary school and as a teenager she had sex with older men. At 18 she had a son; when 20 she had a daughter with a different father who was physically and sexually abusive to her.

Around the birth of her son, Auriel had sporadic contact with mental health services. She felt that her main difficulty was depression, although she also had periods of hearing voices. She received limited counselling and was prescribed antipsychotic medication. When she was 30 she had numerous informal psychiatric admissions; her children went into care.

In Auriel's forensic history there were confusing accounts of psychotic episodes (possibly triggered by cannabis use) in which she had assaulted a neighbour, whom she accused of sexually abusing her, physically attacked her mother and been violent towards her son. At the time of her index offence, Auriel was admitted as an informal patient in a psychiatric hospital; she felt suicidal and feared harming her son further. Anticipating discharge, she threatened to kill herself; she set fire to her home and on return to the hospital set fire to her bedroom. She was arrested and detained at the medium-secure unit.

Therapeutic aims

Auriel agreed to meet for seven sessions and then review the work. My aims were to assess her ability to build a therapeutic relationship and engage with dramatherapy. I saw her once a week for an hour in the dramatherapy room.

Session one

During handover, the nursing staff reported that Auriel had been caught smoking cannabis brought in by her son. We walked in silence to the room; I was conscious of needing to slow down to keep pace with her. Auriel chose to lie on the cushions. 'All my treats are being taken away'; she explained that the nurses were preventing her from drinking Coca-Cola due to her diabetes and weight gain. She carefully watched and waited for my responses.

I then read out the story *Lifting the Sky* (Gersie 1992: 49), a story which had themes of holding weight and responsibility. Auriel was attentive; she thought that the story was about 'people working together'. I felt compelled to move off the cushions and Auriel tentatively copied my body movements.

136

We held up blue cloth to represent the sky and spoke out loud. We pushed our hands against the walls, exploring the boundaries of the space.

She suddenly stopped and sat down at the table. When invited, she rolled some black plasticine that she had been looking at. She commented that it was 'hard to work' and made a black figure saying that it was her. She flattened a layer of yellow plasticine to be the sky, she put this on top of the black figure. She asked if she could 'deviate' from the story, making a green palm tree and placed the yellow sky on top.

She was quiet as if she was waiting for me. She then said that the tree was like her father, he was 'a provider'; he would bring her Coca-Cola and protect her. She likened the restrictiveness of the nurses to her mother who sabotaged things that she wanted to do. She didn't mention the cannabis incident.

My counter-transference

There was a sense of collusiveness, as if 'we' were the 'outsiders' sharing time away from the ward; I was the 'good' therapist and the nursing team was 'bad'. During the silences I felt that Auriel was waiting for me to take the lead – to hold up the heaviness of the sky for her as she held on to her secrets.

Vignette discussion: splitting in the team

The splitting of her idealised 'good' provider father and the 'bad' punitive mother was unconsciously projected onto and played out in the care team. Just as I had felt compelled to move away from Auriel's heaviness during the session, I wondered if the nursing staff also found her emotional needs unbearable, choosing to focus on her dietary and physical health needs instead. Adshead (2002) emphasises how the staff's conflicting roles of 'control and care' can easily replicate patients' abusive or neglecting early care-givers.

During the fourth session, Auriel started to have one-to-one appointments with her male doctor and then cancel dramatherapy; my counter-transference was jealousy. Later on, Auriel revealed how she would dote on her father (the doctor in the transference) to make her mother (me) jealous. I raised this dynamic with the doctor, who changed the session time. Regular reflective practice in forensic settings helps staff to think together rather than acting out and splitting (Stamp 2000).

Session two

Auriel said that she was coping with drinking diet coke and felt 'laid back and cool' without smoking cannabis. She felt isolated as the only black woman on the ward and had also experienced this in the community. I suggested that she choose objects to explore this isolation; this became a time-line, mapping her experiences between the ages of 4–18 years.

Auriel placed the objects on the floor along a tape measure, which related to her mother's constant criticisms about her weight – 'never measuring up'. The turkey was about remembering happy family gatherings at Christmas. Auriel spoke quietly about how a pair of thick joke-glasses reminded her of being bullied at school for being black and wearing 'goggles'.

She then became very animated. She chose a dolphin and a watch to represent living with her maternal grandmother in the relaxed atmosphere of the Caribbean, where 'time didn't matter'. She told stories of playing with her cousins, stealing mangos and being 'walloped' by her grandmother. I was struck by her elated tone as she explained how 'Over there I was called "the English girl" but I got attention and I could manipulate the tourists'.

This Caribbean period ended with her return to England; a calculator reminded her of being good at maths. Whilst holding a figure of an American Indian with an axe and gun, she described how a white South African school friend had corrected her pronunciation of the word 'Indyan' to 'Indian'.

My counter-transference

I could not see Auriel's eyes behind her 'rose-tinted' glasses and I did not believe her idealised stories of 'happy families' in the Caribbean. They contrasted with the sadness I felt when she spoke about the racism and bullying that she'd experienced in this country. I empathised with her desire 'to belong'; even in the Caribbean she was seen as 'different'. I feared that she saw me as a white woman, who like her school friend would not understand her.

Vignette discussion: internalised racism and false self

Whether Auriel had actually lived in the Caribbean or not, she was communicating about her identity as a black woman, her experiences of racism and her desire to belong within her family and community:

> Basically in white culture black women get to play two roles. We are either the bad girls, the 'bitches', the madwomen (how many times have you heard folks say that a particularly assertive black woman is 'crazy') seen as threatening and treated badly, or we are the supermamas, telling it like it is and taking care of everybody, spreading our special magic wherever we go.
>
> (hooks 1990: 91)

The pressure to 'fit in' or 'fight against' racist stereotypes makes it difficult to keep hold of what you yourself think, feel or want. When white people choose to see blackness as 'exotic', they continue to reside within the safe confines of colonial/racist thinking. Auriel chose to show the more 'exotic' aspect of being black. 'It may be difficult for a black person to explore negative feelings about themselves if they feel the need to defend a positive view of their blackness' (Barber and Campbell 1999: 26).

Was Auriel testing whether I was one of the white 'tourists' who would be seduced by the funny 'supermama' stereotype? I noticed the weapons that the 'Ind-yan' was holding, to defend his people from being murdered; was Auriel holding up this stereotype as a defence against the hostility of racism? This 'performance' was Auriel's 'false self'; Winnicott explains how when a baby's needs are not valued, the child will adopt a 'false self' in order to be accepted, meanwhile the 'true self' is shrouded in shame (Gomez 1996).

Session 3

Returning to the time-line, Auriel chose the thick joke-glasses to create a character which she embodied called 'Odd'. We did 'odd' movements in the space. I then interviewed 'Odd from Planet Odd'. Auriel abruptly came out of role and chose to sit at the table. I was concerned that she had become overwhelmed whilst in character. To enable digestion and establish some distance I suggested that she could write about Odd:

> Odd
> Different
> Uncomfortably, comfortable
> Weird, wired
> Quietly noisy
> Non-conformist

She then added 'funny' and 'hard trier' to the poem. She described her frustration with not 'fitting in' on the ward, not wanting to be too loud, watching what she ate, how many times she washed – 'I just want to be normal'. Although she appeared to have much to say, she then stopped speaking. She sat hugging herself, looking up at at the clock, waiting for the session to end.

My counter-transference

I felt that Auriel was angry at me, as if I did not understand her. Auriel and I were orientating ourselves to the secure unit (she had been detained for only 8 months and I had been working there for 6), which was a 'Planet Odd' with its own culture. Auriel felt like 'an alien' as the only black patient on the ward, and I was an 'outsider' to the women's in-house MDT, aware that dramatherapy was not seen to be as important as the dominating medical model.

Vignette discussion: racism and splitting as an internal process

Difference in ethnicity and cultures can become a vehicle into which good and bad feelings are projected (Lowe 2008). In session one I was the 'good' object and the team 'bad', later the doctor was 'good' and I was 'bad'.

> . . . at the level of the social world . . . racism is a form of organising peoples, commodities and the relationships between them by utilizing a notion of race. The second description begins in the world of the emotions and says that racism consists of the feelings of hatred, disgust, repulsion and other negative emotions felt and expressed by one group towards another.
>
> (White 2006: 11)

This process of splitting is intensified for black and white people by the history of colonialism and the enslavement of black people by whites. I wondered if Auriel was experiencing racism on the ward and struggling to acknowledge her anger. As a member of staff I was part of the oppressive system, Auriel's anger was passively directed at me within the transference. Before encouraging the client to deal directly with anger, Wilt (1993) uses a developmental approach to assess the early mother–baby attachment and the child's development of defence mechanisms such as denial, splitting and projection.

> When a baby has experienced her mother as threatening she 'cuts herself off' from feeling both angry and fearful in relation to her mother, on whom she totally depends; she has learnt to dissociate.
>
> (de Zulueta 1998: 179)

Dissociating and splitting are often survival mechanisms for victims of childhood sexual abuse who are attempting to understand how someone they love (good) can hurt them (bad). This idealisation and denigration can be acted out within the therapeutic relationship (Adshead and Van Velsen 1998).

Session 4

Auriel was initially asleep, her hair was neglected, she looked unkempt. She walked reluctantly along the corridor, describing her bed as 'my good friend'. She told me that she had enjoyed watching a play on the ward, about a patient with delusions who believed he was a theatre director; his secretary was really his consultant. I asked if she wanted to do some role play. She instantly announced that she would like to be Prince Charles' girlfriend. She would 'direct' and I was to 'assist'.

Wearing a shawl and beaded silver headdress, she created a character called Fifi who was born in 'the tropics' but educated in England. Fifi had travelled the world and met Prince Charles at a geisha house. Fifi was at a 'quintessentially English garden party with topiary, a lawn, a table with canapés and champagne'. She embodied the role for about 10 minutes, parading her 'sexy walk' in an elated way, and then she suddenly stopped, collapsing into the chair saying that she felt 'self-conscious and silly'.

Auriel talked about how she often wanted to please others and then she said, 'I just want to run away with Prince Charles and have sex'. She reflected that she had 'plenty to run from but nowhere to run to'. She laughed, saying that the Fifi part of her would bring out Prince Charles' 'naughty and rebellious side'. She added that she had slept with many men but they had often betrayed her.

My counter-transference

I was concerned that Auriel's unruly and 'wild' hair would be perceived as 'mad' by the white staff; I felt protective, wanting to oil and braid her hair. In recounting the content of the play I felt Auriel was questioning our roles as client and therapist. I was surprised by her sudden burst of energy as she initiated the drama. The theme of power was very alive as she took control of the session.

Vignette discussion: gender, sexuality and power

Auriel's reluctance to attend, then her creation of a more distanced fantasy world, suggested that she did not want to revisit her vulnerability. Instead she portrayed a white, upper class, 'English' image of herself from a colonial era; here her difference would be seen as 'exotic' and attractive rather than 'odd' and painful. Auriel could feel powerful using her sexuality to dominate men. This contrasted starkly with Auriel as a black, clinically obese, working-class woman. Studies have shown that obesity is often more common in women from a lower socio-economic status who have been sexually abused.

Session 5

Auriel was late and wanted a story from me. I asked about stories she knew; she remembered *Jack and the Beanstalk*. By alternating sentences we created a new version called *Jackie and her Mother*:

141

Jackie had no shoes because they were poor. Mother beat Jackie telling her she was lazy. On the way to the market to sell the clothes they made, Jackie met a well dressed woman who granted her three wishes. Jackie requested and received her coach to paradise, a sunny land where everyone wore shoes. Here a lemonade fountain scattered sweets which magically turned into gold coins . . .

Auriel fell asleep, leaving the story unfinished.

Session 6

Auriel took off her shoes and lay on the cushions; she had just had lunch. She reached for some chiffon scarves, stroking her face and watching them move as she breathed. She slowly played a rhythm, which I mirrored on another drum. She watched and listened carefully. There was little talking and then I watched her fall asleep.

My counter-transference

In these sessions I noticed my opposing maternal responses. As the 'critical' mother I refused to 'feed' Auriel another story, I wanted her to stop 'being lazy' and disapprovingly watched her overweight belly as she slept. As the 'nurturing' mother, I felt protective towards Auriel, wanting to affirm her presence by mirroring.

Vignette discussion: mothering, destructive eating and regression

The play–drama continuum (Jones 2007) defines a series of stages from concrete to symbolic levels of functioning, relevant to clients diagnosed with schizophrenia who often have difficulty in functioning symbolically (McAlister 2000). In session six, Auriel's preverbal explorations of the materials related to the sensorimotor stage, where she was struggling to think, verbalise and share her thoughts. Auriel uses her mouth to eat away the 'bad' feelings.

> The inability of a parent to distinguish between infant needs for food versus other emotional needs is thought to contribute to the infant's subsequent inability to discriminate between hunger and other states, such as fear, anxiety and anger.
>
> (Russell and Shirk 1993: 176)

Orbach (1998) suggests that a woman may unconsciously choose to be fat in order to: hide, protect herself, contain feelings, experience warmth and desexualise herself. Obesity in women is linked to how they relate to their emotions, particularly anger; the symbolic meaning of fat is 'fuck you!'. Fletchman Smith (2000) found that Caribbean clients often have difficulty in expressing their dis-ease in 'mentalistic' terms, instead communicating psychosomatically.

Session 7

Although this was our last session, I reminded Auriel that she could continue. When I asked her what she had remembered, she replied: the 'Odd' character, Fifi and the quiet sessions. She said that she had found it difficult to feel. She had recently attended a psychosocial group on the ward about assertiveness; she emphasised that she had to be 'very assertive' to get what she wanted. When I asked her what she wanted from dramatherapy she replied, 'a place to be passive' and fell asleep.

My counter-transference

I felt disempowered as a dramatherapist. How could I keep the drama and therapeutic relationship alive? How would I explain the work to the MDT? I had to ensure that I didn't project my sense of failure onto Auriel as the 'bad client'.

Vignette discussion: sleep as avoidance and dissociation

I understood Auriel's sleepiness as an 'acting in', a non-verbal expression of anger. She was attempting to regulate her overwhelming feelings of vulnerability, sadness and rage.

Conclusions from clinical practice

Auriel's index offence of arson was a projection of rage that could not be contained or thought about. I have emphasised how unconscious processes of rage and splitting are not just internal processes (Dalal 2006) but need to be understood as part of the structure of racism which exists within individuals and organisations (Lowe 2008).

During the assessment, Auriel engaged with story, projective objects, and created and enacted roles. Her struggles to stay in role indicate that they were too close to overwhelming feelings held in her body. Using the play-continuum as an evaluation tool, I noticed that Auriel could represent aspects of her inner world symbolically and she also regressed into more concrete functioning. She slowly 'killed off' the 'drama' with her unconscious attacks of sleep, a defence mechanism to fend off new experiences (Mann, 1990).

Auriel's 'inner drama' became located within the therapeutic relationship. As she regressed, I embodied a 'nurturing mother', where a state of dependency rather than individuation was initiated. My intention was that Auriel would be able to internalise the 'good enough' attachment. Only when trust was established could she begin to think about how her traumas had affected her behaviour and what this meant (Levine 1997).

11

FROM TRANSITIONAL OBJECT TO SYMBOL: SPIDERMAN IN A DRAMATHERAPY GROUP WITH MENTALLY DISORDERED OFFENDERS

Maggie McAlister

Brief overview of chapter

This chapter explores the role of symbolism in a dramatherapy group for mentally disordered offenders in a psychiatric medium-secure unit. The group members created work around the character of 'Spiderman' to explore issues relating to their offending behaviour and psychosis, before speaking more directly about their offences. My suggestion is that the creative work on Spiderman created a transitional space, and a bridge between concrete and symbolic levels of functioning. Theoretical links between dramatherapy and psychoanalytic theory are discussed to illustrate how dramatherapy can enhance therapeutic engagement with extremely resistant clients, and support the recovery of symbolic processes in offenders with a psychotic illness.

Introduction

This chapter concerns a group who, over a period of several months, used Spiderman to explore mental illness and violent offending long before they were able or willing to talk directly about themselves. Until this point it had been very difficult, if not impossible, for the group to discuss issues to do with their offences or the reason they were in a secure hospital, largely due to resistance and/or lack of insight. My proposal is that the group's collective use of Spiderman functioned as a transitional object in the sense defined by Winnicott (1971: 2) as something 'outside, inside and at the border', an intermediate area of experience, which antedates symbolisation. This is especially important for the client group with whom I work, as one way of thinking about both their mental illness and their offending behaviour is that their capacity to symbolise has broken down. Therefore, the rationale for using dramatherapy as a psychological therapy with such a client group is important and is explored in this chapter.

Introduction to setting and client group

I work in a large medium-secure psychiatric unit in the NHS, with mentally disordered offenders detained on forensic sections of the Mental Health Act (2007). The clients who come to our service have all committed a crime, usually violent, referred to as an 'index offence' (the offence under which they are held), and have either a psychiatric disposal from court (diminished responsibility/unfit to plead) or alternatively are sentenced and subsequently transferred from prison, due to acute mental health problems. The degree of dangerousness they pose to others means that they often remain in our service for several years, due to the severity of their offences and/or mental illness. The need for a long process of treatment and risk assessment means that the Ministry of Justice will often take several years to authorise their discharge under the recommendation of the consultant psychiatrist. There is a very strong emphasis on multidisciplinary team (MDT) work, which gathers regularly in ward rounds and clinical discussion groups. The arts therapies are part of this, and form part of the formal psychological therapies on offer to clients, alongside forensic psychotherapy and psychology.

The clients mainly suffer from psychosis and in most cases the index offence has occurred as a result of their illness. Two important factors in recovery are the extent to which 'insight' and 'remorse' are present. However, both of these states of mind depend on the ability to conceive of a 'third position', one where another point of view can be accommodated. With clients with a psychotic mental illness, this third position can be very difficult to achieve. At the heart of this difficulty is the process of symbolisation. There has been an almost total collapse of the capacity to symbolise in this client group, leading not only to the very concrete states characteristic of schizophrenia, but also to the index offence itself (Cordess and Cox 1996). What is particular to forensic work is that one is working with people who have not only had psychotic, murderous phantasies but have actually acted them out. Murray Cox (1978: 13) states, 'Offender therapy provides a unique clinical arena in which fact and fantasy merge. The offence may take many forms but it always involves action'. The emphasis is on action or acting out, rather than on thought or symbolisation. Therefore, the offence itself can be seen as an enactment, or a wish to evacuate overwhelmingly intolerable states of mind (Morgan and Ruszczynski 2007).

The five members of the dramatherapy group all had a diagnosis of paranoid schizophrenia, and their index offences involved serious psychotic violence (instigated by paranoia). Two of the group members had killed their victims. At the time of the following piece of work, the group members had already been in the dramatherapy group for over 2 years. They came from different rehabilitation wards in order to attend the group, which took place once a week for an hour in a designated dramatherapy room in the secure unit. The group was run by myself and a music therapist, and had a long-term, psychodynamic focus. The aim was to increase the client's insight into their destructive behaviour, using exploration of the transference, the dramatherapy medium and interpersonal group processes.

Frameworks of understanding

Process of enquiry

This chapter takes the form of a single case study design (Yin 1994). My proposition is that dramatherapy can be useful with violent offenders with a psychotic illness because of the role of symbolisation in mental health restoration. The criteria I use to interpret the findings are based on clinical outcome within the group itself (e.g. an increase in personal disclosure and greater engagement with therapeutic aims of the unit). My study is focused on in-depth exploration and description, with the view of presenting a 'critical case' where the dramatherapy practice within this group can be replicated and seen as applying generally to offenders with a psychotic illness in similar settings.

Clinical theory/practice framework

First I would like to briefly describe psychoanalytic theories that enable us to understand psychosis and the importance of symbolisation, before turning to Winnicott's transitional object and the relationship this has to the development of symbolisation and dramatherapy practice.

Much has been written in the field of psychoanalysis about the idea of 'the third', a concept first developed by Ron Britton (1989: 87) when his memorable borderline patient told him to 'stop that fucking thinking' when she could not tolerate his thoughtful silences. Britton understood this as her inability to tolerate his mind having creative 'intercourse', as it were, with psychoanalytic theory. What this vignette illustrates is the enormous difficulty some patients have with what Britton calls 'triangular space', a 'third other' in relationship with the object, from whom one is excluded. This original triangle forms the core of the Oedipus complex, where the infant must accept a (parental) relationship of which he is a part, yet from which he is also excluded. However, it is the capacity to deal with this state of exclusion that leads to symbol formation, where thought develops from a frustration, a tolerance of absence (Bion 1962). In *A Theory of Thinking*, Bion describes this using sexual imagery, of preconceptions 'mating' with a frustration. In normal Oedipal development, Bion linked the development

147

of verbal thought and the ability to form symbols with the capacity to tolerate the state of loss in relation to the Oedipal pairing. This is because by accepting a triangular viewpoint, one can perceive reality from both a subjective and objective perspective, which is crucial to reality testing and symbolisation. In triangular space there can be separateness, leading to other viewpoints and 'as if' quality. These ideas are also highly relevant to Bateman and Fonagy's (2004) concept of 'mentalisation', a process by which one develops a theory of one's own mind and the mind of others.

In psychosis there is a deficit in the capacity to symbolise, leading to the omnipotence and destructive attack on reality we see in illnesses such as schizophrenia. Rusbridger (1999: 491) writes: 'In psychotic states we attack the parental couple and then identify with this destroyed alliance, destroying at the same time our ability to use our mind'. This leads to splitting, concrete thinking, absolute truths, delusional states of mind and results in extreme concreteness. There is no experience of separateness, only inter-changeable 'sets' where thoughts are the same as actions, love is the same as hate and the subject and object become interchangeable. One enters the world of what Segal (1957) calls 'concrete symbols' and 'symbolic equation'. An example of this is a time I knocked on the door of a client to remind him that it was time for his dramatherapy group. He appeared to experience this reminder in an overwhelmingly intrusive, paranoid way telling me to leave because 'your arsehole is sucking up my body'. His experience that I was invading him with my demands was equivalent to trying to suck him up in an anally sadistic way and converted to a concrete symbol in his mind. Instead of one thing being 'as if' it is another thing ('my door *feels like* an extension of my body and you knocking on it *feels like* a shitty attack on me, *as if* I'm going to be annihilated by your demands!'), it *is* the same thing ('your hand/arsehole *is* attacking/annihilating my door/body'). Segal (1991; Quinodoz 2008) demonstrates that symbolic equation underlines schizo-phrenic concrete thinking. Without an 'as if' quality, one lives in a world of concrete, black and white absolutes, where ambivalence cannot exist, only the co-incidence of love and hate.

Winnicott's (1951, 1971) unique contribution to this field is to suggest that before symbolisation (triangular space) can occur, there is a transi-tional object, a pre-curser of the symbol. The transitional object is still in the realm of two persons relating; it is an intermediate area of experience between the infant and the mother. Winnicott's description of the tran-sitional object is as the infant's first 'not-me' possession. Essentially it defends against anxiety, and enables the infant to cope with the absence of mother through the creation of an object which is mother/not mother, me/ not me. It allows for a blurring of boundaries in the process of separation where what can exist is an external object in the real world, but within the complete control of the infant. The important qualities I wish to highlight for the purposes of this chapter are that in 'good enough mothering' it is allowed to be controlled and manipulated by the infant, it is a neutral area of experience which is not challenged, it has a direct relationship to creativity and its fate is to be gradually allowed to be decathected, that is to say lose meaning.

These psychoanalytic concepts are valuable in dramatherapy where aspects of the work are involved in helping the client to have a greater capacity to represent aspects of their inner world symbolically (for links between Kleinian and Winnicottian theories and dramatherapy, see McAlister 2000, 2002; Dokter 1994; Jenkyns 1996). I suggest that, in dramatherapy, the use of the art form can be allowed to function as a transitional object, something not quite me/not-me, something not quite concrete but not fully symbolised either. Destructive, dangerous phantasies can be safely managed through the containment of the medium. This is important for clients who are anxious about their capacity for destructiveness, especially when this has led to catastrophic acts in the past. As well as creating a container for projections, we also provide a triangular relationship/space between the therapist, the client and the drama medium. This space can offer safety and distance. However, with forensic clients there is a danger that this indirect mode of expression can bypass difficult issues and become therapy in the 'pretend mode', a mentalisation-based term used to describe a state of mind where clients remain superficial in treatment, despite having the appearance of meaningful contact (Bateman and Fonagy 2004: 85). In this case dramatherapy can be recruited in the service of the client's (and therapist's) defences. For this reason, I see one of the therapist's main tasks as offering translations and interpretations of creative material and to sensitively make links in the work over time.

Clinical observations amd discussion

The dramatherapy group for this study was made up of long-standing members. They were familiar with the structure of the group and had gradually taken responsibility for deciding what ideas to explore and what roles to play. Therapists always used de-roling exercises and grounding techniques after any imaginative work as well as holding clear boundaries, in terms of setting, timing and personal non-disclosure. We adopted the stance that anything brought to the sessions was material to be worked with. None of the group members had voluntarily brought up any issues to do with their illness or offences and were extremely resistant to thinking about these issues. However, a basic premise of forensic psychotherapy is that the index offence is dynamically expressed in the transference/counter-transference with the client and what my co-therapist and I largely worked on were issues to do with group dynamics and anxieties, and paranoid ideation around transference issues. To protect their identities, I shall call the clients Les, Tommy, Joe and Chris.

Before this series of sessions, a favourite drama scene for the group was one where they role-played bosses of various status. My co-therapist and I often linked this to anxieties they might have about group hierarchy. There was often a power struggle between two group members in particular, Les and Tommy. Les' mental state was the most fragile of the group members'. He was often grandiose and had the delusion that all females were in love with him.

At the beginning of this series of sessions, Les announced that he had had an idea of a role to play, the 'Incredible Hulk.' This was met by interest from the others.

In a hot-seating exercise, Joe asked Les, 'What does it feel like when you transform?'

Les replied, in role, 'It feels good. My clothes burst and I throw people around . . .'

Tommy asked, 'Do you ever cry?'

Les said, 'No never, I only ever get angry . . .'

This led to other group members thinking about characters who transform. Joe suggested, 'There could be a fight between superheroes!', which we linked to a feeling of fighting for power within the group. The group continued to explore the Hulk for a few weeks. Joe remembered that it was a failed scientific experiment with 'gamma rays' that changed David Banner. They created a storyline of David Banner being jostled in a bar before transforming into the Hulk . . . but running away. An undercurrent of tension continued until Les and Tommy had a verbal confrontation, instigated by Les's paranoid remark that Tommy was looking at him. Tommy became angry and requested to be taken back to the ward. When I returned, the group were unresponsive to the therapists' comments about what had just happened. However, Chris suggested an idea for drama: David Banner was on an aeroplane hijacked by terrorists and changed into the Hulk to save the passengers.

Tommy didn't return to the group for 3 weeks. In his absence, the group continued the storyline of 'the hijacked plane'. Central to this work were two sets of group feelings: 'attacking' and 'frightening', which my co-therapist and I linked to the confrontation. What started to emerge were 'good' roles and 'bad' ('wicked') roles. Les found it increasingly unbearable to play what he described as 'bad' roles. This coincided with a noticeable deterioration in his mental state. After one session, he made an inflated, sexual comment to me about whether I'd noticed how tight his trousers were, and following some other worrying material observed by nurses, his Consultant decided to stop his ground leave. We reflected on these events in the group. My co-therapist and I commented on the difficult feelings left after the confrontation and the feelings Les, in the role of the Hulk, was holding for others. Joe helpfully suggested that the group members should rotate the role of the Hulk, and Les was much relieved by this.

The group returned to the idea of 'transforming'. In the third session of Tommy's absence, they individually worked on the idea of a superhero of their own choice, using paper and pens and working in different areas of the room. We returned to a circle where they took it in turns to read out their idea and, much to everyone's surprise, they had all chosen exactly the same superhero.

'Spiderman: Brave, helpful, strong, bright, calm, his own boss, kind, not interested in money.'

'When I was a child, I used to like watching Spiderman. What I remember is when he got bitten by a spider and he became like a spider, climbing buildings. He had a spider suit. He was just a normal person before that happened.'

'Spiderman is nimble, quick, clever, acrobatic and very cool. A jeweller's is being robbed by two thieves and Spiderman comes and captures them with his web.'

The following session marked an important development. At the beginning Chris said, 'I've been thinking through the week . . . he wasn't Spiderman all the time'. This was met with a dawning realisation in the rest of the group. 'Peter Parker' emerged, first as a hazy half-forgotten figure, then slowly becoming clearer and more defined. Chris remembered his curly hair and leather jacket. Other group members remembered he was a photographer and lived in New York City. The 'Peter Parker Story' began. Joe wrote:

> It all began when Peter Parker was bitten by a radio-active spider in his biology class. He gained superhuman strength, acrobatics and the ability to cling to walls and ceilings. He got a chance to appear on a TV show where he could show his powers. After the show some thieves stole some money from the studio. He didn't take any notice, being more interested in the money he could earn. Peter Parker got home to find that the thieves had stolen from his aunt and uncle and had killed his uncle: the same thieves. From that day on he developed some webbing – he already had a costume and became Spiderman . . . the superhero.

At this point, the group were more interested in the character of Peter Parker than Spiderman. They collectively remembered many details . . . he was poor, he wasn't popular at school, he had no parents, he had girlfriend problems. My co-therapist and I were struck by 'loss' as a theme; we mulled over the idea that Peter Parker could be thought of as being unable to process and think about loss, resorting instead to an omnipotent defence via Spiderman.

Next week, Tommy returned. He and Les were unable to speak about their confrontation, but Tommy was interested in the work on Spiderman.

He willingly joined in the discussions of ideas. They created a story line about a jeweller's shop being mugged by thieves. Les said he wanted to play the 'assistant manager', suggesting that someone else could play the manager. Tommy told Les he should play 'the thug'. I intervened, commenting on what roles people were choosing for themselves and others and wondering how this linked to what was happening in the group. The group ignored this, but Tommy said he would play the thug and Les chose to play the owner of the shop.

Les and Tommy then staged a stylised fight. Les laughed explosively and wanted Chris (who was playing Spiderman) to come and save him. Tommy anxiously said, 'Well come and save him now then, come and save him.' Chris finally arrived.

On de-roling, we reflected on the 'violence' within the scene and Les said, 'It's only acting – but I'm glad I wasn't playing a bad role.' I said that although the violence was only acting, maybe there were other ways one could feel battered in the group. Tommy and Les nodded at this. I also picked up on the idea of something having been 'stolen' in the group, linking these comments back to the confrontation. Both Tommy and Les agreed but didn't say any more. Chris said, 'It was good to be resolving something. It was nice to play the good guy'.

Over the next few sessions work continued, separating good and bad aspects of Spiderman and Peter Parker. We began deeper explorations of the split within Spiderman, choosing chairs to represent his 'good' and 'bad' aspects. Some of the good aspects emphasised Spiderman's power, e.g. 'swinging from building to building', 'giving to the poor'.

However, the bad aspects of Spiderman far outweighed the good. Group members highlighted: 'Trouble with the police', 'The police think he's a vigilante', 'The police think he's a menace to the city', 'He has to deal with unsavoury characters', 'Getting bitten by a spider', 'Being too sensitive because of his superhero powers'.

Out of these thoughts, the therapists suggested exploring Spiderman's relationship to the police. This was accepted by the group and they devised a scene where Peter Parker was in a restaurant with his girlfriend, Gwen, when outside there was a mugging in the street. He secretly changed into Spiderman in the toilets, and apprehended the muggers until the police arrived. They acted out this scene with obvious enjoyment, with the victim telling the police that the robber was 'a crazy man'. After de-roling, we reflected on the scene. Tommy rather thoughtfully said that Peter Parker broke the law by taking the law into his own hands. I asked him what he meant by this and he said, 'He becomes a superhero and doesn't let the police get on with it themselves'.

At this stage, my co-therapist and I felt that it was possible to begin making clear links between this material and their own lives. This was a crucial turning point, as previously it hadn't felt possible to do this. The following week, at the beginning of the session, Les made a comment that Spiderman was 'normal' when he was Peter Parker. He followed this by saying that he (Les) was about to get town leave, which was good, as it made him feel normal. Other group members agreed with this and said it was good to go out and feel 'normal'. I linked this theme to work within the group, reflecting that what we had been exploring was a 'superhero state' vs. 'a normal state'. I made more links between illness and normality, inside and outside. Chris then announced to the group that he had been granted overnight stay. The rest of the group exclaimed that he must be close to discharge. Chris movingly spoke about his plans for moving on and his hopes that his illness wouldn't relapse. This was the first time that a member had voluntarily talked about how frightening his illness and offence experiences had been.

The next week, group members wrote down some of the private, inner thoughts of Peter Parker and shared them in a circle.

'I wish people appreciated Spiderman.'

'Why do the police think of Spiderman as a dangerous vigilante?'

'Sometimes I would prefer not to be Spiderman.'

'Peter Parker thinks he is a hero and he feels bad about the police. He is full of shit.'

In later weeks, this was followed by work, led by Tommy, of the group acting out a fictional arrest. Les linked this to their own experiences of having been arrested by the police before being brought into the hospital. At this point the work moved away from Spiderman and into their personal experiences.

Discussion

What was the purpose of 'Spiderman'? My proposition is that the group members used the dramatherapy medium to explore difficulties at a point before they were able to fully symbolise. The links between their own lives and the inner world of Peter Parker/Spiderman are striking and are indicative of the paradox between me/not me, which Winnicott (1971: 2) describes as a 'third part of the life of the human being, where inner and outer reality are separate and yet interrelated'. The emergence of Spiderman allowed a transitional space where the group members' destructiveness could be safely contained and brought into therapy. This was first evident when Les chose the Incredible Hulk, the timing of which coincided with the deterioration in his mental state. Part of our technique was always to de-role and orientate the group after role-play; however, it was noticeable that Les started to choose roles that were beginning to express his grandiosity and it was clear that he was struggling to distinguish reality from fantasy. Therapists linked his difficulties with difficulties in the group and the suggestion from Joe that the role should rotate was very helpful. Les' choice of role to express something disturbing in his mental state was also evident in the group's choice of drama about terrorists hijacking a plane. This use of the medium operated as a container of projections, where not only could violent, destructive feelings be held, but also 'flawed' or 'damaged' internal objects (David Banner's gamma rays, Peter Parker's spider bite). Both superhero stories involve persecuting and toxic elements coming in from the outside, which creates a psychotic defence, 'a gift and a curse', an inflated, omnipotent state. At his most paranoid, Les used the Hulk as a concrete symbol, communicating something of his inflated, grandiose state with all the resonances of paranoia inherent in the image of 'gamma rays'. This reminds me poignantly of Bion saying to one of his grandiose patients, in the face of overwhelming anxiety, that he was *reduced* to being omnipotent' (Grotstein 2007; my italics).

As the work progressed, the clients were able to engage fully in an intermediate area of experience where Peter Parker/Spiderman represented their own splits between omnipotence and vulnerability, violence and care, offending and policing. During this time, Spiderman had a vitality and reality of its own, and the group were deeply engaged in the dramatherapy work. They talked about the group outside and would plan ideas in the gaps between sessions. Despite the omnipotence of Spiderman, the group began to see problems in this inflated position above the law – as well as a superhero they could also see a dangerous vigilante, a menace to society. Tommy's comment that Peter Parker becomes a superhero and doesn't allow the police to get on with it themselves was an important realisation. A 'third position' was coming into the work and this allowed us to link their own lives with the material.

An important feature of this work was the co-therapy relationship. My co-therapist and I had a highly attuned relationship where we communicated openly with each other and shared thoughts in the group. Our 'good enough mothering' was present in our intuitive understanding that the primary task was to let the work unfold. Interpretation would have been a premature injection of 'too much reality', foreclosing any experiencing of Spiderman as a transitional object. Winnicott (1971) picks up on this as a vital quality:

> It is a matter of agreement between us and the baby that we will never ask the question: 'Did you conceive of this or was it presented to you from without?' The question is not to be formulated.
>
> (Winnicott 1971: 12)

The transitional object is allowed to be on the border between what is created and what is already there. It is allowed to remain in the control of the subject until it is no longer needed.

Once the work was under way, the group's destructiveness, over time, could move from the concrete to the symbolic, finally become more available to treatment until we ended up with something that could be named, borne and thought about. At this stage Spiderman was quietly dropped; he had fulfilled his purpose. The group moved into a greater relationship with shared reality – a direct acknowledgment of their destructiveness, offences and illness.

Evaluation and areas for further research

As I stated at the beginning of this chapter, the criteria I use to interpret the findings are based on clinical outcome within the group itself, for example, an increase in personal disclosure and greater engagement with therapeutic aims of the group, both of which demonstrated greater insight. The rationale for using dramatherapy with these clients is that it provides a means by which destructive processes can be held and explored through the safety of the medium. This is because the medium acts as a transitional object, where the boundary between me/not me can be safely blurred in order to allow exploration of separation in the area of potential space. Furthermore, the arts medium provides a safe container of projections and a place where symbolisation and triangular space can be encouraged, through the triangular relationship of client, therapist and medium. Finally, in very disturbed clients with a history of early damage and attachment disorders, arts therapies may provide an opportunity for the transitional state to be reached and enjoyed for the first time. This positive experience is vital to the creativity of the individual, which Winnicott (1951: 14) states is retained throughout life in the intense experiencing that belongs to imaginative living.

Les, Chris and Joe were eventually successfully discharged into the community, although this of course is attributable to many therapeutic interventions of which dramatherapy was only one part. Areas for further research in similar studies could use a pre- and post-group questionnaire to consider the client's own views on the benefit of the dramatherapy medium in exploring the role of symbolisation and how this helps with insight.

Summary of key findings

In this chapter I explore how dramatherapy material operated as a safe container for destructive processes in a psychodynamic dramatherapy group for mentally ill offenders.

As the group became more able to symbolise, an important finding was that the work led to personal disclosures about violence and offending, topics previously out of bounds. This increased capacity went hand in hand with greater therapeutic engagement, and was synonymous with the development of insight. I argue that in this case the use of dramatherapy resembled a transitional object where there was a separating out of similarity and difference and clients were able to safely express disturbing aspects of themselves. However, this work involves negotiating the area between inner and outer, phantasy and reality, therefore potential negative side-effects may involve a decompensation into psychosis when anxiety is too severe. It is therefore important that therapists work with consistent boundaries and use structures that help the group orientate towards reality after any imaginative work. In this sense, the dramatherapy setting can become 'potential space', an area where playing and creativity can lead to insight and remorse, and paradoxically a greater awareness of risk and destructiveness.

12

SURVIVING SUICIDE: THE BOOK OF LIFE AND DEATH

Pete Holloway

Brief overview of chapter

This chapter describes and discusses an adaptable dramatherapy process, *The Book of Life and Death*, for working with people who have survived a recent suicide attempt. Originally developed in an acute day treatment unit serving as an alternative to hospital admission, it has also been used in outpatient psychotherapy and community mental health contexts with groups and individuals. The chapter will tentatively evaluate the experience of using this form of work in a variety of contexts, using simple clinical indicators, such as relative length of stay and admission rates, and drawing on the anecdotal feedback of a range of participants in the process.

Introduction to clinical process

It was not until the Suicide Act of 1961 that attempts at killing oneself were no longer considered a crime by the British Government. Whilst there was something deeply ironic in the possibility of being prosecuted for *failing* to take one's own life, there is also something metaphorically illuminating, and etymologically correct, about such a view of suicide: 'sui-cide' – the murder of self. In their seminal paper, based on 500 interviews conducted in casualty departments with individuals who had made a suicide attempt and 20 analytical cases of suicidal individuals, Campbell and Hale (1991) concluded that the suicidal act involves (at least at the level of fantasy) the killing off of the body and a desire for a 'surviving self'. They argued a compelling case that one or more elements of 'the self' are involved in a murderous attempt on other physically embodied elements of 'the self'. This simple, although psychologically contentious, idea was the inspiration for the dramatherapy process detailed in this chapter. When coupled with Yalom's striking assertions about the human being's problematic relationship with death and her/his mortality (Yalom 1980, 1991, 2008), a further theoretical underpinning to the work began to emerge.

157

The clinical process discussed in this chapter was developed whilst working in a day treatment unit where a significant number of clients at any given time had made a recent attempt on their life. The unit's main aim was to offer an alternative to psychiatric hospital admission for individuals with acute mental health problems, by involving them in intensive 5 days/week treatment programmes for 6–8 weeks. The unit was staffed by occupational therapists, mental health nurses, arts therapists and visiting psychiatrists. The group dramatherapy process was, importantly, only a part of a much wider intensive milieu therapy. The treatment programme on offer involved a variety of psycho-educational and diversional and recreational, as well as exploratory, groups, alongside short-term intensive individual therapy.

Defining suicide

Whilst the etymological understanding of suicide may be straightforward, as in 'self-murder', there is little agreement amongst suicidologists about what constitutes suicide or suicide acts. Fairbairn (1995: 57), in his discourse on the language and ethics of self-harm, points out that from a medico-legal perspective it is the *consequence* of the act (i.e. death, or serious likelihood of death) that makes a suicidal act 'real'. Leenaars (2003), however, concludes from a thorough historical, cultural and multimodal review that there is no clear and universal definition of what constitutes suicide or a suicidal act. Both Fairbairn and Leenaars agree, however, that any such definitions must include the *intention* behind the act, rather than simply being based upon the relative success or failure of its outcome. Thus, Fairbairn proposes a definition of suicide as:

> . . . an act, whether of commission or omission, and whether performed by himself or others, by means of which he autonomously intends to bring about his death because he wants to be dead or wants to die the death he enacts.
>
> (Fairbairn 1995: 84)

Leenaars attempts to prove empirically (through reference to age, gender, method, 'attempters' versus 'completers', cross-culture and cross-time) an earlier definition by Shneidman:

> Suicide is a conscious act of self-induced annihilation, best understood as a multidimensional malaise in a needful individual who defines an issue for which suicide is perceived as the best solution.
>
> (Shneidman 1985: 203)

Through his empirical study of suicide notes, matched to the demographic sampling detailed above, Leenaars revises Shneidman's definition, thus:

Suicide can best be understood as a multidimensional malaise. It is constituted, at least, by intrapsychic aspects (unbearable pain, cognitive constriction, indirect expressions, inability to adjust, and ego) and interpersonal aspects (interpersonal relations, rejection-aggression, identification-egression). It is perceived, consciously and unconsciously, as the best solution to a problem.

(Leenaars 2003: 61)

Elements of these three definitions will be considered in the clinical discussion that follows.

Clinical themes

Suicide and mental illness

None of the definitions above make any reference to mental illness in general, or depression in particular – the most common mental illness diagnosis (World Health Organization 2008). Nonetheless, both in the popular imagination and in medical-model psychiatry, there is a pervasive sense that if someone *wants* to die they *must* be depressed, or psychotic; and that suicidal ideation, planning or action are seen as significant indicators of risk and severity in Mental State Examinations (see Gelder et al. 2005: 171–2). Similarly, epidemiological and demographic studies (Miles 1977; Goldring and Fieve 1984; Weissmann et al. 1989) suggest that the suicide rates amongst people diagnosed with 'depression', 'alcoholism', 'bi-polar disorder' and 'schizophrenia' are significantly higher than amongst the general population. Such studies give rise to the popular belief that the wish to die by one's own agency is axiomatic with 'irrationality' or 'mental illness'.

For the medical and paramedical professions, who dedicate their professional existence to *preserving* life, such attempts at 'self-induced annihilation' (Fairbairn 1985: 84) may run counter to their very *raison d'être*. However, most major suicidologists do not accept such a clear view that suicidal ideation, intent or action is *de facto* a signifier of mental illness. Leenaars' empirical review of suicide notes (2003) and Campbell and Hale's clinical interviews (1991) both discern highly rational processes, often scrupulously reflected upon and considered, which lie behind the suicidal act. Further, as the Samaritans organisation points out through its own research, the higher incidences of suicide amongst those diagnosed with mental illness may have as much to do with their access to the effective means of ending their own lives – older style antidepressants [tricylics and monoamine oxidase inhibitos (MAOIs)] and anti-psychotic medications – rather than a direct causal correlation with the diagnosis itself (Samaritans 2010).

One of my earliest experiences as a dramatherapist on an acute admission ward was to be told, by a very experienced consultant psychiatrist, that the time to worry about suicide risk was not when someone was profoundly depressed, or floridly psychotic or in a highly disorganised manic state. The time to think about risk was when those states had resolved: either as a result of treatment (i.e. clinical features of anergia, anhedonia, psychomotor retardation and cognitive disorganisation had started to improve) or as a result of 'a needful individual . . . defin[ing] an issue for which suicide is perceived as the best solution' (Shneidman 1985: 203). This was supported in no small measure just a few weeks later by my first-ever patient in individual dramatherapy arriving at the session in an uncharacteristically highly distressed state. He attributed his distress to the fact that after a lifetime of abandonment, trauma and depression, he had started to experience a sense of hope. This hopefulness was very quickly followed by a distressing anxiety that such optimism might prove to be misplaced, or cruelly snatched away. Paradoxically for him, it was not his depressive experience of the world that became his 'defined issue' (Shneidman) or 'perceived problem' (Leenaars), but the fragility of his emergent optimism. In this particular case, the tension between hope and depression (the desire to live and the lack of trust that life could meet his new-found hopes) did not result in a suicide act. For others, however, such tensions and contradictions may be what drives them to such a radical 'solution to a problem' (Leenaars).

Suicide and the fear of death, or fear of living

We have seen in preceding chapters that many theorists within the psychoanalytic tradition view the struggle between life and growth, and death and decay as an integral dynamic within the human being as a psychological and physiological organism. Everything that is born will at some time die, and therefore the processes of living and dying coexist, often in tension with each other or, as Samuel Beckett (1956) pithily puts it, 'We are born astride the grave' (Beckett, *Waiting for Godot*). Yalom (1980) suggests that there is a fundamental tension between an attempt to live and make meaning, and a profound but often covert awareness of our own mortality. He further proposes that it is precisely this tension which serves as the primary driver of our 'being in the world' and of many psychopathological presentations.

Within the existential psychotherapy tradition, much human behaviour can be seen as an attempt to make meaning of our lives and relationships, which when challenged or punctuated by intimations of our own mortality are rendered fragile or inadequate, leading to a breakdown in our personal sense of meaning and an experience of existential crisis. Underlying this perilous ontological state, they argue, is a fundamentally irreconcilable epistemological contradiction between what we know on an abstract, general, intellectual level ('all men [sic] are mortal'), and that which we actively try to banish from our own awareness ('I am mortal'): the ego, Yalom (1980, 1991) compellingly argues, is simply not programmed to conceive of its own non-existence.

This dialectic of knowing and not-knowing is directly confronted by the actuality of mortality, such as loss of a loved one, a serious illness or the end of a relationship. At such times we can no longer avoid the unsettling awareness that death (in the guise of finitude) is a certainty. However, the manner and timing of one's own death remains fraught with uncertainty. This contradiction between certainty and uncertainty gives rise to existential anxiety, which in turn leads us to a variety of largely unconscious strategies that are best described by Yalom as 'death denial' (1991). Such strategies may be largely affirmative – projecting our genes and identity beyond our own lifetime through procreation, contributing to the collective knowledge and culture of human existence – but they may equally involve a more perverse or self-constraining logic, such as the depressive response to existential anxiety: 'all that lives will die, therefore if I don't *really* live, I can't *really* die'. In similar vein, he discerns a strategy that relies on the futile logic of immunising oneself against death by facing it down in controlled 'doses', such as death-defying extreme sports and the more extreme forms of sado-masochistic sexuality, including auto-erotic asphyxiation; or, in more mundane ways, even smoking, heavy drinking and other forms of self-injurious behaviour may be seen as a way of experiencing a 'little death' which our body builds up a resistance to or neutralises, and hence we can be reassured that we *can* survive death.

With this notion of 'death denial' in mind, we could see both the fantasy of suicide – as well as an actual attempt – as a radical and desperate way to resolve existential anxiety by literally 'taking one's life in one's own hands'. Whilst such a view may seem counter-intuitive, given that so many suicide survivors categorically state that they have no fear of death, as we will see in the clinical observations and reflections below, there is also a more profound theme about the absolute intolerability of the idea that their death is as much out of their direct control as their lives appear to be. Such issues of meaning, mortality and authorship keep on emerging in unholy trinity in the clinical space – or, as Annie Lennox sings it, 'Dying is easy, it's living that scares me to death' (Lennox, *Cold*, 1992).

Suicide as murder of the self

Whether viewed as 'a multidimensional malaise' (Shneidman 1985; Leenaars 2003), an 'enacted death' (Fairbairn 1995) or a signifier of mental illness or of existential crisis, suicide retains its etymological roots as a form of murder. Unlike other forms of murder, however, the victim and perpetrator exist within the same person. For those who continue to live after a suicide attempt there is also the reality of having survived a near-death experience. Thus, within the same client we may experience a complex triad of selves: that which 'needed' to be murdered; that which had the intention or motive to murder; and that which has faced the likelihood of death and (by luck or design) has survived. For the time being, however, I will focus solely on the relationship between self-as-victim and self-as-murderer, and will consider the complexities of surviving a near-death experience in my discussion of the clinical practice.

In an echo of Nitsun's (1996) conceptualisation of the 'anti-group', Firestone (1997) develops the idea that the movement towards, and execution of, the suicidal act involves a potentially mortal struggle between self and 'anti-self'. Firestone locates such a radical splitting in our experience of our identity as a response to parental ambivalence (in relation to their selves, their relationship with each other, their role and capacity as parents and their relationship to the developing child). Following Laing, Firestone suggests that in response to such experiences of parental ambivalence we develop an 'infernal dance of false dualities' (Laing 1967: 75), thus:

> Under painful circumstances, children tend to depersonalize in an attempt to escape from painful emotions. Simultaneously, they internalize or incorporate the attitudes and feelings that are directed toward them. These negative parental introjects or voices lead to an essential dualism within the personality. This 'division of the mind' reflects a primary split between forces that represent the self and those that oppose or attempt to destroy the self. These propensities can be conceptualised as the *self system* and the *anti-self system*. The two systems develop independently; both are dynamic and continually evolve and change over time.
>
> (Firestone 1997: 24)

Firestone goes on to argue that at times of suicidal crises these 'negative parental introjects or voices' in the form of the *anti-self* gain dominance and convince the individual that the 'best solution to the problem' (Leenaars 2003: 61) is to finally kill off the suffering, vulnerable *self*. Whilst Firestone's hypothesis clearly has its roots in psychodynamic theory, he conceptualises the anti-self as an essentially 'here and now' experience of which the individual is (for the most part) conscious. His proposed therapeutic focus is, therefore, to make cognitively explicit the content of the voices and to 'explore ways to move away from negative attitudes and restrictions' (Leenaars 2003: 265) – a therapeutic strategy, which has clear resonances with latter-day 'schema-focused CBT' (Rafaeli et al. 2010).

Campbell and Hale (1991) draw their understanding of the 'divided self' from a more clearly orthodox psychoanalytic source. They see the mortal conflict as one between a 'surviving self', one which aims for 'the pleasurable survival of an essential part of the self . . . in another dimension' (Campbell and Hale 1991: 291), and the physical body experienced as the repository of all that is bad, shameful or worthy of rejection. This conflict, they suggest, relates directly to the infant's experience through projective identification and regression to the desire to merge with the primitive omnipotent care-giver and the consequent fear of annihilation and/or rejection. Despite their insistence that all suicidal acts are a regression to an unresolved infantile 'core complex' (Glasser 1979), Campbell and Hale offer two crucial corner-stones of understanding for the more integrative dramatherapist: the idea of the 'surviving self' and the importance of transgressing the 'body barrier' – whereby we no longer just have 'murder in mind'. In this physical act of potentially fatal embodiment, Firestone's *antiself* 'voice' finds its murderous expression. It is in this dramatic conflagration of mind, voice and body that we may find an explanation for Fairbairn's strange phrasing in his definition: that the suicidal individual 'wants to die the death he enacts'.

Before we consider the importance of the enactment of the 'murder', I would like to consider in more detail Campbell and Hale's conclusions about that part of the self which aims to benefit from the act of 'self-murder'.

The surviving self

Drawing on an avowedly psychoanalytic perspective, Campbell and Hale (1991: 295–298) suggest that the suicidal individual is engaged in a struggle to resolve primitive anxieties of annihilation of engulfment or abandon-ment, related to Glasser's (1979) notion of the 'Core Complex' – see also Seebohm and McAlister, above. When these anxieties cannot be managed by means of more sophisticated ego defences, we resort to a physical enactment of the violent fantasy against our own body, which has become associated 'with the engulfing or abandoning mother who is perceived as someone who would kill by suffocation or starvation. The body must be killed if the self is to survive' (Campbell and Hale 1991: 294) – hence the *body barrier* is crossed:

> In intra-psychic terms, this is homicide, justifiable homicide. Just as there is a split between the good self and the bad body, there is a split between the hated and engulfing or abandoning primal mother, now identified with the body, and the idealised one with which the self will fuse once the bad mother/body has been eliminated.
>
> (Campbell and Hale 1991: 295)

Following this theoretical formulation, Campbell and Hale suggest that there are at least five fantasies of what may happen to the 'surviving self' once the bad object has been destroyed. Such fantasies may co-exist in a variety of combinations within each suicidal individual.

Merging fantasy

This fantasy aims to achieve a state of blissful oblivion – akin maybe to a return to the womb – in which self and other remain undifferentiated in a fused, eternal state of tranquil nothingness. In such a fantasy we may hear echoes of Freud's (1920) 'Nirvana' (see also Chapter 1). By destroying the 'bad' body, the suicidal individual believes that they are removing an 'impediment to the fulfilling of the merging fantasy' (Campbell and Hale 1991: 295).

Revenge fantasy

This suggests a primarily sadistic attack on those who are left behind, accompanied by the more or less conscious thought of 'They will be sorry' (Campbell and Hale 1991: 295). Campbell and Hale (1991: 295) link this fantasy directly back to Menninger's (1938) observation that 'a son or daughter who takes his or her own life robs their parents of their dearest possession'. This fantasy, however, may be embellished and elaborated into the dramatic scenario of 'the surviving self' watching the 'guilty' tears of loved ones (be they parents, partners, children or other associates) at his/her own funeral.

Self-punishment fantasy

Campbell and Hale (1991: 296) suggest that this 'fantasy is dominated by guilt, frequently associated with masturbation, which aims to gratify, in fantasy, incestuous wishes, and an erotisation of pain and death'. They suggest a link here with the *revenge fantasy*, whereby the object of revenge has become internalised and identified with one's own body.

Elimination fantasy

In this fantasy, the body becomes the repository of shameful impulses, which has to be destroyed in order for the 'surviving self' to transcend such conflicted and/or conflictual impulses. Citing Laufer and Laufer (1984), Campbell and Hale (1991) suggest that:

> Adolescents, as well as adults, may experience their bodies as a source of madness when unacceptable regressive infantile wishes are felt to be located in their sexually maturing body, which then

seems confusing, alien, and threatening. The self in their suicide fantasies 'survives', paradoxically, by killing a body that is driving them mad.

(Campbell and Hale 1991: 297)

They go on to discuss this fantasy as drawing upon primitive self-preservative instincts, as opposed to the sadistic and malicious intent of the *revenge* and *self-punishment* fantasies.

Dicing-with-death fantasy

Finally, Campbell and Hale discern a fifth fantasy (which interestingly has less theoretical and clinical material attached to it in order to substantiate it). They suggest that in this fantasy

. . . the patient who is compelled to dice with death actively puts his body, or a symbolic representative of it, at risk in order to both attract and attack the primary object.

(Campbell and Hale 1991: 297)

The surviving self – an empirical critique

Whilst Campbell and Hale's theoretical formulation is illuminating, there is (for this integrative dramatherapist, at least) an off-putting reductionist certitude to their interpretive desire to locate all suicidal acts back to the 'core complex' or 'primal scene'. There is an obvious risk in the analytic perspective of seeing all 'acting out' as a regressive process back into Oedipal or pre-Oedipal concerns, in that it marginalises the very real dilemmas of relational and existential experience as they manifest in the 'here and now'. Such a purely analytically orientated view posits a great deal of knowledge and understanding of the client's 'unconscious' experience within the therapist. My experience of working with suicide survivors, however, suggests that the survivors in retrospect have a very strong sense of their own 'motives', fantasies and hopes, which also relate to material 'here-and-now' relationships and which come into full consciousness *in the moment* of the suicidal act. In the clinical process, therefore, it seems important for the therapist to keep in mind the theory that suicide involves a regression to more primitive states, whilst also respecting and attending to the often much more 'here-and-now' content of the fantasy of the surviving self made manifest in the planning and execution of the 'murder'.

Therefore, from direct clinical experience of using the process discussed in this chapter, these fantasies may take on a distinctly more conscious and immediate focus, located in the awareness of the client, rather than in the interpretative mind of the therapist. Thus, the *merging fantasy* often reveals

165

itself as the straightforward desire for 'peace and quiet', or 'an end to pain and suffering'. The *revenge fantasy* is frequently heard as a direct response to intrafamilial abuse, or the ignoring or minimising of disclosures of such experience, where 'then they'll be sorry' becomes the last word in retribution. The *self-punishment fantasy* may find its direct expression in those facing court cases and/or serving sentences for transgressive crimes against other bodies (paedophiles, child pornographers, child murderers and the like) – it may be worthy of note that this category of successful suicides (for those on bail, in remand or serving sentences) is the one with the greatest statistical growth. Likewise, the *elimination fantasy* frequently occurs amongst those individuals for whom physical and sexual urges, once enacted, are experienced as entirely ego-dystonic and/or beyond social taboos – by killing off the body, therefore, they are aiming to transcend their very real and present confusion in relation to eroticism, sexual orientation or gender identity. The *dicing-with-death fantasy* (possibly the least compelling and most sketchily described of Campbell and Hale's fantasies) seems to relate directly to Yalom's description of attempting to immunise oneself against mortality and also the more nonchalant and/or dissociative process described as 'Russian roulette' in the para-suicide section, below.

Whether or not such fantasies exist at the level of unconscious regressive processes which become 'acted out', or have a more material focus to them involving a distinct level of conscious awareness, may seem like an abstract theoretical debating point. However, when we come to thinking about the question of the body and the 'aesthetics' of the death to be enacted, the level of conscious awareness of the suicidal individual and their sense of their own autonomous agency is anything but an abstract theoretical point.

The murder scene and 'the death enacted'

I have been consistently struck in my experience within this clinical process about just how much conscious thought, contrivance and planning goes into the question of who will (or will not) find the body that the 'surviving self' leaves behind, and what kind of a state it will be in. Similarly, a great deal of energy is expended on ensuring that material affairs are in order, both for the benefit of those that are left behind and for the 'self' that will transcend such material worries.

Furthermore, in a number of cases – particularly in those that Campbell and Hale would refer to as expressing more sadistic and malicious intent – the *impact* of the murder scene is a crucial consideration. Thus, signifying revenge and retribution, or self-punishment, in the *mis en scene* of the act means that the image of the dead body carries an emotional potency. So we hear of plans and acts that hint at the Tarot image of 'the hanging man' on public display; or the broken body in the public square; or the brutal 'look what you've done to me' of the distinctly violent domestic laceration or shooting; or the calm serenity (Ophelia-like) of the peaceful, sleeping death. In an early experience as a newly qualified dramatherapist, I was asked to see the adoptive parents (white, middle-class) of a young black man who had hanged himself in their conservatory with a dog lead. They were sure that the symbolism of his use of the dog lead (rather than a cable or rope) had been well considered as an image – it was this detail that was seared into their minds.

Para-suicide: acting out and ambivalence

Elsewhere in this volume, Dokter (Chapter 6) has considered the relationship between self-harm and suicide, and has pointed out that self-harming behaviour is a clear risk factor in determining subsequent successful suicide attempts. This link, although it is acknowledged within the NICE guidelines on managing self-harm (NICE 2008), remains a contentious one within the medical and paramedical professions – with serial self-harmers frequently seen as the *bêtes noirs* of accident and emergency departments and mental health services. Professional responses to such presentations may be at best ambivalent and at worst dismissive or punitive. If, however, we weave together some of the insights from the theoretical perspectives outlined above, we may construe acts of deliberate self-harm not just as 'cries for help' or 'half-hearted' attempts where the individual should 'try harder next time', but as rehearsals for and/or a 'working through' of ambivalent existential conflicts. Thus, following Firestone, in any act of self-harm there is a clear splitting of the self into victim and perpetrator. There is also, in the act and image of self-harm, an echo of Fairbairn's 'death enacted [or rehearsed]'. Most importantly, however, there is the reality of Campbell and Hale's 'body barrier' having been crossed, in which intrapsychic conflict no longer remains an emotional or psychological entity but finds its concrete physical realisation. Furthermore, Yalom's notion that death is simply a 'given of existence' and not ultimately within our control may help us to understand that self-harm is sometimes a 'Russian Roulette' during which we cut too deep, take just too many tablets, or are not 'rescued' quite in time – with fatal consequences.

Whilst these four domains of understanding may go some way to explaining the heightened incidence of completed suicide in individuals who have previously self-harmed, it seems crucial in individual cases to consider Fairbairn's, Shneidman's and Leenars' definitions that the suicidal act is about *intent* rather than *consequence*. When thinking about risk, therefore, which must always be in the mind of the professionals working with the suicidal or para-suicidal individual, there is always a delicate balancing act between a clear appraisal and understanding of the intent behind an action and the unpredictable consequences of an action. In the description of clinical practice to follow, the role of the multidisciplinary team, in constantly assessing risk and (where necessary) taking appropriate action, was a vital component. In the case of the group-work this meant that I was able to focus much more directly on exploring the intent or 'motive' of the 'murderous' self, in the full knowledge that the risk of such actions towards the 'victim' self was being considered by the wider team.

Practice framework

Group structure

This process was developed within the framework of a twice-weekly closed group conducted over 6–8 weeks with four to six participants. All group members had been referred to this group as part of their treatment pro-gramme within the unit because they had recently made significant attempts to kill themselves. Prior to starting the group, I would meet with each prospective participant to outline the purpose of the group, acknowledge the significance of their suicide attempt and propose a viewpoint through which we could think about and process the 'meaning' of their attempt. This viewpoint involved:

- An explicit acceptance of the reason why people were in this group (by both therapist and participant).
- An understanding that there may be different motives for suicide, and a willingness to explore their own honestly and openly, whilst attempting to avoid blame and judgement.
- The group was not about risk-assessment or 'catching them out' if they were contemplating a further attempt (that could be monitored else-where within the multidisciplinary team).

The dramatherapy process

Alongside the theoretical underpinnings detailed above, the content of the group was adapted from a structure devised by Sue Jennings in her work at the Infertility Clinic at the London Hospital (Jennings 1987). In its earliest manifestation the process involved creating an eight-page book, as follows:

- Book cover – an image of goodbye: the emotional 'landscape' immedi-ately preceding the suicidal act.
- Page one: *life in all its glory* – written words or phrases which detail objects, qualities, events, people without which life would be a lesser thing. Participants share their lists and are encouraged to add other people's ideas to their list.

168

- Page two: *the common sense of death* – written words or phrases based on associations to the clichés, cultural associations, lines from poems, book/song/film titles, images of death, which serve to euphemise, sanitise or keep the reality of death 'at arm's length'. Again, participants are encouraged to share their associations.
- Page three: *the after-death* (I purposely used this phrase, rather than 'after-life', in an attempt to side-step religious associations) – participants are invited to fantasise about what the experience of being dead may be like for them. It is not to be seen as a statement of faith or ideology, but a private contemplation of what they were hoping to achieve for the 'surviving self' had their act resulted in death. This page is not shared with the group.
- Page four: *filling the gap* – participants are asked to consider the tension between the certainty of their mortality and the uncertainty of its timing – what hopes/wishes/desires/goals for the present and future can they put into action in their life? When completed, they may share as much or as little as they want to.
- 'Dedication' – inside the front cover, participants are invited to dedicate the work of the book to something or someone.
- 'Epilogue' – inside the back cover, the invitation is to write or use images to summarise their experience of the process and/or where they are now.
- Revisiting the image of goodbye – is there anything that can be added to give or suggest a sense of life/growth/potential in the 'landscape'?
- The final act is to then give the completed book a title.

In this earliest phase of development the process remained cognitively distanced, relying heavily on words and conceptual associations. At the same time, however, there was a real energy generated when the group members began to share their associations. These were often humorous and irreverent, going beyond the apparent seriousness and gravity of their recent circumstances. Initially, in supervision, I wondered whether such humour was a defence against the 'murderousness' they had so recently visited. Even if this was the case, we began to see that such an energy had a truly therapeutic function in terms of establishing connections within the group and transforming a slow, subdued and morose inertia which frequently accompanied the opening phase of the group process.

In response to participant feedback over the first 6 months of running this group, we developed two further phases to the work, which moved it beyond a simple cognitive and/or projective process and introduced the idea of the therapist taking on the role of 'Detective Columbo' and (more importantly) facilitating the participants in reconnecting to the body that they had attempted to kill off.

Group development

The humorous response to particular phases of the work gave rise to a sense that the development of this structure was a truly collaborative process – thus, in my initial planning of the group I had anticipated that participants would struggle to identify anything in the first phase of work (*Life in All its Glory*) which gave their life meaning. Instead, what would emerge when group members started sharing their associations was a very broad range of experiences, themes and objects from the deeply spiritual to the thoroughly mundane and profane; so 'love', 'a beautiful sunset' sat alongside 'Guinness', 'nice knickers' and 'long, slow sex'. The same dynamic would occur in relation to the second phase of the work (*The Common Sense of Death*), with participants bringing both very dark images and reminding each other of some of the more weird and wonderful euphemisms and metaphors for death ('pushing up the daisies', 'worm food', and so on). In a later group, one of the participants introduced the idea of being 'a coffin dodger', which then became the informal title for the work we were involved in, and this process became the 'Coffin Dodgers group' amongst its participants. This particular moment of self-referential irreverence really brought home for me, as the therapist, the idea that we were working with a trinity of selves – not just the potential murderer and potential victim, but also a 'surviving self' that had survived in reality, not just in fantasy. This acknowledgement of having faced and survived a mortal threat, and the ambivalence which that gave rise to (regret and/or relief at still being alive; guilt at what the survivors had put other people through, alongside a reappraisal of relationships; a sense of being out of control and a fantasy of immortality/invincibility) enabled therapist and participants to explore these tensions through dramatic play.

One such way that this dramatic play developed as the process became more established and incorporated ideas and feedback from the participants was in the exploration of the moment of the suicidal act itself. In the third roll-out of this process, we introduced the idea of 'the murder of the self', as usual – to which one of the participants responded that this wasn't so much a 'whodunnit', rather a 'whydunnit'. This idea resonated with the other group members and with the therapist (as I try to approach all clinical work from a position of respectful curiosity). The group played for some time with the idea of detective and murder mystery genres, until we hit on the character and format of Columbo, as inhabited by the actor Peter Falk. Unlike the loftier, omniscient Inspector Morse or the provocative Fitz in *Cracker* (both of whom were dominating TV ratings at the time these groups were running), Columbo seemed a much more personable and relational character. In the format of the much-repeated films and TV shows, Columbo operates at a simple level of curiosity, coupled with a respect for the 'chief suspect', whom he gets alongside to the point where the murderer becomes Columbo's accomplice in solving the crime. During the unfolding narrative there is something very human in the relationship between the two characters, Columbo sometimes endearing, sometimes infuriating, but always openly and honestly musing with the murderer about developments in the case. It is through this relationship that surface realities and rationales are slowly unpicked and the truth is revealed.

These key features of the format seemed to illuminate a potential position for me as a therapist in relation to the destructive reality of the self-as-murderer: maintaining curiosity and respect in equal measure, and avoiding taking an 'expert' position or imposing a particular reality or interpretation on someone's suicidal behaviour, meant that we were able to get to an apparently more honest and open appreciation of what was being expressed in the act than adopting a more remote, evaluative and risk-assessing stance may have done. This phase of collaborative detective work slowly became a key element embedded in the structure between *The After Death* and *Filling the Gap* sections, in which we would forensically investigate the planning of the act, what was it hoped to achieve, and what went 'wrong' (or how ambivalence manifested itself). Insights gained from this work seemed to broadly support Campbell and Hale's notion of the fantasy of the surviving self, Firestone's 'anti-self' and Fairbairn's idea of suicide as a well thought-through and very particular 'death enacted'.

A further development in the process inspired by one of the participants was to take the cognitive and collective explorations of the work back into the body. It started with a group member experiencing a panic attack in relation to *The After Death* section of the work. In her quiet contemplation of what she believed existed after death, she started to speculate that she might, in fact, already be dead and how would she know. According to her account, this led to a disassociative episode in which she was sure she had stopped breathing altogether (although she hadn't) and of a complete paralysis in this 'frozen' state. It took some time in the session to enable the individual to ground herself back in the group and in her own physical reality – by working on her breathing and on her sensory and physical perceptions within the space, the panic slowly subsided and she returned to present reality. When reflecting on the session as a whole, this particular participant talked of how the moment of dissociation had taken her right back to her overdose attempt, when she was sure that her next breath would be her last, and how that sense had stayed with her despite her physical recovery from the overdose. In the grounding exercise we had done using breathing, we focused on both life-giving oxygen coming into the body and fuelling the organs and muscles with the in-breath, and on the poisonous, toxic carbon dioxide being expelled from the body through the out-breath. In that experience of just being with her breath, she had started to experience her body as a 'finely balanced' and 'miraculous' organism that 'contained both life and death', and 'It's mine, I mean it's me, it should be looked after, 'cos it's the only one I've got!'.

The experience of this particular client led to the structure incorporating a new phase of work where participants revisited the themes of life, mortality, after death and possibility within their own bodies. Thus, the central process became a physical exploration of all their associations of *Life in All its Glory*, focusing on movement to the in-breath; *The Common Sense of Death* involved movement led by the out-breath and the expulsion of deadly carbon dioxide; *The After Death* became a point of absolute stillness in the body; followed by an exploration of the impulse to breathe again and how that breath leads to movement and momentum to make meaning, establish hope and take us back into life. As this phase of work became more established within the overall structure, the effect on participants appeared profound, as if they were rediscovering and re-inhabiting the body, which they had contemplated and/or nearly succeeded in killing off. This in turn led to a greater investment in the final phase of the work, whereby individual group members incorporated some of their discoveries, needs and desires back into their 'dedication', 'epilogue' and images of hope.

Adaptations for individual work

In subsequent years, following the amalgamation of this unit into an in-patient facility and my move to an exclusively community-based setting, I have continued to use the structure and insights gained from these group experiences in work with individual clients. Unlike the day treatment unit, which was able to see suicide survivors relatively quickly after their first attempt, my work in the community tends to be with individuals who have exhausted community mental health team resources and/or optimism by virtue of their chronic self-harm and/or numerous suicide attempts. My experience of working individually with such clients has involved a recalibration of some of the dynamics highlighted above.

Firstly, the absence of a group programme and wider containing structure has meant that there is a tendency (in the early phases of therapy at least) for a greater sense of shame and failure to be present for the client. At the same time I have noticed that, without a clear and coherent containing structure of a multi-disciplinary team surrounding the work, I have become much more aware of (and organised by) issues of risk assessment and risk management. This in turn has led to a paradoxical position with many of the chronic self-harmers and suicide survivors. With such clients, rather than inviting them to establish trust in me, I suggest that I may need to extend my trust to them – in terms of their expertise in knowing how deep to cut, or how many tablets to take and still get away with it. A consequence of this is an overwhelming sense of responsibility in my role as the therapist not to be *too* provocative or *too* irreverent in order not to amplify risk and ensure that the concrete concerns and potential for 'acting out' of these clients is treated seriously. At the same time, however, the importance of the gallows humour, the image of Columbo's bumbling naïve enquirer, and a reframing of the experience of their own relationship to their body remain illuminating ideas. All of these considerations lead to a more gentle, but painstaking exploration of moments of ambivalence in their fantasy of, planning for, execution of and ambivalence within the suicidal act – what manages and maintains my position and approach within that far more intense process is that early client-generated image of Detective Columbo.

Observations and reflections

Given the reservations and very different dynamic described above in relation to individual work, the following observations and reflections relate to the experience of using this structure with groups. A central feature of this work was the sheer sense of communality, which all groups very quickly developed – this may be in part due to the collaborative nature of the early phases of the structure where ideas and associations were readily shared and equally readily begged, borrowed and stolen between group members. On a deeper level the honest appraisal of common experiences tended to produce 'no bull-shit' challenges between group members and a ready willingness to accept more quirky and idiosyncratic suggestions about what gave life its meaning and the personal euphemisms by which death and mortality were kept at 'arm's length'. Further, the dramatic conceit suggested by one of the group members of the Detective Columbo motif enabled a playfully couched, though honestly negotiated, exploration of the motive behind the murderous act. Given the common experience of all of the 'survivors' within the group, this tended to move very quickly beyond obvious responses of shame and failure. Similarly, whether or not individuals shared their reflections on *The After Death*, group members very quickly established a respect for each other's individual (and often idiosyncratic) beliefs. This was only partially modelled by me in my role as therapist, because at the same time I strived to maintain a position of respectful but doubting scepticism in relation to any individual beliefs. I was keen to keep in focus Yalom's notion that mortality and finitude, when acknowledged, are intimately bound up with uncertainty and doubt.

For me, however, the moment that the structure really began to deepen and explore experiences, which had previously been diminished, conceptualised away or simply played with, was in the revisiting of the body. Individual participants' response to this phase of the work ran the whole gamut of reactions, from manifest discomfort (in the form of childlike self-conscious giggling, particularly in the phase of stillness/contemplation of *The After Death*) to profoundly poignant tears, loud sobbing and a newly tolerable sense of disorientation and uncertainty.

Evaluation and areas for further research

It is difficult to consider the effectiveness of this intervention alone, given the fact that for much of its life it was primarily delivered alongside other interventions – intensive individual key-worker support; counselling or psychotherapy over 8–12 weeks; attendance at the 5 days/week group programme (diversional, recreational and psycho-educational groups, weekly medication review by the psychiatrist). Also, as a group experience for this particular client group, it was delivered within the day unit setting in the mid-1990s, as the evidence-based practice movement was only just starting to emerge. Whilst on-going client feedback and evaluation was a key component of the ethos of the unit, robust quantitative data was not systematically collected. Thus, whilst admissions following suicide attempt became virtually non-existent (the default position being that people with recent suicide attempts would be referred directly to the day unit, rather than to the inpatient ward), this was attributable to the unit being able to respond, not to this particular intervention. Similarly, although very low recurrence of attempts followed participation in the group, it is not possible to isolate the group as the only factor that may have affected this outcome.

What we do have are anecdotal reports of participants, and some rudimentary client feedback and outcome data. Thus, of 26 respondents to a questionnaire conducted over the course of 1 year at the unit, about what they had found 'most helpful' through to 'not helpful' (all of whom had attended this particular dramatherapy group), eight cited this group structure as 'most helpful' – which was exactly the same figure as those who cited intensive individual support/counselling/therapy, or 'the whole range of activities at the unit' as 'most helpful'. A further 12 rated it as 'helpful'. No respondents rated it as 'least helpful/not helpful'. From a follow-up study of 68 participants in the group in 2 consecutive years in the mid-1990s, there had been one reported completed suicide within the subsequent 2 years, although we have no figures for further attempts amongst those individuals.

In individual work, the structure itself appears less useful. This may be due to the lack of milieu and communality. Alternatively, it may also be a result of the current caseload, which comprises more complex and chronic presentations with much longer histories of serious self-harm, suicidal acts, violence against others and primary diagnoses of borderline personality disorder and complex trauma. What does continue to be helpful is the theoretical and attitudinal perspectives that underpin the model and enable me to get alongside the individual clients without blame or shame or a desire to label as 'mad'.

Theoretically, however, there appears to be sound benefit from an honest non-judgemental appraisal of what the attempt meant, acknowledging moments of ambivalence and resolution, and the darker fantasies beyond release into punishment and retribution, also holding in mind that the individuals we were seeing were victims–perpetrators–survivors and acknowledging these different experiences/propensities. Most importantly, reconnecting to the body, and transforming the relationship from something that has to be killed off to something that can contain all possibilities.

Part III

TOWARDS AN EVALUATION OF THE EVIDENCE BASE SO FAR

13

PLAYING WITH THANATOS: BRINGING CREATIVITY TO DESTRUCTIVENESS

Pete Holloway, Ditty Dokter and Henri Seebohm

Knowledge, practice and evidence

In the Introduction we outlined our aims for this book. In general we wished to explore the phenomenon of destructiveness and how this is worked with in the therapeutic encounter. Specifically we wished to explore:

- Dilemmas of human existence as represented by our clients, both when their lives have been shaped by destructive forces and when they enact their destructive potential on themselves or others.
- Whether a therapeutic practice based on enactment serves only to encourage the 'acting out' of violent, aggressive or dangerous material or whether, in playing out destructiveness, it reduces its internal momentum and its dynamic can be transformed.
- How and where manifestations of destructiveness are woven into the clinical problems faced by clients and staff, and the relationship between destructiveness and a range of clinical diagnoses.

Whilst a number of individual chapters rely on a broadly psychodynamic theoretical framework, the thinking behind the volume in its entirety is avowedly eclectic. Initially we draw on thinking and practice from the fields of cultural theory, psychotherapy and arts therapies. In the opening chapters the authors interrogate different ways of understanding destructiveness and propose alternative artistic views, based on the aesthetics of destructiveness and its multilayered relationship to artistic creativity. We wanted to define destructiveness by its internal momentum, rather than simply by its effect when enacted upon the external world. Destructiveness is thus regarded primarily as a propensity within the psyche and within relationships between people. The subtitle of this book and the title of this closing chapter are influenced by classical psychoanalytic understandings of destructiveness, but we have also clearly attempted to integrate post-modern theory and contemporary critiques of psychoanalytic 'certainty' into our understanding of the phenomenon. We have therefore attempted to move beyond a position whereby destructiveness is merely characterised as the bipolar opposite of the creative drive towards growth. Throughout, we have attempted to appreciate the potency and toxicity of destructive acts, whilst maintaining a dialectical position through which manifestations of destructiveness can also be seen as a force that *can* be engaged with and survived, and its positive potential unleashed.

When considering the difference between destructiveness as an act or as an internal momentum, it is vital to appreciate the relationship between thought and action. In Chapter 1 the editors discussed whether to understand this relationship in the context of primary and secondary processes of mental development (Bion 1967), analytic notions of 'acting out'; or developmental notions of relational attachment patterns (de Zulueta 2006; Skogstad 2004) and a failure to 'mentalise' (Bateman and Fonagy 2004). Storr's (1991) suggested connection of destructiveness with the imagination provides a link to the potential for destructiveness as a transformative force to identity. Similarly, Nitsun's (1996) idea that destructive potential exists in a complex dialectical relationship with creativity and growth enables the editors to argue that there is not a straightforward oppositional relationship between destructiveness and creativity, or between thought and action. When considered through the aesthetic frame, the relationship becomes more problematic and it is this frame that may provide the final pillar of the containing thought. Does the artistic act enable the reframing or reconstruing of a potentially destructive impulse, enabling thought (via symbolisation and reflection) to start *anticipating* action? Within this final chapter, we want to explore whether the book's contents really support this hypothesis and, if so, to what extent? If not, what type of research is needed to further substantiate or refute this?

Jones in Chapter 2 posits the importance of the social constructionist question about whose meaning we are looking at: acknowledging the relativity of the spectator or witness. From this perspective, destructiveness can hold more than one meaning or significance in any one encounter, depending on whose perspective you are looking from, or who the dominant narrator is in a situation. He shows how destructiveness and creativity have become dominant themes in contemporary art (Grenier 2005) and how the arts can facilitate the exploration of the multiplicity of meanings in this relationship. The complexity and ambiguity in this relationship is illustrated in the 'illegal' creativity of the exploding shed, but also the destructiveness of 'legal' colonialism and, depending on whose perspective, whether destructiveness is seen as a force of resistance and/or survival. From this social constructionist and artistic perspective, Jones analyses dramatherapy discourse about destructiveness (looking at the therapist rather than the client) in the areas of the embodiment–projection–role paradigm; myth, symbol and metaphor; and role. His analysis highlights the transformative, bridge-building function of drama, movement and symbol (Hougham 2006; Jennings 1990, 1995, 1997, 1998), but also the potential of role-theory to help the 'actor' understand the roles she or he plays (Landy 1993, 1995, 1997, 2008) to mediate destructive and creative pressures.

Chapter 3 considers the BADth Systematic Review of published evidence in client groups who display destructive behaviours as part of their presenting problems, and also considers the demands and tensions within the evidence-based practice agenda. The individual clinical chapters which form Part II of this volume present a series of clinical vignettes and practice-based discussions. They represent an initial, tentative attempt to detail the work of dramatherapists when faced with the phenomenon of destructiveness in a variety of clinical contexts. The stories, observations and discussions of the authors are testimonial evidence to the creative possibilities of dramatherapy's inherent potential to stage and reflect upon conflict. The editors acknowledge that such testimony, as presented in this book, remains a long way from the kind of objective, quantitative evidence of effectiveness or efficacy that is currently the vogue amongst the majority of service commissioners and policy makers; and this could be seen as an inherent weakness of any book of this kind. Before entirely negating the conclusions drawn from practice about the potential effectiveness of dramatherapy, however, it may be worth interrogating further the current nature and status of dominant views of what constitutes 'evidence'. The first section of Chapter 3 discusses the framework around evidence-based practice in the arts therapies and provides examples of how professional associations aim to address the need for evidence, whilst emphasising the importance of practice-based evidence.

The issue remains, however, that in terms of the NICE hierarchy of evidence discussed in Chapter 3, we are unable to deliver the large-scale randomised control trials favoured by NICE. This inability relates to structural and practical impediments as well as some of the philosophical issues outlined below. This places discussions about dramatherapy practice in a strange position where, on the one hand, we are clearly developing ideas, processes and interventions from our own practice, which have some relevance and validity, and demonstrate anecdotal effectiveness of drama-therapy's use across a range of presenting problems. On the other hand, due to the holistic and eclectic stance that many dramatherapists take, and the nature of the clinical problems we tend to deal with, our ability to identify (let alone measure), simple single diagnosis-linked outcomes remains elusive. Nowhere is this more the case than in the complex multifaceted phenomenon of destructiveness. Thus, whilst in Chapter 3, Dokter considered those diagnostic categories where destructiveness may present as one of the clinical features, in none of those areas is destructiveness co-terminous with the diagnosis. A structural impediment here to delivering the kind of quantitative evidence required by NICE, is the fact that the

NICE guidelines adhere tightly to distinct categories of medical diagnosis (with the exception of the guidelines on self-harm, which offers guidelines on the *management* of the presenting behaviour). BADth's review of the working practice of its members showed that only 43% of dramatherapists work in medical settings. The majority of dramatherapists, therefore, work in a variety of non-medical settings and the way they describe their case study work is not necessarily in relation to psychiatric diagnoses. The way they perceive a client's problems is influenced by their psychotherapeutic orientation and their wider philosophical and epistemological position. Furthermore, dramatherapists, like many of their arts therapy and psycho-therapy colleagues, do not offer standardised protocol-based interventions, aimed at remedying discrete symptoms or particular facets of behaviour, as such the replicability and generalisability of dramatherapy as an inter-vention is difficult to prove when it relies, in essence, on a creative improvisation between therapist and client(s). All the work documented in this book is essentially an exploration of complex, often contradictory, multidimensional experiences, beliefs and desires which manifest in a variety of different ways in a variety of different contexts.

In this final chapter, therefore, we aim to summarise the findings from each of the chapters in an attempt to consider how far the question of dramatherapy's effectiveness in relation to destructiveness can be and has been addressed. We will then briefly revisit some of the findings from the BADth Systemic Review in order to link the new practice-based evidence included in this volume to that which has already been evaluated through the systematic review. It is worth noting that none of the chapters in this book indicates the medical diagnosis of the clients discussed; where there is a relatively clear relationship between the presenting problems considered and a distinct psychiatric diagnosis, we have included them in the subject index so that the reader looking for diagnostic categories can locate the evidence provided. Finally, whilst this volume has attempted to deconstruct destructiveness as an unambiguously negative phenomenon, when we attempt to link its manifestation to diagnostic categories it inevitably falls back into a negatively-construed 'problem' located within the psycho-pathology of the individual, rather than the far more complex, relational and systemic phenomenon we have attempted to illuminate.

Conclusions from clinical practice

In her consideration of a young boy diagnosed with ADHD, who had experienced intergenerational violence and trauma, Ramsden (Chapter 4) concludes that non-verbal play was key in developing the child's sense of his own agency in a difficult parenting environment. Further, she asserts that through using role-play to revisit narratives of experience, there was an observable sense of him working through some of the difficulties that had been identified in his behaviour. It is important to note that this took place in a group setting, where children were able to connect and explore shared themes generating playful expression of difficult emotions. She also considers, through the lens of attachment, brain development and systemic perspectives on complex family cases, how there is a mutual influence on the developing self, which can be contained and transformed through an innovative dramatherapy process which did not simply focus on the deficits of the individual child, but also involved engaging with the transgenerational system around him.

In her presentation of dramatherapy work in a challenging school for excluded and 'statemented' adolescents, Eleanor Zeal (Chapter 5) describes a process that has, at its centre, the idea of engaging and tolerating manifest chaos. She suggests that, due to the responsiveness and improvisational qualities of the dramatherapist and the multidimensional nature of dramatherapy as a medium, the therapy process can both reflect back and contain the adolescents' tumultuous process. Further, she argues that despite the challenges for the dramatherapist, staying with the hostility, aggression and ambivalence of this client group and maintaining a playful optimism enables the potential to revisit earlier developmental gaps and allows the possibility of a process of maturation.

In Chapter 6, Ditty Dokter reports on the findings of a piece of research which she conducted as a visiting researcher, rather than as the facilitating dramatherapist. She considers the impact of arts therapies interventions on an adolescent with an emergent diagnosis of borderline personality disorder, exhibiting self-harm. She proposes some conclusions and challenges from the research which highlight the importance of long-term group therapy that emphasises the relationship between peers as well as the relationship between client and therapist. She is mindful of the ambivalence within this client group with respect to seeking and accepting help, which may explain a high attrition rate in treatment. She highlights that such ambivalence may be a particular challenge for the dramatherapist who is attempting to offer action methods and the possibility of symbolic play. Dokter's conclusion stresses the importance of not moving into action simply as a way of filling the void of difficult feelings or an impasse in therapy, as this can lead to a struggle within the transference and countertransference as to who is in control.

Chapter 7 is also written from the perspective of a researcher rather than a practitioner, in which Jane Jackson considers other dramatherapists' understanding of self-harm in clients with severe to profound learning disabilities. She discusses practitioners' experiences of working with self-harming clients to explore the meaning that they make of their clients' actions. She concludes that the idea of simply viewing self-harm in this client group as 'challenging behaviour' does not do justice to the complexity of the act as a form of communication or as a response to past trauma or present stress. She suggests that the range of interventions that are open to the dramatherapist may help to negotiate a more positive, stable and trusting therapeutic relationship, in which what is being communicated through the self-harm can be acknowledged and integrated into an understanding of the client's life beyond the therapy space.

Chapter 8 considers the tensions and possibilities that may arise when a dramatherapy process is used alongside some of the concepts of the Narcotics Anonymous (NA) approach. Working with a small group in private practice, all of whom were members of NA, Zografou describes the use of Rebillot's (1993) Hero's Journey within a brief dramatherapy process. She acknowledges that within the experience of the addict is a struggle between resilience and relapse, between hope and destructiveness. In animating the Hero (hope) and the Demon (destructiveness), she argues that resistance within dramatherapy can be transformed into a 'disguised friend' and become a catalyst in moments of immobility and cognitive stagnation. She also considers the importance of the dramatherapist maintaining their own hope and resilience in the face of her client's imminent relapse.

In Chapter 9, Henri Seebohm offers a series of vignettes considering some of the difficulties of working individually with highly disturbed and dangerous clients through the medium of an improvisational dramatic process. She argues that attending to the here and now of what is happening in the play space is as important as the conceptual understanding of the client's personal history and offending behaviour. Through her vignettes, she highlights a number of significant moments when the play space collapses, either as a result of the client's resistance or of the therapist's response. She highlights the importance of maintaining access to a 'third' within such intense therapeutic encounters, whether that is the medium, the therapeutic relationship or the supervisory process. Further, she concludes that through an imaginative and responsive use of either the medium or the collaborative relationship, possibilities for development and transformation can be maintained even in the face of manifest destructiveness.

Chapter 10 explores an extended assessment process with a woman in a medium-secure unit. Rose Thorn considers the stories that emerged within the process and also those which developed around this woman amongst the wider staff team. This includes stories of culture and racism, which resonated in different ways with the dramatherapist. Through her exploration of the impact of race, gender and power – both in the therapeutic relationship and in the clinical setting – Thorn posits the possibility of negotiating a 'good enough' holding and containment, even when the medium of drama is 'killed off'.

Maggie McAlister, in Chapter 11, discusses the use of dramatic play with a group of forensic patients experiencing psychosis. In the unfolding narrative of the group experience, she hypothesises that creative work with a fictional character (Spiderman) enables a bridge to be slowly built between concrete and symbolic levels of functioning. Her conclusions support this hypothesis, equating the dramatherapy process with Winnicott's (1951) 'transitional space', in which symbolisation led directly to personal disclosures about violence and offending. This in turn provided for a greater degree of insight and an acknowledgement of remorse in these previously disowned, disturbing aspects amongst the offender patients.

Chapter 12 presents a dramatherapy structure developed with clients who had survived suicide attempts. Pete Holloway discusses the theoretical underpinnings for this work and considers the importance of incorporating participant feedback and their responses to the structure, so that the process builds as a collaborative venture over time. Rudimentary evaluation of the dramatherapy process suggests some effectiveness in terms of reducing the recurrence of further suicide attempts, although it is acknowledged that this may be as much due to the wider treatment framework of the unit in which the work took place, as to the dramatherapy intervention itself. He concludes that the attitudinal stance of the therapist towards the murderous self, as well as the 'surviving self', is of crucial importance in this work if the level of destructiveness to self and others is to be tolerated and ultimately transformed.

The clinical chapters as a whole suggest that there can be positive outcomes when dramatherapy meets destructiveness; or at least the *possibility* of positive outcomes, even if the realisation of such outcomes demands an enormous amount of the therapist. In each chapter the importance of the dramatic medium as a way of containing and mediating the potency of the destructive momentum is stressed. The dramatic medium, the ability to move into 'as if' realities and to engage playfully with destructive forces may be crucial in enabling both the therapist and clients to withstand and work through such forces. The improvisational quality and multi-media nature of drama as an artistic process is the key factor (identified by many of the contributors) in the dramatherapists' effectiveness in these clinical contexts. Their findings on the centrality of the dramatic process would seem to support our initial hypothesis that 'enactment' of destructiveness moves clients beyond an 'acting out' state of evacuation and intolerability, and provides the space for gradual reflection upon and re-incorporation of such destructive potential.

Emerging clinical themes

When taken together with the reader group evaluations of the BADth Systematic Review, we can discern that there are a number of clinical themes which this practice-based evidence is struggling with and attempting to address. Some of these themes are a direct echo of the reader group findings and some are a further development, which may indicate areas for on-going consideration, research and evaluation.

Symbol, thought and action

We have suggested in both Chapter 1 and the introduction to this chapter that symbolic play and dramatic representation may enable the client to move from 'acting out' to reflection and thought. This theoretical argument appears to be borne out in the majority of the chapters, particularly those by Ramsden, Zeal, Zografou and Holloway, who all demonstrate that the use of dramatic process appears to enable previously impulsive, 'mindless' or self-destructive behaviour to be mediated and processed through revisitation and enactment in the therapeutic space. Some of the chapters, however, add an important caveat to this argument in relation to psychotic and borderline presentations. Thus, Seebohm and McAlister clearly highlight the difficulties confronted by the therapist when the capacity for symbolic thought has been severely compromised in the experience of psychotic concrete thinking. Meanwhile, Dokter in Chapter 6 discusses the difficulties arising from the ambivalent responses to therapy (and the therapist) in the classic borderline presentation, whilst cautioning against the dramatherapist's tendency to *do something* (that is, move into dramatic structure or action) as a way of side-stepping and simplistically alleviating the experience of overwhelmingly turbulent or devoid feelings. These findings are generally consistent with many of the prior publications considered in the Systematic Review (particularly those of Grainger 1992; Johnson 1980; Johnson and Quinlan 1985; Johnson et al. 1999; Spencer et al. 1983). An important further consideration from the discussions in this volume, however, relates to the gradual development of the dramatic process. The earlier research cited above tended to emphasise the relief of primary and secondary symptoms of the presenting disorder (psychosis for example) as the main preoccupation of the therapists' focus; thus treatment was focused on a remedial approach to perceived 'deficits' in the client. We would argue that many contributors in this volume start with the clients' immediate presentation and gradually build the capacity to symbolise by finding ways to work with their tendency to concretise and their apparent 'resistance' to dramatise. Thus, Zeal's use of 'tags' and postcodes, Dokter's account of unselfconsciously showing scars in the sunshine, Zografou's awareness of the absolute fear of relapse into substance abuse, Seebohm's discussion of introducing a shared viewing of a film in order to 'get alongside' one of her clients, McAlister's acceptance that some insights were simply taboo in the early stages of group life and Holloway's acknowledgement that there was 'murder in mind' – all demonstrate the importance of starting with and responding to the often very concrete concerns of the client group. We would suggest that without such an acknowledgement and acceptance of what preoccupies these client groups on a concrete level, any enforced move to encourage them to move into symbolisation and reflection would be experienced as potentially overwhelming, resisted and ultimately doomed to fail.

186

Experience and making meaning

What seems to be important for the dramatherapist here is to move beyond the perspective which simply sees the presenting problem as a manifestation of 'illness', 'deficit', 'bad/challenging behaviour' and so on. Instead, we may begin to see psychotic concerns, suicidal and self-harming behaviour, aggression and anxiety as arising from real, lived experiences which themselves carry meaning and significance for the particular client groups. From the Systematic Review it was noted that Casson (2004) and Yotis (2006) discussed an approach to working with schizophrenia, whereby its 'symptoms' were reconstrued as a meaningful human experience and engaged with as such. A number of contributors echo this finding. This is most clearly demonstrated in Jones' discussion of dramatherapists' discourse about their work (Chapter 2), and in Jackson's research into how dramatherapists understand self-harm in clients with profound learning disabilities (Chapter 5). Such a view, however, is also implicit in the work detailed by Zeal, Dokter, Zografou, Seebohm, McAlister and Holloway, who all suggest the importance of acknowledging and understanding the here-and-now, concrete concerns and presenting behaviours of the client group as a given reality which have their own intrinsic meaning. We would argue that such a shift from a problem-based view of 'symptoms', subjective concerns and behaviours that have to be treated or remedied to one that sees them as a form of communication enables the dramatherapist to work directly with 'resistance' and 'sabotage', rather than being frustrated or paralysed by it. The focus of the work undergoes a subtle shift: rather than dramatic distance, symbolisation and play being vehicles to create, restore or impose more normative or functional meanings and 'insight', the dramatic process and the improvisation between therapist and client become a way of making meaning of the clients' direct experience. As such, the work becomes an heuristic collaboration where meaning emerges, rather than being imposed or structured *onto* the clients *by* the therapist. This may involve (as discussed by Dokter and demonstrated by Zeal, Seebohm, McAlister and Holloway) *not* moving straight into dramatic action, but staying with discomfort, resistance and the concrete reality of destructiveness until primitive symbolisation, dramatic embodiment and reflection begin to emerge; only then can clients begin to reframe and reintegrate destructive impulses, rather than feeling overwhelmed by them and/or acting them out.

The power of the group, the intensity of individual work

Much has been written in the group psychotherapy and group analytic traditions about the potential of the group to generate positive change (Yalom 1995) and to contain and harness destructive potential (Nitsun 1996). Similarly, much of the evidence considered in the BADth Systematic

Review had been delivered through group work, and this mode of delivery of dramatherapy was seen as important and effective in the reader group evaluation. In this volume, both group and individual interventions have been discussed. Seebohm illustrates the particular challenges placed on the therapist when working at an intense level with disturbed individuals. Thorn discusses the depth of identification and resonance that can develop in the transference/countertransference in individual therapy and the demands experienced by the therapist in attempting to provide a 'good enough' holding of the potentially destructive clients. Holloway suggests that the intensity of the relationship in individual therapy with suicide survivors may intensify shame and humiliation and therefore increase a guardedness against exploration of underlying destructive feelings and experiences. He contrasts this with a more open and collaborative process in the collective sharing and challenging within the same process when used in a group, whereas Zografou hints that a group setting may amplify feelings of shame and humiliation for an individual group member when they are in crisis. McAlister suggests that the group members begin to hold and represent qualities and attributes for each other as a precursor to individuals developing their own capacity to symbolise and reflect. This suggestion is also borne out in Zeal's description of her adolescent group, although she does document individual work in which the relationship between adolescent and therapist takes on a much more regressive and nurturing rhythm than that encountered in the group. Dokter raises the potentially important point that client peer-to-peer relationships within a group setting may be as beneficial (if not more so) than the client–therapist relationship. From the work included in this volume and the relative paucity of individual work considered in the Systematic Review, it is not possible to conclude which mode of dramatherapy is most effective. It is clear that both have elements which either intensify certain processes or provide the opportunity for challenge and different possibilities to emerge.

Embodiment and physicality

Despite our editorial stance, that destructiveness relates to an internal momentum within the psyche and within relationships, it is nonetheless striking that much destructiveness only becomes evident through physicalisation. This may take the form of attacks on other bodies or one's own body, attempts at sexualizing the therapeutic relationship, falling asleep in sessions, or physically absenting oneself from a session. If this is true of manifestations of destructiveness, we would also argue that a different kind of embodiment within the therapeutic space is a crucial factor in the potential reintegration of our internal destructive momentum. Holloway's experience of clients revisiting their bodies through breath and movement and stillness – bodies which they had previously attempted to kill off –

demonstrates how that self-destructiveness can be reframed and construed differently. Similarly, the work detailed by the majority of contributors suggests that there is an added dimension within dramatherapy that involves the physicality of both clients and therapist in relation to the therapeutic space. Sometimes this may take the form of dramatic embodiment of alternative roles or characters; sometimes it may simply be the physical proximity or distance between therapist and client, or the clients' relationship to the space; sometimes it may be the sensory and physical experience of being with others or exploring materials. A hypothesis here is that the inherent physicality of dramatherapy may serve to raise the implicit awareness of bodies in space and their relationship to each other from the very outset of a process. When we relate this observation back to destructive potential, it may be that such awareness for therapist and client alike presents a dialectical possibility: transgression, vulnerability and the potential of attack are present (as in Seebohm's and Zeal's chapters), but so is the real responsibility to maintain and respect physical boundaries, personal safety and the life of the group (as in McAlister's chapter). Further, when dramatic embodiment and representation of destructive acts occur, therapists need to be clear about the 'rules of play' and clients, in response to such clarity – playing within the rules – may begin to see that they can police and mediate their own destructiveness.

Improvisational play and irreverence

The concept of play is clearly integral to dramatherapy, both as a noun (a theatrical event) and as a verb (to play). All contributors identify the importance of developing a degree of playfulness within and between the clients. Some contributors, such as Ramsden, Jackson and McAlister, utilise a developmental notion of play, derived from Winnicott (2005), which enables participants to rehearse and rework (through symbolic play) undigested emotional material in order to absorb gradually that which has been overwhelming. Such a notion is essentially located in the playfulness of the client as a corrective or reparative process. There is, however, another emergent theme within some of the chapters, which locates playfulness as equally necessary for therapist and client alike. So in Zeal's work with turbulent adolescents, Holloway's observations about the use of humour in the groups for suicide survivors, and Seebohm's discussion of what may have been possible in moments of apparent impasse, we may begin to see a certain position that is, or could be, adopted by the therapist. In such a position the therapist is also required to develop a sense of playfulness in response to their clients. No longer just holding a structure or facilitating the development of playfulness amongst the clients, the dramatherapist herself becomes a 'play object' and uses her own playfulness and engagement with the client's material as the vehicle for facilitation. Such a 'use of self' in the therapeutic process is a well-established idea within systemic family therapy, inspired by Satir and Baldwin (1987) and further developed by Cecchin (1993) to incorporate the idea of therapist and client joining in a collaborative irreverence towards the apparently overwhelming difficulties and problems. In theatrical terms, the therapist adopts a position like that of Harlequin in the commedia del arte tradition or (in its more contemporary guise) of Boal's 'Joker' (2002), the function being to adopt a mercurial stance that both keeps the improvisational quality of the unfolding drama alive, whilst simultaneously serving as an *agent provocateur* in terms of linking the contents of the drama (be they concrete or symbolic) back to what can be a deeply serious and troubling reality. Such a position, albeit drawing upon different cultural traditions, in some ways parallels Read Johnson's 'Developmental Transformations' work (in Jones 2010) in the USA, developed in response to clients with complex post-traumatic stress disorder (PTSD). The effectiveness (or otherwise) of the dramatherapy intervention in both the chapters in this volume and in Read Johnson's USA-based approach appears to relate directly to the openness, responsiveness and improvisational qualities of the dramatherapist. If that *is* the case, then the issue of researching and evidencing what is potentially a new paradigm shift in dramatherapy practice becomes a more challenging one, as we have to embrace the improvisational uniqueness of each clinical encounter, rather than relying on replicable and generalisable models of intervention.

Areas for further consideration and research

Theoretical considerations

• The individual chapters in this book have demonstrated that dramatherapists draw on a wide range of psychodynamic, group analytic, cultural, arts therapies and aesthetic theories to underpin their practice of working with destructiveness. This may be both a strength and weakness within the profession's ability to make coherent sense of its work. Without a defining discourse that integrates all of the above influences, we may simply find ourselves reaching for psychoanalytic certainty to justify our practice. On the other hand, given the wide variety of settings and diagnoses where destructiveness may manifest, prioritising particular discourses and frameworks of understanding where they are most appropriate or helpful may be important. There are, however, current strands within contemporary psychotherapy theory which aim to integrate attachment theory, cognitive development and the concept of 'mentalisation' (Fonagy et al. 2002), which may serve to inspire an integrative dialogue amongst dramatherapists.

• Within the clinical chapters in this book, there is a relative absence of Jungian thought. A question remains as to what we can learn from an appreciation of Jung's notion of 'the Shadow' and a need for mature integration of Shadow material. The Drama and Movement Therapy *Sesame* orientation of Jackson's dramatherapists has a strong Jungian underpinning (Karkou and Sanderson 2006), whilst McAlister is also a Jungian analyst, so it would be a useful further area of research to draw on these interdisciplinary strengths in dramatherapy to develop this area of thinking.

- Are all manifestations of destructiveness to be interpreted as regression to infantile concerns, such as Glasser's (1979) 'core complex', or is there another view that acknowledges the 'here-and-now', relational and self/ personality/identity features of the phenomenon? If the different perspectives detailed above become integrated into a coherent discourse for dramatherapists working with particular problems, this question may become superfluous. The primary to secondary process development (Bion 1967), the development of the capacity to mentalise (Fonagy et al. 2002), the developmental bridge from thought to action (Winnicott 1971) need to be translated into the here and now of the multilayered dramatherapeutic relationship.

- Arts therapies theory has, over time, developed from the dyadic relationship (involving the client–therapist relationship) to the triadic relationship (including the importance of the artistic medium). But maybe there is need to develop a fourth dimension, a quadratic equation – therapist, client, medium + collective sense/solidarity of the group (and anti-group) – that *socialises*. The concepts of the group matrix (Nitsun 1996) and the four dimensions of functioning to be considered when working with refugees – political, cultural, interpersonal and intrapsychic (Blackwell 2005) – may provide vehicles to conceptualise this in an arts therapeutic context.

Practice considerations

- Rather than simply pathologising or minimising the significance of destructive behaviour, there appears to be a real need to hear, take seriously and make meaning from such apparently negative, resistant or sabotaging behaviour.

- There is a further need in training and in developing practice to consider the therapist maintaining playfulness *in relation to* destructiveness, not despite it. We also need to develop a confidence in not jumping into action in order to impose positive possibilities or deflect negative consequences. Instead, we may need to develop ways in which to tolerate, frame and play with destructive impulses and by so doing invite the client to take a similar position to their own destructiveness.

- Further to the point above – there is an obvious risk in moving to action in order to fill the void. Dramatherapists may have a belief in action, which can curtail the possibility of client agency and development. It is important to adjust practice to client needs. The various clinical chapters in this book each provide ideas and suggestions for adjustment, but a crucial factor in this is avoiding defensive action initiated from a defensive therapist's need to fill the void (see Schwartz-Salant in Chapter 6).

Further research

There is clearly a need for both further outcome-based and qualitative case study research into how dramatherapists work with destructiveness and the effectiveness of such work. A major obstacle to this remains the fact that destructiveness does not fit into a simple, single, diagnostic category. Its complexity does not lend itself to being isolated as a standardised variable to be measured and monitored. As Seebohm points out, it cannot stand as a phenomenon in isolation from context, relationship and history. Similarly, as a phenomenon in clinical practice it does not straightforwardly correlate with any single, specific dimension on accepted outcome measures. Standardised outcome measures such as CORE are increasingly used by dramatherapists (Dokter and Winn 2009). They include assessment of risk in relation to suicide and self-harm, but need to be used in the context of the clinical setting and therapeutic relationship, rather than as absolute indicators. Most importantly, we have seen that the phenomenon of destructiveness is not simply an attributable *behavioural* signifier of individual pathology or illness, but exists in a relational and/or systemic context. However, there are elements of destructive and self-destructive presentations that seem to occur frequently in certain identifiable clinical groups (Winter et al. 2009; see earlier in this chapter). Therefore, the challenge may be for us to think more creatively about how we highlight particular features of destructiveness and self-destructiveness within standard outcomes measures that are used and developed, and how we formulate presenting problems that we are working with in ways that do fit more neatly into traditional diagnostic profiles.

In facing this challenge, dramatherapists are not alone – all of the non-standardised, non-manualised psychotherapies are grappling with the dominance of the current evidential heirarchy. This has recently been acknowledged within the Department of Health in its publication *New Ways of Working for Psychological Therapists*. The evidence-base working group within that project 'encourage a greater dialogue with NICE to . . . consider including a broader range of evidence and methodologies, and embrace a more psychologically-orientated approach to mental and physical health conditions than its current medical and diagnostically-based approach' (National Institute for Mental Health in England 2010).

Conclusion

There were two crucial questions for dramatherapists that provided the rationale for initiating this book. The first was whether a therapeutic practice based on enactment serves only to encourage the 'acting out' of violent, aggressive or dangerous material. The case material presented as practice-based evidence in this book, as well as that evaluated in the Systematic Review, indicate that this is not the case. In fact, there are indications that a form of therapy based on enactment and embodiment, which takes into account both the creative and destructive possibilities of 'acting out', may facilitate a possible answer to our second question – this being, does the art form enable reframing or reconstruing of a potentially destructive impulse, enabling thought to start anticipating action? Whilst this question has been partially answered anecdotally in a number of the chapters in their discussion of symbolisation, reflection and reintegration of experience, the evidence is not definitive. Given the complexity of this phenomenon and its occurrence across a number of client groups, it may be particularly optimistic to consider that such empirical proof is possible in one definitive publication. The practice-based evidence in the case material with particular client groups and presenting problems provides clear indications for smaller-scale pieces of research, be it in the form of cumulative single case studies (Smeijsters 1997; Aldridge 2005) or quantitative research along the lines of the art therapy and psychosis randomised control trial currently being conducted. As editors, we hope to have provided sufficient inspiration for further research to be developed and conducted, thus enabling further development of the evidence base to 'play with Thanatos'.

BIBLIOGRAPHY

Abram, J. (1996). *The Language of Winnicott – A Dictionary of Winnicott's Use of Words*. London: Karnac.

Adshead, G. (2002). Three degrees of security: attachment and forensic institutions. *Criminal Behaviour and Mental Health 12*, 31–45.

Adshead, G. (2010). Thereby hangs a tale . . . . Invited response to Annual Isaac Ray Lecture by Professor Ezra Griffiths. American Academy of Psychiatry and Law, Tucson, AR, USA, 23 October 2010.

Adshead, G. and Van Velsen, C. (1998). Psychotherapeutic work with victims of trauma. In C. Cordess and M. Cox (eds), *Forensic Psychotherapy – Crime, Psychodynamics and the Offender Patient*. London: Jessica Kingsley.

Aigen, K. (1995). Principles of qualitative research. In B. Wheeler (ed.), *Music Therapy Research. Quantitative and Qualitative Perspectives*. Phoenixville, AR: Barcelona.

Alcoholics Anonymous. (2001). *The Story of How Many Thousands of Men and Women Have Recovered from Alcoholism*. New York: AA World Services.

Aldridge, D. (1993). Music Therapy Research I: a review of the medical research literature within a general context of music therapy research. *The Arts in Psychotherapy 20*(1), 11–35.

Aldridge, D. (1996a). *Music Therapy Research and Practice in Medicine*. London: Jessica Kingsley.

Aldridge, D. (1996b). The development of music therapy research as a perspective of complementary medicine. In S. Olesen and E. Hog (eds), *Communication In and About Alternative Therapies*. Odense: Odense University Press.

Aldridge, D. (2005). *Case Study Designs in Music Therapy*. London: Jessica Kingsley.

Anderson-Warren, M. and Grainger, R. (2000). *Practical Approaches to Dramatherapy: The Shield of Perseus*. London: Jessica Kingsley.

Apollinari, C. (1996). Dramatherapy and personality disorder. Echoes of abuse. In S. Mitchell (ed.), *Dramatherapy Clinical Studies*. London: Jessica Kingsley.

Banks-Wallace, J. and Parks, L. (2001). So that our souls don't get damaged: the impact of racism on maternal thinking and practice related to the protection of daughters. *Issues of Mental Health Nursing 22*, 77–98.

Bannister, A. (1995). Images and action: dramatherapy and psychodrama with

194

sexually abused adolescents. In S. Jennings (ed.), *Dramatherapy with Children and Adolescents*. London: Routledge (pp. 169–185).

Bannister, A. (2003). *Creative Therapies with Traumatized Children*. London: Jessica Kingsley.

Barker, C. and Galasinski, D. (2001). *Cultural Studies and Discourse Analysis*. London: Sage.

Barnes, B., Ernst, S. and Hyde, K. (1999). *An Introduction to Groupwork. A Groupanalytic Perspective*. London: Macmillan.

Bateman, A. and Holmes, J. (1995). *Introduction to Psychoanalysis*. London: Routledge.

Bateman, A. and Fonagy, P. (2004). *Psychotherapy for Borderline Personality Disorder: Mentalisation Based Treatment*. Oxford: Oxford University Press.

Barber, V. and Campbell, J. (1999). Living colour in art therapy – visual and verbal narrative of black and white. In J. Campbell, M. Liebmann, F. Brooks, J. Jones and C. Ward (eds), *Art Therapy, Race and Culture*. London: Jessica Kingsley.

Becker, C. (1992). *Living and Relating: An Introduction to Phenomenology*. London: Sage.

Beckett, S. (1956). *Waiting for Godot*. London: Faber and Faber.

Benson, J. F. (1995). The secret war in the dis-united kingdom: psychological aspects of the Ulster conflict. *Group Analysis 28*(1), 47–62.

Berger, J. (2008). *Ways of Seeing*. London: Penguin Modern Classics.

Bergman, J. (2001). Using drama therapy to uncover genuineness and deception in civilly committed sexual offenders. In *The Sexual Predator, vol. 2, Legal Issues, Clinical Issues, and Special Populations*. New York: Civic Research Institute Inc.

Bion, W. R. (1959). Attacks on linking. *International Journal of Psychoanalysis 40*(5,6), 308–315.

Bion, W. R. (1961). *Experiences in Groups*. London: Tavistock.

Bion, W. R. (1962). *Learning from Experience*. London: Karnac.

Bion, W. R. (1967). *Second Thoughts*. London: Heinemann.

Blackman, N. (2003). *Loss and Learning Disability*. London: Worth.

Blackman, N. (2008). Making space for thought: supervision in a learning disability context. In P. Jones and D. Dokter (eds) *Supervision of Dramatherapy*. London: Routledge (pp. 185–198).

Blackwell, D. (2005). *Counselling and Psychotherapy with Refugees*. London: Jessica Kingsley.

Bloch, H. S. (1995). *Adolescent Development, Psychology and Treatment*. New York: International University Press.

Blos, P. (1962). *On Adolescence*. New York: Free Press.

Boal, A. (1992). *Games for Actors and Non-actors*. London and New York: Routledge.

Boal, A. (2002). *Theatre of the Oppressed*. London: Pluto Classics.

Bolton, A. and Adams, M. (1983). An investigation of the effects of music therapy on a group of profoundly mentally handicapped adults. *Research News: International Journal of Rehabilitation 6*(4), 511–512.

Bowlby, J. (1975). *Attachment and Loss, vol. 2, Separation, Anxiety and Loss*. Harmondsworth: Penguin.

Bowlby, J. (1998). *A Secure Base*. London: Routledge.

Bowlby, J. (2009). *A Secure Base*, 2nd re-issue edn. London: Routledge Classics.

Brem, A. (2002). The creative container between sessions. Helping self harming patients to endure solitude. *Dramatherapy 24*(2), 16–22.

Brezo, J., Paris, J., Dylan Barker, E., Tremblay, R., Vitaro, F., Zoccolillo, M., Hébert, M. and Turecki, G. (2007). Natural history of suicidal behaviours in a population-based sample of young adults. *Psychological Medicine 37*, 1563–1574.

British Association of Dramatherapists (BADth). (2005). *Code of Practice*. Available online: www.badth.org.uk/code/index.html#cop (accessed 1 August 2009).

British Association of Dramatherapists (BADth). (2008). *Equal Opportunities dictionary*. Available online: www.badth.org.uk/downloads/information/Equal%20Opportunities%20Analysis%2015.4.08.PDF (accessed 21 February 2009).

British Association of Dramatherapists (BADth). (2009). Available online: www.badth.org.uk (accessed 1 August 2009).

Britton, R. (1989). The missing link: parental sexuality in the Oedipus complex. In J. Steiner (ed.), *The Oedipus Complex Today*. London: Karnac.

Brooker, J., Cullum, M., Gilroy, A., McCombe, B., Ringrose, K., Russell, D., Smart, L. and Waldman, J. (2005). *The Use of Art Work in Art Psychotherapy with People Who Are Prone to Psychotic States*. London: Goldsmiths' College and Oxleas NHS Trust.

Bruscia, K. E. (1998). *Defining Music Therapy*, 2nd edn. New Hampshire: Barcelona.

Bucher, R. and Strauss, A. (1961). Professions in process. *American Journal of Sociology 6*(4), 325–334.

Cambridge Online Dictionary: cambridge.dictionary.org

Campbell, D. and Hale, R. (1991). Suicidal acts. In Holmes, J. (ed.), *Textbook of Psychotherapy in Psychiatric Practice*. Edinburgh: Churchill Livingstone.

Campbell, J. (1993). *The Hero with A Thousand Faces*. London: Fontana.

Casson, J. (2004). *Drama, Psychotherapy and Psychosis: Dramatherapy and Psychodrama with People Who Hear Voices*. Hove and New York: Brunner-Routledge.

Cattanach, A. (ed.). (1999). *Process in the Arts Therapies*. London: Jessica Kingsley.

Cecchin, G. (1993). *Irreverence: A Strategy for Therapists' Survival*. London: Karnac.

Chasen, L. R. (2005). Spectacle and ensemble in group dramatherapy treatment for children with ADHD and related neurological syndromes. In A. Weber and C. Haen (eds), *Clinical Applications of Dramatherapy in Child and Adolescent Treatment*. New York and Hove: Brunner-Routledge.

Chesner, A. (1994). An integrated model of dramatherapy and its application with adults with learning disabilities. In S. Jennings, A. Cattanach, S. Mitchell, A. Chesner and B. Meldrum (eds), *The Handbook of Dramatherapy*. London: Routledge.

Chesner, A. (1995). *Dramatherapy for People with Learning Disabilities: A World of Difference*. London: Jessica Kingsley.

Clarke, L. and Whittaker, M. (1998). Self-mutilation: culture, contexts and nursing responses. *Journal of Clinical Nursing 7*, 129–137.

Clarkson, P. and Nuttall, J. (2002). Working with countertransference. In P.

Clarkson (ed.), *On Psychotherapy 2*. London, UK, and Philadelphia, PA: Whurr.

Collins, D. (1996). Attacks on the body: how can we understand self-harm? *Psychodynamic Counselling 2*(4), 463–475.

Comtois, K. A. and Linehan, M. M. (2006). Psychosocial treatments of suicidal behaviours: a practice-friendly review. *Journal of Clinical Psychology: In Session 62*(2), 161–170.

Cordess, C. and Cox. M. (eds). (1996). *Forensic Psychotherapy: Crime, Psycho-dynamics and the Offender Patient*. London: Jessica Kingsley.

Cordess, C. and Hyatt Williams, A. (1996). The criminal act and acting out. In C. Cordess and M. Cox (eds), *Forensic Psychotherapy Crime, Psychodynamics and the Offender Patient*. London: Jessica Kingsley.

Cossa, M. (2006). *Rebels with a Cause: Working with Adolescents Using Action Techniques*. London: Jessica Kingsley.

Costello, S. J. (2002). *The Pale Criminal: Psychoanalytic Perspectives*. London and New York: Karnac.

Cottis, T. (ed.). (2009). *Intellectual Disability, Trauma and Psychotherapy*, Hove: Routledge.

Count Me In Census. (2008). Commission for Healthcare Audit and Inspection. Available online: www.cqc.org.uk/_db/_documents/Count_me_in_2008_Results _of_the_2008_national_census_of_inpatients_in_mental_health_and_learning_ disability_services_in_England_and_Wales.pdf (accessed 20 November 2009).

Cox, M. (1978). *Structuring the Therapeutic Process: Compromise with Chaos*. Oxford: Pergamon (p. 13).

Cox, M. (1988). *Structuring the Therapeutic Process*. London: Jessica Kingsley.

Crouch, W. and Wright, J. (2004). Deliberate self harm at an adolescent unit: a qualitative investigation. *Clinical Child Psychology and Psychiatry 9*(2), 185–204.

Cummings, J. L. and Mega, M. S. (2003). *Neuropsychiatry and Behavioural Neuro-science*. Oxford: Oxford University Press.

Dalal, F. (2002). *Race, Colour and the Processes of Racialization*. Hove: Brunner-Routledge.

Dalal, F. (2006). Racism – processes of detachment, dehumanization and hatred. In K. White (ed.), *Unmasking Race, Culture, and Attachment in the Psycho-analytical Space*. London: Karnac.

Davidoff, F., Haynes, B., Sackett, D. and Smith, R. (1995). Editorial. In *Evidence Based Medicine 1*(1), 5.

Davidson, K., Livingstone, S., McArthur, K., Dickson, L. and Gurnley, A. (2007). An integrative complexity analysis of CBT sessions for borderline personality disorder. *Psychology and Psychotherapy: Theory, Research and Practice 80*, 513–523.

Davies, R. (1998). The inter-disciplinary network and the internal world of the offender. In C. Cordess and M. Cox (eds), *Forensic Psychotherapy – Crime, Psychodynamics and the Offender Patient*. London: Jessica Kingsley.

Davis, J. (2010). *And When the Smile Gets Just too Tired* [unpublished].

Dent-Brown, K. and Wang, M. (2004). Pessimism and failure in six-part stories: indicators of borderline personality disorder? *The Arts in Psychotherapy 31*(5), 321–333.

Department of Health. (1999). *Saving Lives: Our Healthier Nation*. London: Stationary Office.

Department of Health. (2001). *Valuing People: A New Strategy for Learning Disability for the 21st Century*. A White Paper. Available online: www.archive. official-documents.co.uk/document/cm50/5086/5086.htm (accessed 15 January 2008).

de Zulueta, F. (1993). *From Pain to Violence: The Traumatic Roots of Destructiveness*. London: Whurr.

de Zulueta, F. (1998). Theories of aggression and violence, In C. Cordess and M. Cox (eds), *Forensic Psychotherapy – Crime, Psychodynamics and the Offender Patient*. London: Jessica Kingsley.

de Zulueta, F. (2006). *From Pain to Violence: The Traumatic Roots of Destructiveness*, 2nd edn. London: Wiley-Blackwell.

Dintino, C. and Johnson, D. R. (1997). Playing the perpetrator. Gender dynamics in developmental dramatherapy. In S. Jennings (ed.), *Dramatherapy Theory and Practice 3*. London and New York: Routledge.

Doctor, R. (1999). Understanding the erotic and eroticised countertransference. In D. Mann (ed.), *Erotic Transference and Countertransference: Clinical Practice in Psychotherapy*. London: Routledge.

Doctor, R. (2003). The role of violence in perverse psychopathology. In R. Doctor (ed.), *Dangerous Patients: A Psychodynamic Approach to Risk Assessment and Management*. London: Karnac.

Dokter, D. (1988). Acting out: a dialogue between dramatherapy and group analysis. In P. Jones (ed.), *State of the Art Conference Proceedings*. Hertfordshire College of Art and Design, St. Albans.

Dokter, D. (ed.). (1994). *Arts Therapies and Clients with Eating Disorders: Fragile Board*. London: Jessica Kingsley.

Dokter, D. (1996). Dramatherapy and clients with eating disorders. In S. Mitchell (ed.), *Dramatherapy: Clinical Studies*. London: Jessica Kingsley.

Dokter, D. (ed.). (1998). *Arts Therapists, Refugees and Migrants – Reaching Across Borders*. London: Jessica Kingsley.

Dokter, D. (2001). Arts therapies in the asylum. In L. Kossolapow, S. Scoble and D. Waller (eds), *Arts-Therapies-Communication*. Munster: Lit Verlag (pp. 180–191).

Dokter, D. (2003). Exile. Arts therapies and refugees. In L. Kossolapow, D. Waller and S. Scoble (eds), *Arts-Therapies-Communication 3*. Munster: Munster Verlag.

Dokter, D. (2005–2006). The fool and stranger anxiety; creative and destructive possibilities. *Dramatherapy 27*(4). 9–14.

Dokter, D. (2008). Immigrant mental health: acculturation stress and the response of the UK host. In M. Finklestein and K. Dent-Brown (eds), *Psychosocial Stress in Immigrants and Members of Minority Groups as a Factor of Terrorist Behaviour*. Amsterdam: IOS Press.

Dokter, D. (2010). Helping and hindering processes in creative arts therapy group practice. In *GROUP 34*(1), 67–84.

Dokter, D. and Hughes, P. (2007). *Equal Opportunities Survey*. Available online: www.badth.org.uk

Dokter, D. and Hughes, P. (2009). Evidence-based practice systematic review database. Available online: www.badth.org.uk

Dokter, D. and Winn, L. (2009). Evidence based practice, a dramatherapy research project. *Dramatherapy 31*(1), 3–9.

DSM-IV. (2000). *Diagnostic and Statistics Manual*, 4th edn. Washington, DC: American Psychological Association.

Duncan, E., Nicol, A. S., Ager, M. M. and Dalgleish, L. (2006). A systematic review of structured group interventions with mentally disordered offenders. *Criminal Behaviour and Mental Health* 16(4), 217–241.

Edwards, D. (1999). The role of the case study in art therapy research. *Inscape 4*(1), 2–9.

Ellens, J. H. (2004). *The Destructive Power of Religion: Violence in Judaism, Christianity, and Islam*. Westport, CT: Praeger.

Ellis, A. (2001). *Overcoming Destructive Beliefs, Feelings, and Behaviors*. Amherst, NY: Prometheus Books.

Emerson, E., Felce, D., McGill, P. and Mansell, J. (1994). Introduction. In E. Emerson, P. McGill and J. Mansell (eds), *Severe Learning Disabilities and Challenging Behaviours. Designing High Quality Services*. London: Chapman and Hall.

Emunah, R. (1994). *Acting for Real: Drama Therapy Process, Technique, and Performance*. New York: Brunner-Routledge.

Emunah, R. (1995). From adolescent trauma to adolescent drama: group drama-therapy with emotionally disturbed youth. In S. Jennings (ed.), *Dramatherapy with Children and Adolescents*. London: Routledge (pp. 150–168).

Emunah, R. (2005). Drama therapy and adolescent resistance. In A. Weber and C. Haen (eds), *Clinical Applications of Dramatherapy in Child and Adolescent Treatment*. New York and Hove: Brunner-Routledge (pp. 107–120).

Fairbairn, G. J. (1995). *Contemplating Suicide: The Language and Ethics of Self-harm*. London: Routledge.

Favazza, A. R. (1987). *Bodies Under Siege. Self-mutilation in Culture and Psychiatry*. Baltimore, MD: Johns Hopkins University Press.

Fenichel, O. (1946). *The Psychoanalytic Theory of Neurosis*. London: Routledge and Kegan Paul.

Fernando, F., Ndegwa, D. and Wilson, M. (1998). *Forensic Psychiatry, Race and Culture*. London: Routledge.

Fields, B., Reesman, K., Robinson, C., Sims, A., Edwards, K., McCall, B., Short, B. and Thomas, S. P. (1998). Anger of African American women in the South. *Issues of Mental Health Nursing 19*, 353–373.

Finklestein, M. and Dent-Brown, K. (eds). (2008). *Psychosocial Stress in Immigrants and Members of Minority Groups as a Factor of Terrorist Behaviour*. Amsterdam: IOS Press.

Firestone, R. W. (1997). *Suicide and the Inner Voice*. London: Sage.

Fisher, S. and Cooper, C. (1990). *On the Move: The Psychology of Change and Transition*. London: Wiley.

Fletchman Smith, B. (1993). Assessing the difficulties for British patients of Caribbean origin in being referred for psychoanalytical psychotherapy. *British Journal of Psychotherapy 10*(1), 50–61.

Fletchman Smith, B. (2000). *Mental Slavery – Psychoanalytic Studies of Caribbean People*. London: Rebus.

Flores, P. J. (1997). *Group Psychotherapy with Addicted Populations: An Integrated 12-Step Approach*. New York: Haworth.

Fonagy, P. and Target, M. (1999). Towards understanding violence: the use of the body and the role of the father. In R. J. Perelberg (ed.), *Psychoanalytic Understanding of Violence and Suicide*. London: Routledge.

Fonagy, P., Gergely, G., Jurist, E. and Target, M. (2002). *Affect Regulation, Mentalization, and the Development of the Self*. New York: Other Press.

Foulkes, S. H. (1964). *Therapeutic Group Analysis*. London: George Allen and Unwin.

Frankl, R. (1998). *The Adolescent Psyche. Jungian and Winnicottian Perspectives*. London: Routledge.

Freud, S. (1895). Reply to the criticisms on anxiety-neurosis. In J. Reviere (ed.), *Sigmund Freud Collected Papers*, vol. 1. New York: Basic Books.

Freud, S. (1920). *Beyond the Pleasure Principle*, standard edn 18. London: Hogarth.

Fromm, E. (1973). *The Anatomy of Human Destructiveness*. New York: Holt, Rinehart and Winston.

Fromm, E. (1974). *The Anatomy of Human Destructiveness*. New York: Henry Holt and Co.

Gardner, F. (2001). *Self-harm. A Psychotherapeutic Approach*. Hove: Brunner-Routledge.

Gelder, M., Mayou, R. and Geddes, J. (2005). *Psychiatry*, 3rd edn. Oxford: Oxford University Press.

Gerard, R. (1952). The biological basis of imagination. In B. Ghiselin (ed.), *The Creative Process*. New York: Mentor.

Gerhardt, S. (2004). *Why Love Matters*. London: Routledge.

Gersie, A. (1992). *Earthtales – Storytelling in Times of Change*. London: Greenprint.

Gersie, A. and King, N. (1990). *Storymaking in Education and Therapy*. London: Jessica Kingsley.

Gilbody, S. and Sowden, A. (2000). Systematic reviews in mental health. In N. Rowland and S. Goss (eds), *Evidence Based Counselling and Psychological Therapies*. London: Routledge.

Gilligan, J. (1996). *Violence: Reflections on Our Deadliest Epidemic*. London: Jessica Kingsley.

Gilroy, A. (2006). *Art Therapy, Research and Evidence-based Practice*. London: Routledge.

Gilroy, A. and Lee, C. (1995). *Art and Music. Therapy and Research*. London: Routledge.

Glass, I. P. (ed.). (1991). *The International Handbook of Addiction Behaviour*. London: Routledge.

Glasser, M. (1979). Some aspects of the role of aggression in the perversions. In I. Rozen (ed.), *Sexual Deviation*. Oxford: Oxford University Press.

Glasser, M. (1985). The weak spot – some observations on male homosexuality. *International Journal of Psychoanalysis 79*, 405–414.

Glyn, J. (2002). Drummed out of mind. In E. Richards and A. Davies (eds), *Sound Company: Group Work in Music Therapy*. London: Jessica Kingsley.

Goertz, K. (1998). Transgenerational representations of the holocaust: from memory to 'post-memory'. *World Literature Today 72*(1), 33.

Gomez, L. (1996). *An Introduction to Object Relations*. London: Free Association Books.

Goldring, N. and Fieve, R. R. (1984). Attempted suicide in manic-depressive disorder. *American Journal of Psychotherapy 38*, 373–383.

Grainger, R. (1990). *Drama and Healing: The Roots of Drama Therapy*. London: Jessica Kingsley.

Grainger, R. (1992). Dramatherapy and thought disorder. In S. Jennings (ed.), *Dramatherapy: Theory and Practice 2*. London: Tavistock/Routledge (pp. 164–180).

Grainger, R. (1999). *Researching the Arts Therapies – A Dramatherapists Perspective*. London: Jessica Kingsley.

Greenwood, H. (2000). Captivity and terror in the therapeutic relationship. *Inscape: The Journal of the British Association of Art Therapists 5*(2), 53–61.

Grenier C. (2005). *Big Bang: Creation and Destruction in 20th Century Art*. Paris: Editions du Centre Pompidou. Available online: www.studio-international. co.uk/reports/big_bang (accessed 9 September 2009).

Grimshaw, D. (1996). Dramatherapy with children in an educational unit: the more you look, the more you see. In S. Mitchell (ed.), *Dramatherapy Clinical Studies*. London: Jessica Kingsley.

Gross, R. D. (1991). *Psychology: The Science of Mind and Behaviour*. London: Hodder and Stoughton.

Grotstein, J. S. (2007). *An Intense Beam of Darkness: Wilfrid Bion's Legacy to Psychoanalysis*. London: Karnac.

Gruen, A. (2007). *The Insanity of Normality: Toward Understanding Human Destructiveness*. Berkeley, CA: Human Development Books.

Guggenbuhl-Craig, A. (1971). *Power in the Helping Professions*. Dallas, TX: Spring Publications.

Guillén, M. F. (2001). Is globalization civilizing, destructive or feeble? A critique of five key debates in the social science literature. *Annual Review of Sociology 27*, 235–260.

Haen, C. (2005). Rebuilding security: group therapy with children affected by September 11. *International Journal of Group Psychotherapy 55*, 391–414.

Halliday, S. and Mackrell, K. (1998). Psychological interventions in self-injurious behaviour. Working with people with a learning disability. *British Journal of Psychiatry 172*, 395–400.

Harding, C. (ed.). (2006). *Aggression and Destructiveness: Psychoanalytic Perspectives*. London: Routledge.

Haste, E. and McKenna, P. (2010). Clinical effectiveness of dramatherapy in the recovery of severe neuro-trauma. In P. Jones (ed.), *Drama as Therapy*, vol. 2. London: Routledge.

Hayden, C. (2007). *Children in Trouble – The Role of Families, Schools and Communities*. Basingstoke: Palgrave Macmillan.

Hawton, K., Townsend, E., Arensman, E., Gunnell, D., Hazell, P., House, A. and van Heeringen, K. (1999). Psychosocial and pharmacological treatments for deliberate self-harm. *Cochrane Database of Systematic Reviews*, Issue 4, Art. No. CD001764; doi: 10.1002/14651858.CD0011764.

Hawton, K., Rodham, K., Evans, E. and Weatherall, R. (2002). Deliberate self-harm in adolescents: self-report study in schools in England. *British Medical Journal 325*, 1207–1211.

Hawton, K., Zahl, D. and Weatherall, R. (2003). Suicide following deliberate self-harm; long-term follow-up of patients who presented to a general hospital. *British Journal of Psychiatry 182*, 537–542.

Herman, J. L. (1997). Good enough fairy tales for resolving sexual abuse trauma. *The Arts in Psychotherapy 24*(5), 439–445.

Herman, J. L. (2001). *Trauma and Recovery: From Domestic Abuse to Political Terror*. New York: Rivers Oram Press.

Hewitt, D. (1999). Points of view: cold dark matter. Available online: www.tate.org.uk/colddarkmatter/texts (accessed 9 September 2009).

Higgins, R. (1996). *Approaches to Research: A Handbook for Those Writing a Dissertation*. London: Jessica Kingsley.

Hill, M. (2006). Children's voices on ways of having a voice: children's and young people's perspectives on methods used in research and consultation. *Childhood 13*, 69–89.

Hillman, J. (1965). *Suicide and the Soul*. Dallas, TX: Spring Publications.

Hillman, J. (1990). *The Essential James Hillman: A Blue Fire*. London: Routledge.

Hillman, J. (2004). *A Terrible Love of War*. Harmondsworth: Penguin.

Hiscox, A. R. and Calisch, A. C. (1998). *Tapestry of Cultural Issues in Art Therapy*. London: Jessica Kingsley.

HMSO (2003). *Every Child Matters*. London: The Stationery Office.

Holmes, J. (2001). *The Search for a Secure Base. Attachment Theory and Psychotherapy*. Hove and New York: Brunner-Routledge.

Holloway, P. (1996). Dramatherapy in acute intervention. In S. Mitchell (ed.), *Dramatherapy: Clinical Studies*. London: Jessica Kingsley.

hooks, b. (1990). *Yearning – Race, Gender, and Cultural Politics*. Boston, MA: Southend Press.

Hoskyns, S. (1982). An investigation into the value of music therapy in the care of patients suffering from Huntington's chorea. Outcome study on short-term music therapy. *Lancet 319*(8283), 1258–1260.

Hougham, R. (2006). Numinosity, symbol and ritual in the sesame approach. *Dramatherapy 28*(2), 3–7.

Huizinga, J. (1955). *Homo ludens*. Boston, MA: Beacon.

James, J. (1996a). Dramatherapy with people with learning disabilities. In S. Mitchell (ed.), *Dramatherapy Clinical Studies*. London: Jessica Kingsley.

James, J. (1996b). Poetry in motion: drama and movement with people with learning disabilities. In J. Pearson (ed.), *Discovering the Self through Drama and Movement: The Sesame Approach*. London: Jessica Kingsley.

James, M. and Johnson, D. R. (1997). Drama therapy in the treatment of combat-related post-traumatic stress disorder. *The Arts In Psychotherapy 23*(5), 383–395.

James, M., Forrester, A. M. and Kim, K. C. (2005). Developmental transformations in the treatment of sexually abused children. In A. Weber and C. Haen (eds), *Clinical Applications of Dramatherapy in Child and Adolescent Treatment*. New York and Hove: Brunner-Routledge (pp. 67–86).

Jenkyns, M. (1996). *The Play's the Thing. Exploring Text in Drama and Drama-therapy*. London: Routledge.

Jennings, S. (1987). Rights and rites? Innovation in the teaching of medical students at the London Hospital. *Journal of Interprofessional Care 3*(4), 185–194.

Jennings, S. (1990). *Dramatherapy with Families, Groups and Individuals*. London: Jessica Kingsley.

Jennings, S. (1995). *Dramatherapy with Children and Adolescents*. London: Routledge.

Jennings, S. (1997). *Dramatherapy. Theory and Practice 3*. London: Routledge.

Jennings, S. (1998). Introduction to dramatherapy: theatre and healing. In S. Jennings (ed.), *Dramatherapy Theory and Practice 3*. London: Routledge.

Jennings, S., Cattanach, A., Mitchell, S., Chesner, A. and Meldrum, B. (1994). *Handbook of Dramatherapy*. London: Routledge.

Jennings, S., McGinley, J. D. and Orr, M. (1997). Masking and unmasking: dramatherapy with offender patients. In S. Jennings (ed.), *Dramatherapy Theory and Practice 3*. London: Routledge.

Johnson, D. R. (1980). Effects of theatre experience on hospitalised psychiatric patients. *The Arts in Psychotherapy 7*, 265–272.

Johnson, D. R. (1982a). Dramatherapy and the schizophrenic condition. In G. Schatner and R. Courtney (eds), *Drama in Therapy*, vol. 2. New York: Drama Book Specialists.

Johnson, D. R. (1982b). Developmental approaches to drama therapy. *The Arts in Psychotherapy 9*, 183–190.

Johnson, D. R. (1999). *Essays on the Creative Arts Therapies*. Springfield, IL: Charles C. Thomas.

Johnson D. R. (2005). *Text for DvT Practitioners* [unpublished].

Johnson, D. R. and Quinlan, D. (1985). Representational boundaries in role portrayals among paranoid and nonparanoid schizophrenic patients. *Journal of Abnormal Psychology 94*(4), 498–506.

Johnson, D. R., Lubin, H. and Corn, B. (1999). Course of treatment during a cohort based inpatient programme for PTSD. *Group 23*(1), 19–35.

Johnson, R. (1991). *Owning Your Own Shadow: Understanding the Dark Side of the Psyche*. San Francisco, CA: Harper San.

Jones, E. (1957). *Sigmund Freud: Life and Work, vol. 3: The Last Phase, 1919–1939*. London: Hogarth.

Jones, G. (2002). *Killing Monsters – Why Children need Fantasy, Super Heroes, and Make-Believe Violence*. New York: Basic Books.

Jones, P. (1996). *Drama as Therapy, Theatre as Living*. London: Routledge

Jones, P. (2005). *The Arts Therapies. A Revolution in Health Care*. London: Routledge.

Jones, P. (2007). *Drama as Therapy: Theory, Practice and Research*. London: Routledge.

Jones, P. (ed.). (2010). *Drama As Therapy*, vol. 2. London: Routledge.

Jones, P., Moss, D., Tomlinson, S. and Welch, S. (2008). *Childhood – Services and Provision for Children*. Harlow, Essex: Pearson Education.

Jones, V., Davies, R. and Jenkins, R. (2004). Self-harm by people with learning difficulties: something to be expected or investigated? *Disability and Society*, *19*(5), 487–500.

Jung, C. G. (1952). *The Answer to Job*. Collected Works No. 11. Princeton, NJ: Princeton University Press.

Jung, C. G. (1964). *Civilization in Transition*. Collected Works No. 10. London: Routledge.

Jung, C. G. (1966). *The Practice of Psychotherapy*. Collected Works No. 16. Princeton, NJ: Princeton University Press.

Jung, C. G. (1970). *Symbols of Transformation*. Collected Works No. 5. London: Routledge and Kegan Paul.

Jung, C. G. (1975). *The Archetypes and the Collective Unconscious*. Collected Works No. 9, Part 1. London: Routledge and Kegan Paul.

Jung, C. G. (2002). *The Undiscovered Self* (first published 1957). London: Routledge Classics.

Kalsched, D. (1996). *The Inner World of Trauma*. London: Routledge.

Kareem, J. and Littlewood, R. (eds). (2000). *Intercultural Therapy*. London: Blackwell Science.

Karkou, V. (1999). Art therapy in education: findings from a nationwide survey in arts therapies. *Inscape: Journal of the British Association of Art Therapists 4*(2), 62–70.

Karkou, V. and Sanderson, P. (2006). *Arts Therapies: A Research Based Map of the Field*. Bodmin: Elsevier.

Kelly, G. (1955). *The Psychology of Personal Constructs*. New York: Norton.

Kernberg, O. F. (1975). *Borderline Conditions and Pathological Narcissism*. New York: Jason Aaronson.

Kernberg, O. F. (1976). *Obect Relations Theory and Psychoanalysis*. New York: Jason Aaronson.

Klein, M. (1946). Notes on some schizoid mechanisms. In *Envy and Gratitude and other Works 1946–1963*. London: Hogarth Press and the Institute of Psychoanalysis.

Lahad, M. (1992). Story-making in assessment method for coping with stress. In S. Jennings (ed.), *Dramatherapy: Theory and Practice 2*. New York: Routledge.

Lahad, M. (1996). Masking the gas mask. In A. Gersie (ed.), *Dramatic Approaches to Brief Therapy*. London: Jessica Kingsley.

Laing, R. D. (1967). *The Politics of Experience*. New York: Ballantine.

Lambert, R. (2004). *Handbook of Psychotherapy and Behavior Change*, 5th edn. New York: Wiley.

Landers, F. (2002). Dismantling violent forms of masculinity through developmental transformations. *The Arts in Psychotherapy*, *29*, 19–30.

Landy, R. (1993). *Persona and Performance: The Meaning of Role in Drama, Therapy, and Everyday Life*. London: Jessica Kingsley.

Landy, R. (1995). The dramatic world view: reflections on the roles taken and played by young people. In S. Jennings (ed.), *Dramatherapy with Children and Adolescents*. London: Routledge.

Landy, R. (1997). The case of Sam: application of taxonomy of roles to assessment, treatment and evaluation. In Jennings, S. (ed.), *Dramatherapy Theory and Practice 3*. London: Routledge.

Landy, R. (2008). The dramatic world view revisited: reflections on roles taken and played by young children and adolescents. *Dramatherapy*, *30*(2), 3–14.

Langenberg, M. and Frommer, J. (1994). From isolation to bonding. Case study of a music therapy process – a qualitative research approach. In H. Smitskamp (ed.), *Proceedings of the Third European Arts Therapies Conference, Ferrara, Italy*. Hatfield: University of Hertfordshire Press.

Langley, D. (2006). *An Introduction to Dramatherapy*. London: Sage: www.nationalstrategies.standards.dcsf.gov.uk/node/132587 (accessed 28 September 2009).

Larkin, M. and Griffiths, M. D. (2002). Experiences of addiction and recovery: the case for subjective accounts. *Addiction Research and Theory 10*(3), 281–311.

Laufer, M. and Laufer, M. E. (1984). *Adolescence and Developmental Breakdown: A Psychoanalytic View*. New Haven, CT: Yale University Press.

Lavender, J. and Sobelman, W. (1995). I can't have me if I can't have you. Working with the borderline personality. In F. Levy (ed.), *Dance and Other Expressive Therapies*. London: Routledge.

Lawes, C. and Woodcock, J. (1995). Music therapy and people with severe learning difficulties who exhibit self-injurious behaviour. In B. Saperston and T. Wigram (eds), *The Art and Science of Music Therapy: A Handbook*. Amsterdam: Harwood Academic.

Leenaars, A. A. (2003). *Psychotherapy with Suicidal People: A Person-centred Approach*. Chichester: Wiley.

Levens, M. (1995). *Eating Disorders and Magical Control of the Body*. London: Routledge.

Levine, P. (1997). *Walking the Tiger*. Berkeley, CA: North Atlantic Books.

Lewith, G. and Aldridge, D. (1993). *Clinical Research Methodology for Complementary Therapies*. London: Hodder and Stoughton.

Littlewood, R. and Lipsedge, M. (1997). *Aliens and Alienists: Ethnic Minorities and Psychiatry*, 3rd edn. London: Routledge.

Livingston, R. B. (1967). Brain circuitry relating to complex behaviour. In G. C. Quarton, T. O. Melnechuck and F. O. Scmitt (eds), *The Neurosciences: A Study Program*. New York: Rockefeller University Press.

Long, K. and Weber, A. (2005). Through the eyes of the therapists and children. Drama therapy during and after September 11th. In A. Weber, and C. Haen (eds), *Clinical Applications of Dramatherapy in Child and Adolescent Treatment*. New York and Hove: Brunner-Routledge (pp. 261–279).

Lorde, A. (1984). *Sister Outsider*. Berkeley, CA: Crossing Press.

Lovell, A. (2007). Learning disability against itself: the self-injury/self-harm conundrum. *British Journal of Learning Disabilities 36*, 109–121.

Lowe, F. (2008). Colonial object relations: going underground, black–white relations. *British Journal of Psychotherapy 24*(1), 20–33.

Luxmore, N. (2006). *Working with Anger and Young People*. London: Jessica Kingsley.

McAdams, D. P. and Pals, J. L. (2006). A new Big Five: fundamental principles for an integrative science of personality. *American Psychologist 61*, 204–217.

McAlister, M. (2000). An evaluation of dramatherapy in a forensic setting. *Journal of Dramatherapy 22*(1), 16–19.

McAlister, M. (2002). Dramatherapy and psychosis: symbol formation and dramatic distance. *Free Associations 9*(3), 353–370.

McGilchrist, I. (2009). *The Master and His Emissary: The Divided Brain and the Making of the Modern World*. New Haven, CT, and London: Yale University Press (first paperback edn, 2010).

McGrath, J. (1996). *A Good Night Out – Popular Theatre: Audience, Class and Form*. London: Nick Hern Books.

McKenna, P. and Haste, E. (1999). Clinical effectiveness of dramatherapy in the recovery from neurotrauma. *Disability and Rehabilitation 21*(4), 162–174.

McLeod, J. (2001). *Qualitative Research in Counselling and Psychotherapy*. London: Sage.

McMillan, M. (2007). Hopelessness evidence. *Psychological Medicine 37*, 769–778.

McNiff, S. (1998). *Art Based Research*. London: Jessica Kingsley.

Malan, D. H. (1997). *Anorexia, Murder and Suicide*. Oxford: Butterworth-Heinemann.

Mann, D. (1990). Art as a defence against creativity. *British Journal of Psychotherapy 7*(1), 5–14.

Mann, T. (1996). Clinical audit in the NHS. In *Using Clinical Audit in the NHS – A Position Statement*. Wetherby: NHS Executive.

Mansell, J. L. (1993). *Services for People with Learning Disabilities and Challenging Behaviour or Mental Health Needs: Report of a Project Group*. London: HMSO.

Mansell, J. L. (2007). *Services for People with Learning Disabilities and Challenging Behaviour or Mental Health Needs: Report of a Project Group*. London: HMSO [first published 1993].

Marquis de Sade, M. Dialogue between a priest and a dying man: www.horrormasters.com/Text/a0293.pdf

Maslow, A. H. (1993). *The Farther Reaches of Human Nature*. Arkana: Penguin.

May, C. (2001). Pathology, identity and the social construction of alcohol dependence. *Sociology 35*(2), 385–401.

Meekums, B. and Payne, H. (1993). Emerging methodology in dance movement therapy research. In H. Payne (ed.), *Handbook of Inquiry in the Arts Therapies*. London: Jessica Kingsley.

Meltzer, H., Harrington, R., Goodman R. and Jenkins, R. (2002). *Children and Adolescents Who Try to Harm, Hurt or Kill Themselves. A Report of Further Analysis from the National Survey of the Mental Health of Children and Adolescents in Great Britian in 1999*. London: Office for National Statistics.

Menninger, K. (1938). *Man Against Himself*. New York: Harvest Books.

Miles, C. P. (1977). Conditions predisposing to suicide: a review. *Journal of Nervous and Mental Disease 164*, 231–246.

Milia, D. (2000). *Self-mutilation in Art Therapy. Violent Creation*. London: Jessica Kingsley.

Milioni, D. (2001). Social constructionism and dramatherapy: creating alternative discourses. *Dramatherapy 23*(2), 10–17.

Mitchell, S. (ed.). (1996). *Dramatherapy: Clinical Studies*. London: Jessica Kingsley.

Moffet, L. A. and Bruto, L. (1990). Therapeutic theatre with personality disordered substance abusers: characters in search of different characters. *The Arts in Psychotherapy 17*, 339–348.

Moore, J. (2006). Theatre of attachment using dramatherapy to facilitate attachment in adoption. *Adoption and Fostering 30*(2), 64–73.

Moore, J. (2009). Dramatherapy and social theatre: necessary dialogues. In D. J. Betts (ed.), *Creative Arts Therapies Approaches in Adoption and Foster Care: Contemporary Strategies for Working with Individuals and Families*. Springfield, IL: Charles C. Thomas.

Morgan, D. and Ruszczynski, S. (eds). (2007). *Lectures on Violence, Perversion and Delinquency: The Portman Papers*. London: Karnac.

Moustakas, C. (1990). *Heuristic Research: Design Methodology and Applications*. Newbury Park, CA: Sage.

Moustakas, C. (1994). *Phenomenological Research Methods*. Thousand Oaks, CA: Sage.

Mulder, J. (1995). Het terugval preventie model als behandelingsmethodiek in een forensische dagbehandelingskliniek [the prevention of recidivism model as a treatment method in a forensic day treatment clinic]. *Tijdschrift voor Psychotherapie 21*(2), 119–133.

Murphy, G. (2003). Information sheet – self-injurious behaviour. Available online: www.thecbf.org.uk (accessed 1 December 2007).

Murphy, G. and Wilson, B. A. (1985). *Self-injurious Behaviour*. Kidderminster: British Institute of Mental Handicap Publications.

Murray, J. (1985). The use of health diaries in the field of psychiatric illness in general practice. In *Psychological Medicine*, 15, 827–840.

National Collaborating Centre for Mental Health. (2004). *Self-harm: The Short-term Physical and Psychological Management and Secondary Prevention of Self-harm in Primary and Secondary Care*. Leicester: British Psychological Society.

National Institute for Mental Health in England (2010). *New Ways of Working for Psychological Therapists* (Overarching Report), London NIMHE/NSP/IAPT. Available online: www.iapt.nhs.uk/wp-content/uploads/nww4pt-overarching-report-final.pdf (accessed 10 September 2010).

Neall, L. (2002). *Bringing the Best Out in Boys*. Stroud, Gloucestershire: Hawthorn Press. Available online: www.Ofsted.gov.uk (accessed 28 September 2009).

NHS Centre for Reviews and Dissemination. (1998). Deliberate self-harm. *Effective Health Care 4*, 1–12.

NICE Guidelines. (2008): www.doh.gov.uk

Nicholas, M. and Forrester, A. (1999). Advantages of heterogeneous group therapy in the psychotherapy of the traumatically abused: treating the problem as well as the person. *International Journal of Group Psychotherapy 49*(3), 323–342.

Nitsun, M. (1996). *The Anti-group: Destructive Forces in the Group and Their Creative Potential*. London: Routledge.

Nitsun, M., Stapelton, J. H. and Bender, M. P. (1974). Drama and movement therapy with long-stay schizophrenics. *British Journal of Medical Psychology 47*, 101–119.

Nordoff, C. and Robbins, R. (1971). *Music Therapy in Special Education*. London: John Day Books.

Ogden, T. H. (1979). On Projective Identification. *International Journal of Psychoanalysis* (Issue 60). London: Institute of Psychoanalysis.

Oliver, C. and Head, D. (1990). Self-injurious behaviour in people with learning disabilities: determinants and interventions. *International Review of Psychiatry 2*(1), 101–116.

Online Medical Dictionary: www.mondofacto.com

Orbach, S. (1998). *Fat Is a Feminist Issue – and Its Sequel*. Reading: Arrow.

Parker, C. (1999). Extract from an interview with Cornelia Parker by Bruce Ferguson. Available online: www.tate.org.uk/colddarkmatter/texts (accessed 9 September 2009).

Parry, G. (1996). Service evaluation and audit methods. In G. Parry and F. Watts (eds), *Behavioral and Mental Health Research*. Hove: Erlbaum (UK) Taylor & Francis.

Parry, G. and Richardson, A. (1996). *NHS Psychotherapy Services in England: Review of Strategic Policy*. Wetherby: NHS Executive.

Payne, H. (ed.). (1993). *Handbook of Inquiry in the Arts Therapies*. London: Jessica Kingsley.

Perelberg, R. J. (1999). A core phantasy in violence. In R. J. Perelberg (ed.), *Psychoanalytic Understanding of Violence and Suicide*. London: Routledge.

Piaget, J. (1983). Piaget's theory. In P. Mussen (ed.), *Handbook of Child Psychology*, 4th edn, vol. 1. New York: Wiley.

Pitruzzella, S. (2004). *Introduction to Dramatherapy, Person and Threshold*. London: Routledge.

Pounsett, H., Parker, K., Hawtin, A. and Collins, S. (2006). Examination of the changes that take place during an art therapy intervention. *International Journal of Art Therapy 11*(2), 79–101.

Practice-based evidence website: www.practisebasedevidence.com

Priestley, M. (1975). *Music Therapy in Action*. London: Constable.

Quinodoz, J.-M. (2008). *Listening to Hanna Segal: Her Contribution to Psychoanalysis*. London: Routledge.

Qureshi, H. (1993). Prevalence of challenging behaviour in adults. In I. Fleming and B. Stenfert Kroese (eds), *People with Learning Disability and Severe Challenging Behaviour: New Developments in Services and Therapy*. Manchester: Manchester University Press.

Qureshi, H. (1994). The size of the problem. In E. Emerson, P. McGill and J. Mansell (eds), *Severe Learning Disabilities and Challenging Behaviours. Designing High Quality Services*. London: Chapman and Hall.

Radmall, B. (2001/2002). The dance between post-modern systemic therapy and dramatherapy. *Dramatherapy, Journal of the British Association for Dramatherapists 23*(3), 16–19.

Rafaeli, E., Bernstein, D. P. and Young, J. (2010). *Schema Therapy (CBT Distinctive Features)*. London: Routledge.

Rasmussen, S. (2000). *Addiction Treatment: Theory and Practice*. Thousand Oaks, CA: Sage.

Rawlinson, B. (1996). The seeds of the pomegranate: images of depression. In S. Mitchell (ed.), *Dramatherapy: Clinical Studies*. London: Jessica Kingsley.

Reason, J. (1988). *Human Inquiry in Action*. London: Sage.

Rebillot, P. (1993). *The Call to Adventure: Bringing the Hero's Journey to Daily Life*. San Francisco, CA: Harper.

Renfrew, C. (1999). Points of view: formation. Available online: www.tate.org.uk/colddarkmatter/texts (accessed 9 September 2009).

Rice, C. A. and Benson, J. F. (2005). Hungering for revenge: the Irish famine, the troubles and shame–rage cycles and their role in group therapy in Northern Ireland. *Group Analysis 38*(2), 219–235.

Rosenfeld, H. (1971). A clinical approach to the psychoanalytic theory of the life and death instincts: an investigation into the aggressive aspects of narcissism. In B. Spillius (ed.), *Melanie Klein Today: Mainly Theory*, vol. 1. London and New York: Routledge.

Roth, A. and Fonagy, P. (eds). (2004). *What Works for Whom: A Critical Review of Psychotherapy Research*. London: Guilford.

Roth, A., Fonagy, P. and Parry, G. (2004). Psychotherapy research, funding and evidence-based practice. In A. Roth and P. Fonagy (eds), *What Works for Whom. A Review of Psychotherapy Research*. London: Guilford.

Rothschild, B. (2000). *The Body Remembers – The Psycho-physiology of Trauma and Trauma Treatment*. London: W. W. Norton.

Rouchy, J. C. (1995). Identification and groups of belonging. *Group Analysis 28*(1), 129–141.

Royston, R. (2006). Destructiveness: revenge, dysfunction or constitutional evil? In C. Harding (ed.), *Aggression and Destructiveness: Psychoanalytic Perspectives*. London: Routledge.

Rozynko, V. and Dondershine, H. E. (1991). Trauma focus group therapy for Vietnam veterans with PTSD. *Psychotherapy Theory–Research–Practice–Training 28*(1), 157–161.

Ruddy, R. and Dent-Brown, K. (2007). Drama therapy for schizophrenia or schizophrenia-like illnesses. In H. I. Spitz and S. T. Spitz (1999). *Group Therapy With the Chronic Psychiatric Patient: A Pragmatic Approach to Group Psychotherapy*. Philadelphia, PA: Brunner/Mazel (pp. 141–152).

Rusbridger, R. (1999). Elements of the Oedipus complex: building up the picture. *British Journal of Psychotherapy 15*, 488–500.

Russell, S. S. and Shirk, B. (1993). Women's anger and eating. In S. P. Thomas (ed.), *Women and Anger*. New York: Springer.

Ryle, A. (1997). *Cognitive Analytic Therapy and Borderline Personality Disorder*. Chichester: Wiley.

Samuels, A. (1985). *Jung and the Post-Jungians*. London: Routledge.

Samuels, A., Shorter, B. and Plaut, A. (1997). *A Critical Dictionary of Jungian Analysis*. London: Routledge.

Satir, V. and Baldwin, M. (1987). *The Use of Self in Therapy*. New York: Haworth.

Schwartz-Salant, N. (1989). The borderline personality. In A. Samuels (ed.), *Psychopathology: Contemporary Jungian Perspectives*. London: Karnac.

Segal, H. (1957). Notes on symbol formation. *International Journal of Psycho-analysis 39*, 391–397.

Segal, H. (1991). *Dream, Phantasy and Art*. London: Routledge.

Schneidman, E. (1985). *Definition of Suicide*. New York: Wiley.

Schore, A. (2001). The effect of early relational trauma on right brain development, affect regulation and infant mental health. *Infant Mental Health Journal 22*, 201–249.

Schore, A. (2003). *Affect Dysregulation and Disorders of the Self*. London: W. W. Norton & Co.

Shakespeare, W. (1952). *Complete Works*. Oxford: Oxford University Press.

Shakespeare, W. (1998). *The Tempest*, F. Kermode (ed.), Arden edn. Surrey, UK, Thomas Nelson Ltd.

Shakespeare, W. (1998). *Julius Caesar*, D. Daniell (ed.), Arden edn. London: Thomson Learning.

Silver, A. L. and Larsen, T. K. (eds). (2003). The schizophrenic person and the benefits of the psychotherapies – seeking a PORT in the storm. *Journal of the American Academy of Psychoanalysis and Dynamic Psychotherapy 31*, 1–10.

Silverman, Y. (2004). The story within – myth and fairytale in therapy. *The Arts in Psychotherapy 31*(3), 127–135.

Simpson, D. and Miller, L. (eds). (2004). *Unexpected Gains: Psychotherapy with People with Learning Disabilities*. London: Karnac.

Sinason, V. (1992). *Mental Handicap and the Human Condition*. London: Free Association Books.

Skogstad, W. (2004). Action and thought: inpatient treatment of severe personality disorders within a psychotherapeutic milieu [unpublished paper].

Smeijsters, H. (1993). Music therapy as psychotherapy. *The Arts in Psychotherapy 20*, 223–229.

Smeijsters. H. (1997). *Multiple Perspectives. A Guide to Qualitative Perspectives in Music Therapy*. Phoenixville, AR: Barcelona.

Smeijsters, H. (2003). Multiple perspectives for the development of an evidence-based creative therapy. In L. Schiltz (ed.), *Epistemology and Practice of Research in the Arts Therapies*. Luxembourg: CRP-Sante Luxembourg.

Smeijsters, H. and van Cleven, G. (2006). The treatment of aggression using arts therapies in forensic psychiatry: results of a qualitative inquiry. *The Arts in Psychotherapy 33*, 37–58.

Solomon, Z. (1992). The Koach project. *Journal of Traumatic Stress 5*, 173–272.

Soyinka, W. (1996). *The Open Sore of a Continent: A Personal Narrative of the Nigerian Crisis*. Oxford: Oxford University Press.

Spencer, P. C., Gillespie, C. R. and Ekisa, E. G. (1983). A controlled comparison of the effects of social skills training and remedial drama on the conversational skills of chronic schizophrenic patients. *British Journal of Psychiatry 143*, 165–172.

Spinelli, V. (1989). *The Interpreted World: An Introduction to Phenomenological Psychology*. London: Sage.

Stamp, S. (1998). Holding on: dramatherapy with offenders. In J. Thompson (ed.), *Prison Theatre: Perspectives and Practice*. London: Jessica Kingsley.

Stamp, S. (2000). A fast-moving floorshow – the space between acting and thinking in dramatherapy with offenders. *Dramatherapy 22*(1), 10–15.

Stamp, S. (2008). A place of containment: supervising dramatherapists in a secure setting. In P. Jones and D. Dokter (eds), *Supervision in Dramatherapy*. London: Routledge.

Stapley, L. F. (2006). *Globalization and Terrorism. Death of a Way of Life*. London: Karnac.

Stern, D. (1985). *The Interpersonal World of the Human Infant. A View from Psychoanalysis and Developmental Psychology*. New York: Basic Books.

Stern, D. (1995). *The Motherhood Constellation: A Unified View Of Parent–Infant Psychotherapy*. New York: Basic Books.

Stern, D. (2008). *Diary of a Baby*. New York: Basic Books.

Storr, A. (1991). *Human Destructiveness. The Roots of Genocide and Human Cruelty*, 2nd edn. London: Routledge.

Temple, N. (1996). Transference and countertransference: general and forensic aspects. In C. Cordess and M. Cox (eds), *Forensic Psychotherapy: Crime, Psychodynamics and the Offender Patient*. London: Jessica Kingsley.

Thompson, J. (1999a). *Drama Workshops for Anger Management and Offending Behaviour*. London: Jessica Kingsley.

Thompson, J. (1999b). *Prison Theatre: Perspectives and Practice.* London: Jessica Kingsley.

Timimi, S. B. (1996). Race and colour in internal and external reality. *British Journal of Psychotherapy 13*(2), 183–192.

Timmer, S. (2000). Delict keten denken binnen dramatherapie [The use of the concepts of the chain of offence in dramatherapy. Dramatherapy in a forensic day treatment clinic]. *Tijdschrift voor Kreatieve Therapie 19*(1), 12–18.

Timmer, S. (2003). *Werkwijzen Dramatherapie in de Forensische Psychiatrie* [Dramatherapy Treatment Modalities in Forensic Psychiatry]. Nijmegen: Kairos-Pompe Stichting.

Timmer, S. (2004). Dramatherapy within a schema oriented treatment for sexual offenders. *Tijdschrift voor Kreatieve Therapie 23*(1), 11–16.

Tomlinson, S. (2008). The politics of childhood. In P. Jones, D. Moss, S. Tomlinson and S. Welch (eds), *Childhood – Services and Provision for Children.* Harlow, Essex: Pearson Education.

Twist, S. and Montgomery, A. (2005). Promoting healthy lifestyles – challenging behaviour. In G. Grant, P. Goward, M. Richardson and P. Ramcharan (eds), *Learning Disability: A Life Cycle Approach to Valuing People.* Maidenhead: McGraw-Hill International.

United Nations (1998/9). *Convention on the Rights of the Child – Adopted by the General Assembly of the United Nations on 20 November 1989.* London: The Stationary Office.

Valery, P. (1919). The crisis of the mind. In *La Nouvelle Revue Française* [from *History and Politics*, trans. D. Folliot and J. Mathews] *10*, 23–36.

Valery, P. (1940). The course in poetics: first lesson. *Southern Review 5*(3), 6.

Vardi, D. (1999). Group therapy with holocaust survivors and second generation. *Mikbaz 4*(2), 11–23.

Vaughn, J. (2003). The drama unfolds. In C. Archer and A. Burnell (eds), *Trauma, Attachment, and Family Permanence: Fear Can Stop You Loving.* London: Jessica Kingsley.

Volkan, V. D. (1997). *Blood Lines: From Ethnic Pride to Ethnic Terrorism.* New York: Farraf, Strauss and Geroux.

Volkan, V. D. (1999). Psychoanalysis and diplomacy, part II: large group rituals. *Journal of Applied Psychoanalytic Studies 1*, 223–247.

Volkan, V. D., Ast, G. and Greer, W. (2002). *The Third Reich in the Unconscious. Trans-generational Transmission and Its Consequences.* New York: Brunner-Routledge.

Waite, T. (1991). In: www.getquote.com

Waller, D. (1991). *Becoming A Profession: the History of Art Therapy in Britain 1940–82.* London: Routledge.

Waller, D. (1998). *Towards a European Art Therapy: Creating a Profession.* Buckingham and Philadelphia: Open University Press.

Ward, J. (2006). *The Student's Guide to Cognitive Neuroscience.* New York: Psychology Press.

Warner, C. (2007). Challenging behaviour: working with the blindingly obvious. In T. Watson (ed.), *Music Therapy with Adults with Learning Disabilities.* Hove: Routledge.

Watkins, J. (1999). Points of view: on cold dark matter. Available online: www.tate.org.uk/colddarkmatter/texts (accessed 9 September 2009).

Watts, P. (1992). Therapy in drama. In S. Jennings (ed.), *Dramatherapy Theory and Practice 3*. London: Routledge.

Watzlawick, P., Weakland, J. H. and Fisch, R. (1974). *Change*. New York: Norton.

Weber, A. and Haen, C. (eds). (2005). *Clinical Applications of Dramatherapy in Child and Adolescent Treatment*. New York and Hove: Brunner-Routledge.

Weinberg, H., Nuttman-Schwartz, O. and Gilmore, M. (2005). Trauma groups: an overview. *Group Analysis 38*(2), 187–202.

Weissmann, M. M., Klerman, G. L., Markowitz, J. S. and Oulette, R. (1989). Suicidal ideation and suicide attempts in panic disorder and attacks. *New England Journal of Medicine 321*, 1209–1214.

Welldon, E. (1988). *Mother, Madonna, Whore*. New York: Guilford.

Welldon, E. V. (1992). *Mother, Madonna, Whore – The Idealization and Denigration of Motherhood*. London: Guilford.

Welldon, E. (1997). Forensic psychotherapy: the practical approach, In E. V. Welldon and C. Van Velsen (eds), *A Practical Guide to Forensic Psychotherapy*. London: Jessica Kingsley.

Welldon, E. V. and Van Velsen, C. (eds). (1997). *A Practical Guide to Forensic Psychotherapy*. London: Jessica Kingsley.

West, J. (1996). *Child Centred Play Therapy*, 2nd edn. London: Arnold.

Wheeler, B. (1995). *Music Therapy Research. Quantitative and Qualitative Perspectives*. Phoenixville, AR: Barcelona.

White, K. (ed.). (2006). *Unmasking Race, Culture, and Attachment in the Psycho-analytical Space*. London: Karnac.

Wilkinson, M. (2006). *Coming Into Mind – The Mind–Brain Relationship: A Jungian Clinical Perspective*. London: Routledge.

Wigram, T. (1993). Observational techniques in the analysis of both active and receptive music therapy with disturbed and self-injurious clients. In M. Heal and T. Wigram (eds), *Music Therapy in Health and Education*. London: Jessica Kingsley.

Wigram, T., Pedersen, I. N. and Bonde L. O. (2002). *A Comprehensive Guide to Music Therapy*. London: Jessica Kingsley.

Wikipedia website: en.wikipedia.org/wiki/Destructiveness_(Phrenology); or www.wikipedia.org

Williams, R. (1971). *Culture and Society*. London: Penguin.

Willig, C. (ed.). (1999). *Applied Discourse Analysis*. Buckingham: Open University Press.

Wilt, D. (1993). Treatment of anger. In S. P. Thomas (ed.), *Women and Anger*. New York: Springer.

Winn, L. (1994). *Post Traumatic Stress Disorder and Dramatherapy: Treatment and Risk Reduction*. London: Jessica Kingsley.

Winn, L. (2008). The use of outcome measures in dramatherapy. Available online: www.badth.org.uk/members/research-project/index.php (accessed 13 October 2009).

Winnicott, C., Shepherd, R. and Davis, M. (eds). (1984). *Deprivation and Delinquency*. London: Tavistock.

Winnicott, D. W. (1947; published 1982). Hate in the countertransference. In *Through Paediatrics to Psycho Analysis*. London: Hogarth Press.

Winnicott, D. W. (1967; published 1991). The location of cultural experience. In *Playing and Reality*. London: Routledge.

Winnicott, D. W. (1951, 1971; published 1991). Transitional objects and transitional phenomena. In *Playing and Reality*. London: Routledge.

Winnicott, D. W. (1989). *The Family and Individual Development*. London: Routledge.

Winnicott, D. W. (2005). *Playing and Reality*. London: Routledge.

Winter, D., Bradshaw, S., Bunn, F. and Wellsted, D. (2009). *Counselling and Psychotherapy for the Prevention of Suicide: A Systematic Review of the Evidence*. Lutterworth: BACP.

Wolverson, M. (2006). Self-injurious behaviour and learning disabilities. Available online: www.naidex.co.uk (accessed 10 December 2007).

Woods, J. (1996). Handling violence in child group therapy. *Group Analysis 29*, 81.

Woods, N. (2006). *Describing Discourse*. London: Hodder Arnold.

Woods, P., Reed, V. and Collins, M. (2001). *Measuring Communication and Social Skills in a High Security Forensic Setting Using the Behavioral Status Index*. London: King's College.

Yalom, I. (1980). *Existential Psychotherapy*. New York: Basic Books.

Yalom, I. (1991). *Love's Executioner*. London: Penguin.

Yalom, I. D. (1995). *The Theory and Practice of Group Psychotherapy*, 4th edn. New York: Basic Books.

Yalom, I. (2008). *Staring at the Sun: Overcoming the Terror of Death*. New York: Piatkus Books.

Yin, R. K. (1994). *Case Study Research: Design and Methods*, 2nd edn. Newbury Park, CA: Sage.

Yotis, L. (2002). Dramatherapy Performance and Schizophrenia. PhD Thesis, University of Hertfordshire.

Yotis, L. (2006). A review of dramatherapy research in schizophrenia: methodologies and outcomes. *Psychotherapy Research 16*(2), 190–200.

Zane, N., Gordon, C., Hall, N., Sue, S., Young, K. and Nunez, J. (2004). Research on psychotherapy with culturally diverse populations. In R. Lambert (ed.), *Bergin and Garfield's Handbook of Psychotherapy and Behaviour Change*, 5th edn. London: Wiley.

Zarkowska, E. and Clements, J. (1988). *Problem Behaviour in People with Severe Learning Disabilities. A Practical Guide to a Constructional Approach*. Beckenham, Kent: Croom Helm.

Zografou, L. (2007). The drama of addiction and recovery. In S. Scoble (ed.), *European Arts Therapies: Grounding the Vision – To Advance Theory and Practice*. Talinn: ECArTE Conference Publication.

Websites

ASBOs: www.antisocial behaviour.org.uk

Association of Dance Movement Therapists UK (ADMPUK): www.admt.org.uk

British Association of Art Therapists: www.baat.org

British Society for Music Therapists: www.bsmt.org

Department for Children Schools and Families: www.dcsf.gov.uk/everychildmatters/ (accessed 28/9/09)

Department of Health: *New Ways of Working for Psychological Therapists*, p.8 and pp.21–23. www.newsavoypartnership.org/docs/NWW4PT-overarching-report. pdf (accessed 10/09/10)

Gangs: www.centreforsocialjustice.org.uk

Hidden Pain? Self-injury and people with learning disabilities: www.bristol.ac.uk/ norahfry/research/completed-projects/hiddenpainrep.pdf

Looked-after children: tameside.gov.uk

Samaritans (2010): www.samaritans.org/your_emotional_health/publications/ depression_and_suicide.aspx (accessed 15/04/10)

SDQs: www.sdqinfo.com

Statements: www.direct.gov.uk

World Health Organization: www.who.int/whosis/whostat/2008/en/index.html (accessed 15/01/10)

INDEX

20584223R00129

Printed in Great Britain
by Amazon